AF568153

Problems and Prospects of Working Women

Problems and Prospects of Working Women

Ms. Kalpana Taing

RANDOM PUBLICATIONS
NEW DELHI - 110 002 (INDIA)

Problems and Prospects of Working Women

ISBN 978-93-5111-309-6

Published in 2014 in India by
RANDOM PUBLICATIONS
4376-A/4B, Gali Murari Lal, Ansari Road
New Delhi-110 002
Phone: +9111-43580356, 23289044
E-mail: randomexports@gmail.com; sales@randompublications.com; info@randompublications.com

Type Setting by: Friends Media, Delhi-110089
Printed at: Sanat Printers

Preface

With the political emancipation of India, the women of free India ushered into a new role. Today the women enjoy equality of status, equality of opportunity with men. She became financially independent and economically sound, she became the major decision maker, and she became the policy maker in various new fields. She ventured into outer field, but the traditional views about her role as home maker, about! Her so called sacred duties of Mother, Sister, Wife, are still kept on demanding on her the women are divided between her official work and home duties. Her duties start from early in the morning with many responsibilities on her shoulder before going to office, like preparing breakfast, lunch, getting kids ready for school etc. During office hours she has to work equally or say more sincerely than her male counterparts. She has to fulfill her duties at home even after office homes. Her pathetic position, working at home as well as at office, is not admired, even by her husband or mother-in-law or father-in-law. The support and cooperation if extended by her husband in household; work is at his sole desertion. Husband is free to take excuses of over burdened work pressure of official exigencies, but wife is expected to be found fresh and amiable all the time. The men consider the household work as sole responsibility of the women. He considers working at home below his dignity and if he does something it is done as per his wish and convenience.

The working atmosphere in the offices, particularly, for the women is also not so congenial. Most of the male counter-part treat the woman an easy scope goat for fulfilling their sexual desires. The incident of intentional touching, double meaning dialogues, unwarranted comments, piercing in her private affairs are some of the common examples which create lot of irritation and make the women unnecessarily defensive. The incidents of one sider sexual advancement by the boss, staring at her body parts, alluring her with quick promotion in return, are generally to be faced by a working woman. With women entering into new fields, she become more vulnerable to the dangers like eve-teasing, sexual advancement, transfers, etc. The women can only explain to have frights and hardships experienced by her while working in office. In the present male dominated, patriarchal society, people find it difficult to accept the women as independent personality. In addition to these hardships, the women are bound to play the traditional role of child bearing and child rearing. She can't desist from her role as a mother and as a wife. So while performing these natural roles, sometimes she had to be out of office for a long period which causes adverse effects on her career, though not openly but in reality. One more peculiar problem, a woman faces while keeping the children with her, in case when her husband is transferred out of town, ·and she is unable to shift being a working woman, as the children prefer to stay with mother. Now she has to play the role of both the parents and her duties are tribled. The problems of a career woman are endless and peculiar and differ from place to place, office to office, and person to person.

The woman has her own personality, more confident, financially independent, accepting any kind of challenge, can no longer remain under the illogical dominance of man, but at the same time she suffers a lot mentally and physically divided between home and office. Our society had been a male dominated society; the changes are gradually being digested. With necessity of time absences of joint families the financial independence of women are making the male absorb the change slowly but gradually. In spite of all the hardships being faced by the working women, it must be noted that women have fought a great battle and are still fighting at their own against the fright and hardships faced by them and got remarkable success in every field of life. Policies and legal mechanisms alone cannot help in curbing the problems faced by women at work place - the overall attitude and acceptance level of the people of needs to change. Just letting women work outside home does not mean that society treats men and women equally. The issues and problems that women face in their workplaces should be put to an end and then only it can be said that men and women have equal status.

This book titled, "Problems and Prospects of Working Women", provides readers with an analysis of the problem of sexual harassment of women at workplace. An introduction to status and attitude of working women is given. The social characteristics of working women and the status of women workers in the unorganized sectors are discussed in detail. A case study of the status of working women in socialist countries is provided herein. Efforts have been made to focus on patterns of women's labour in various situations. In addition, this book also is helpful in discussing the problems of urban working women and the challenges for self-employed women. Efforts are made towards estimating the quality of women's working life. A detailed bibliography, appendix and elaborate index make this publication user-friendly.

—Editor

Contents

1

Analyzing the Problem of Sexual Harassment of Working Women at Workplace

> "If your flirting strategy is indistinguishable from harassment, it's not everyone else that's the problem."
>
> —*John Scalzi*

Generally it seen that sexual harassment is a great problem for working women. Sexual harassment is intimidation, bullying or coercion of a sexual nature, or the unwelcome or inappropriate promise of rewards in exchange for sexual favours. In most modern legal contexts sexual harassment is illegal. As defined by EEOC, "It is unlawful to harass a person (an applicant or employee) because of that person's sex. Harassment can include "sexual harassment" or unwelcome sexual advances, requests for sexual favours, and other verbal or physical harassment of a sexual nature. Harassment does not have to be of a sexual nature, however, and can include offensive remarks about a person's sex. For example, it is illegal to harass a woman by making offensive comments about women in general.

Both victim and the harasser can be either a woman or a man, and the victim and harasser can be the same sex. Although the law doesn't prohibit simple teasing, offhand comments, or isolated incidents that are not very serious, harassment is illegal when it is so frequent or severe that it creates a hostile or offensive work environment or when it results in an adverse employment decision (such as the victim being fired or demoted). The harasser can be the victim's supervisor, a supervisor in another area, a co-worker, or someone who is not an employee of the employer, such as a client or customer.

It includes a range of behaviour from seemingly mild transgressions and annoyances to actual sexual abuse or sexual assault. Sexual harassment is a form of illegal employment discrimination in many countries, and is a form of abuse (sexual and psychological) and bullying. For many businesses and other organizations, preventing sexual harassment, and defending employees from sexual harassment charges, have become key goals of legal decision-making. It is interesting to note that term *sexual harassment* was used in 1973 in a report to the then President and Chancellor of MIT about various forms of gender issues. Rowe has stated that she believes she was not the first to use the term, since sexual harassment was being discussed in women's groups in Massachusetts in the early 1970s, but that MIT may have been the first or one of the first large organizations to discuss the topic (in the MIT Academic Council), and to develop relevant policies and procedures. MIT at the time also recognized the injuries caused by racial harassment and the harassment of women of colour which may be both racial and sexual.

The President of MIT also stated that harassment (and favouritism) are antithetical to the mission of a university as well as intolerable for individuals. In the book *In Our Time: Memoir of a Revolution* (1999), journalist Susan Brownmiller quotes the Cornell activists who in 1975 thought they had coined the term sexual harassment: "Eight of us were sitting in an office ... brainstorming about what we were going to write on posters for our speak-out. We were referring to it as 'sexual intimidation,' 'sexual coercion,' 'sexual exploitation on the job.' None of those names seemed quite right. We wanted something that embraced a whole range of subtle and un-subtle persistent behaviours. Somebody came up with 'harassment.' 'Sexual harassment!'

Instantly we agreed. That's what it was." (p. 281). These activists, Lin Farley, Susan Meyer, and Karen Sauvigne went on to form Working Women's Institute which, along with the Alliance Against Sexual Coercion, founded in 1976 by Freada Klein, Lynn Wehrli, and Elizabeth Cohn-Stuntz, were among the pioneer organizations to bring sexual harassment to public attention in the late 1970s. Still the term was largely unknown until the early 90s when Anita Hill witnessed and testified against Supreme Court Justice nominee Clarence Thomas. In 1991 when Anita Hill testified the number of sexual harassment cases reported in US and Canada increased 58 percent and have climbed steadily ever since.

Harassment Situations

Sexual harassments can occur in a variety of circumstances. Often, but not always, the harasser is in a position of power or authority over the victim (due to differences in age, or social, political, educational or employment relationships) or expecting to receive such power or authority in form of promotion. Forms of harassment relationships include:

- The harasser can be anyone, such as a client, a co-worker, a parent or legal guardian, relative, a teacher or professor, a student, a friend, or a stranger.
- The victim does not have to be the person directly harassed but can be a witness of such behaviour who finds the behaviour offensive and is affected by it.
- The place of harassment occurrence may vary from school, university, workplace and other
- There may be other witnesses or attendances, or not
- The harasser may be completely unaware that his or her behaviour is offensive or constitutes sexual harassment or may be completely unaware that his or her actions could be unlawful.
- The harassment may be one time occurrence but more often it has a type of repetitiveness
- Adverse effects on the target are common in the form of stress and social withdrawal, sleep and eating difficulties, overall health impairment, etc.
- The victim and harasser can be any gender
- The harasser does not have to be of the opposite sex.
- Misunderstanding: It can result from a situation where one thinks he/she is making themselves clear, but is not understood the way they intended. The misunderstanding can either be reasonable or unreasonable. An example of unreasonable is when a man holds a certain stereotypical view of a woman such that he did not understand the woman's explicit message to stop. (Heyman, 1994)

Varied Behaviours

One of the difficulties in understanding sexual harassment is that it involves a range of behaviour, and in most cases (although not in all cases) is difficult for the recipient to describe first to themselves, and then to others, about exactly what they are experiencing, this can be related of difficulty of classifying the situation or could be related to stress and humiliation experienced by the recipient. Moreover, behaviour and motives vary between individual cases.

Behavioural Classes

Dzeich et al. has divided harassers into two broad classes:

- Public harassers are flagrant in their seductive or sexist attitudes towards colleagues, subordinates, students, etc.
- Private harassers carefully cultivate a restrained and respectable image on the surface, but when alone with their target, their demeanor changes.

Langelan describes three different classes of harassers.

- Predatory harasser who gets sexual thrills from humiliating others. This harasser may become involved in sexual extortion, and may frequently harass just to see how targets respond. Those who don't resist may even become targets for rape.
- Dominance harasser: the most common type, who engages in harassing behaviour as an ego boost.
- Strategic or territorial harassers who seek to maintain privilege in jobs or physical locations, for example a man's harassing female employees in a predominantly male occupation.

Prevention

Sexual harassment and assault may be prevented by secondary school, college, and workplace education programs. At least one program for fraternity men produced "sustained behavioural change."

The Injured of Sexual Harassment

Effects of sexual harassment can vary depending on the individuality of the recipient and the severity and duration of the harassment. Often, sexual harassment incidents fall into the category of the "merely annoying." In other situations harassment may lead to temporary or prolonged stress and/or depression depending on the recipient's psychological abilities to cope and the type of harassment, and the social support or lack of it for the recipient. Psychologists and social workers report that severe/chronic sexual harassment can have the same psychological effects as rape or sexual assault. (Koss, 1987) Victims who do not submit to harassment may also experience various forms of retaliation, including isolation and bullying. As an overall social and economic effect every year sexual harassment deprive women form active social and economic participation, and costs hundreds of millions of dollars in lost educational and professional opportunities for mostly girls and women. (Boland, 2002) However, the quantity of men implied in these conflicts is significant.

Coping

Sexual harassment, by definition, is unwanted and not to be tolerated but there often are a number of effective ways for offended and injured people to overwhelm harassment psychological effects, remain or return socialization, regain personal relationship feelings when they were affected by the outside relationship trauma, and regain social approval, return ability to concentrate and be productive in educational, work, etc. environments.

This may include stress management and therapy, cognitive-behavioural therapy, friends and family support, etc. Immediate psychological and legal counselling are suggestive in the happening of the event since self-treatment may not release stress or remove trauma, and simply reporting to authorities may not have the desired effect, be ignored or may further injure the victim at its response, or may lead to harmful social circumstances in relation to creating difficulties in school or workplace, and even firing.

Common Effects on the Victims

Common psychological, academic, professional, financial, and social effects of sexual harassment and retaliation:

- Psychological stress and health impairment
- Decreased work or school performance as a result of stress conditions; increased absenteeism in fear of harassment repetition
- Firing and refusal for a job opportunity can lead to loss of job or career, loss of income
- Having to drop courses, change academic plans, or leave school (loss of tuition) in fear of harassment repetition and/or as a result of stress
- Being objectified and humiliated by scrutiny and gossip
- Having one's personal life offered up for public scrutiny—the victim becomes the "accused," and his or her dress, lifestyle, and private life will often come under attack.
- Becoming publicly sexualized (i.e. groups of people "evaluate" the victim to establish if he or she is "worth" the sexual attention or the risk to the harasser's career)
- Defamation of character and reputation
- Loss of trust in environments similar to where the harassment occurred
- Loss of trust in the types of people that occupy similar positions as the harasser or his or her colleagues, especially in case they are not supportive, difficulties or stress on peer relationships, or relationships with colleagues
- Effects on sexual life and relationships: can put extreme stress

upon relationships with significant others, sometimes resulting in divorce

- Weakening of support network, or being ostracized from professional or academic circles (friends, colleagues, or family may distance themselves from the victim, or shun him or her altogether)
- Having to relocate to another city, another job, or another school
- Loss of references/recommendations

Some of the psychological and health effects that can occur in someone who has been sexually harassed as a result of stress and humiliation: depression, anxiety and/or panic attacks, sleeplessness and/or nightmares, shame and guilt, difficulty concentrating, headaches, fatigue or loss of motivation, stomach problems, eating disorders (weight loss or gain), alcoholism, feeling betrayed and/or violated, feeling angry or violent towards the perpetrator, feeling powerless or out of control, increased blood pressure, loss of confidence and self esteem, withdrawal and isolation, overall loss of trust in people, traumatic stress, post-traumatic stress disorder (PTSD), complex post-traumatic stress disorder, suicidal thoughts or attempts, suicide.

Retaliation and Backlash

Retaliation and backlash against a victim are very common, particularly a complainant. Victims who speak out against sexual harassment are often labelled troublemakers who are on their own *power trips,* or who are looking for attention. Similar to cases of rape or sexual assault, *the victim* often becomes *the accused*, with their appearance, private life, and character likely to fall under intrusive scrutiny and attack. They risk hostility and isolation from colleagues, supervisors, teachers, fellow students, and even friends. They may become the targets of mobbing or relational aggression. Women are not necessarily sympathetic to female complainants who have been sexually harassed. If the harasser was male, internalized sexism, and/or jealousy over the sexual attention towards the victim, may encourage some women to react with as much hostility towards the complainant as some male colleagues.

Fear of being targeted for harassment or retaliation themselves may also cause some women to respond with hostility. For example, when Lois Jenson filed her lawsuit against Eveleth Taconite Co., the women placed a hangman's noose above her workplace, and shunned her both at work and in the community—many of these women later joined her suit. (Bingham et al. 2002). Women may even project hostility onto the victim in order to bond with their male coworkers and build trust. Retaliation has occurred when a sexual harassment victim suffers a *negative action* as a result of the harassment. For example, a complainant be given poor evaluations or low grades, have their projects sabotaged, be denied work or academic opportunities, have their work hours cut back, and other actions against them which undermine their productivity, or their ability to advance at work or school, being fired after reporting sexual harassment or leading to unemployment as they may be suspended, asked to resign, or be fired from their jobs altogether.

Retaliation can even involve further sexual harassment, and also stalking and cyberstalking of the victim. Moreover, a school professor or employer accused of sexual harassment, or who is the colleague of a perpetrator, can use their power to see that a victim is never hired again, or never accepted to another school. Of the women who have approached her to share their own experiences of being sexually harassed by their teachers, feminist and writer Naomi Wolf writes,

> "I am ashamed of what I tell them: that they should indeed worry about making an accusation because what they fear is likely to come true. Not one of the women I have heard from had an outcome that was not worse for her than silence. One, I recall, was drummed out of the school by peer pressure. Many faced bureaucratic stonewalling. Some women said they lost their academic status as golden girls overnight; grants dried up, letters of recommendation were no longer forthcoming. No one was met with a coherent process that was not weighted against them. Usually, the key decision-makers in the college or university—especially if it was a private university—joined forces to, in effect, collude with the faculty member accused; to protect not him necessarily but the reputation of the university, and to keep information from surfacing in a way that could protect other women. The goal seemed to be not to provide a balanced forum, but damage control."

Another woman who was interviewed by Helen Watson, a sociologist, reported that, "Facing up to the crime and having to deal with it in public is probably worse than suffering in silence. I found it to be a lot worse than the harassment itself." (Watson, 1994) which directs to the nature of reexperiencing of the situation and baring negativism of group opinion.

Organizations Policies, Procedures, Effects

Most companies have policies against sexual harassment, however these policies are not designed and should not attempt to "regulate romance" which goes against human urges and therefore sexual harassment may always happen. Act upon a report of harassment inside the organization should be:

The investigation should be designed to obtain a prompt and thorough collection of the facts, an appropriate responsive action, and an expeditious report to the complainant that the investigation has been concluded, and, to the full extent appropriate, the action taken.

—Mark I. Schickman, Sexual Harassment.
The employer's role in prevention.
American Bar Association

When organizations do not take the respective satisfactory measures for properly investigating, stress and psychological counselling and guidance, and just deciding of the problem this could lead to:

- Decreased productivity and increased team conflict
- Decreased study / job satisfaction
- Loss of students / staff. Loss of students who leave school and stuff resignations to avoid harassment. Resignations/firings of alleged harassers.
- Decreased productivity and/or increased absenteeism by staff or students experiencing harassment
- Decrease in success at meeting academic and financial goals
- Increased health care costs and sick pay costs because of the health consequences of harassment and/or retaliation
- The knowledge that harassment is permitted can undermine ethical standards and discipline in the organization in general, as staff and/or students lose respect for, and trust in, their seniors who indulge in, or turn a blind eye to, or treat improperly sexual harassment
- If the problem is ignored or not treated properly, a company's or school's image can suffer
- High jury awards for the employee, attorney fees and litigation costs if the problem is ignored or not treated properly (in case of firing the victim) when the complainants are advised to and take the issue to court (Boland 1990).

Studies show that organizational climate (an organization's tolerance, policy, procedure etc.) and workplace environment are essential for understanding the conditions in which sexual harassment is likely to occur, and the way its victims will be affected (yet, research on specific policy and procedure, and awareness strategies is lacking). Another element which increases the risk for sexual harassment is the job's gender context (having few women in the close working environment or practicing in a field which is atypical for women). According to Dr. Orit Kamir, the most effective way to avoid sexual harassment in the work place, and also influence the public's state of mind, is for the employer to adopt a clear policy prohibiting sexual harassment and to make it very clear to their employees.

Many women prefer to make a complaint and to have the matter resolved within the workplace rather than to "air out the dirty laundry" with a public complaint and be seen as a traitor by colleagues, superiors and employers, adds Kamir. Most prefer a pragmatic solution that would stop the harassment and prevent future contact with the harasser rather than turning to the police. More about the difficulty in turning an offence into a legal act can be found in Felstiner & Sarat's (1981) study, which describes three steps a victim (of any dispute) must go through before turning to the justice system: naming – giving the assault a definition, blaming – understanding who is responsible for the violation of rights and facing them, and finally, claiming – turning to the authorities.

Evolution of Sexual Harassment Law in Different Jurisdictions

In India, the case of Vishaka Vs. State of Rajasthan in 1997 has been credited with establishing sexual harassment as illegal. In Israel, the 1988 Equal Employment Opportunity Law made it a crime for an employer to retaliate against an employee who had rejected sexual advances, but it wasn't until 1998 that the Israeli Sexual Harassment Law made such behaviour illegal. (Kamir, 2005). In May 2002, the European Union Council and Parliament amended a 1976 Council Directive on the equal treatment of men and women in employment to prohibit sexual harassment in the workplace, naming it a form of sex discrimination and violation of dignity.

This Directive required all Member States of the European Union to adopt laws on sexual harassment, or amend existing laws to comply with the Directive by October 2005. In 2005, China added new provisions to the *Law on Women's Right Protection* to include sexual harassment. In 2006 "The Shanghai Supplement" was drafted to help further define sexual harassment in China. The United Nations General Recommendation 19 to the Convention on the Elimination of all Forms of Discrimination Against Women defines sexual harassment of women to include:

> "such unwelcome sexually determined behaviour as physical contact and advances, sexually coloured remarks, showing pornography and sexual demands, whether by words or actions. Such conduct can be humiliating and may constitute a health and safety problem; it is discriminatory when the woman has reasonable ground to believe that her objection would disadvantage her in connection with her employment, including recruitment or promotion, or when it creates a hostile working environment."

While such conduct can be harassment of women by men, many laws around the world which prohibit sexual harassment recognize that both men and women may be harassers or victims of sexual harassment. However, most claims of sexual harassment are made by women. There are many similarities, and also important differences in laws and definitions used around the world. After covering one country in some detail (the United States), approaches in other countries are covered alphabetically.

Australia

The Sex Discrimination Act 1984 defines sexual harassment as "... unwanted conduct of a sexual nature, in circumstances in which a reasonable person, having regard to all the circumstances, would have anticipated that the person harassed would be offended, humiliated or intimidated."

Czech Republic

Undesirable behaviour of a sexual nature at the workplace if such conduct is unwelcome, unsuitable or insulting, or if it can be justifiably perceived by the party concerned as a condition for decisions affecting the exercise of rights and obligations ensuring from labour relations.

Denmark

Sexual harassment is defined as, when any verbal, non-verbal or physical action is used to change a victim's sexual status against the will of the victim and resulting in the victim feeling inferior or hurting the victim's dignity. Man and woman are looked upon as equal, and any action trying to change the balance in status with the differences in sex as a tool, is also sexual harassment. In the workplace, jokes, remarks, etc., are only deemed discriminatory if the employer has stated so in their written policy. Women are viewed as being responsible for confronting harassment themselves, such as by slapping the harasser in the face. Law number 1385 of December 21, 2005 regulates this area.

France

Article 222-33 of the French Criminal Code describes sexual harassment as, "The fact of harassing anyone using orders, threats or constraint, in order to obtain favours of a sexual nature, by a person abusing the authority that functions confer on him..." This means the harasser can only be someone with authority on the harassed (basically, there can't be sexual harassment between coworkers of the same rank). However, moral harassment occurs when an employee is subjected to repeated acts (one is not enough) the aim or effect of which may result in a degradation (deterioration) of his conditions of employment that might undermine his rights and his dignity, affect his physical or mental health or jeopardize his professional future. Sexual as well as the moral harassment is recognized by the law.

India

Sexual harassment in India is termed "Eve teasing" and is described as: unwelcome sexual gesture or behaviour whether directly or indirectly as sexually coloured remarks; physical contact and advances; showing pornography; a demand or request for sexual favours; any other unwelcome physical, verbal/non-verbal conduct being sexual in nature. The critical factor is the unwelcomeness of the behaviour, thereby making the impact of such actions on the recipient more relevant rather than intent of the perpetrator.

According to India's constitution, sexual harassment infringes the fundamental right of a woman to gender equality under Article 14 of the Constitution of India and her right to life and live with dignity under Article 21 of the Constitution. Although there is no specific law against sexual harassment at workplace in India but many provisions in other legislations protect against sexual harassment at workplace, such as Section 354, IPC deals with "assault or criminal force to a woman with the intent to outrage her modesty, and Section 509, IPC deals with "word, gesture or act intended to insult the modesty of a woman.

Poland

There is no special provision in the employment law that provides for moral or sexual harassment; however it is commonly accepted by the jurisprudence, that sexual harassment occurs when the employee is subjected to acts of another person in order to obtain favours of a sexual nature. Moral harassment occurs when en employee is subjected to acts which may result in a deterioration of his conditions of employment or undermine his rights and dignity as well as affect his physical or moral health. These definitions are not legal ones, but definitions accepted by the jurisprudence.

Israel

The 1998 Israeli Sexual Harassment Law interprets sexual harassment broadly, and prohibits the behaviour as a discriminatory practice, a restriction of liberty, an offence to human dignity, a violation of every person's right to elementary respect, and an infringement of the right to privacy. Additionally, the law prohibits intimidation or retaliation that accommodates sexual harassment. Intimidation or retaliation thus related to sexual harassment are defined by the law as "prejudicial treatment". (Kamir, 2005)

Pakistan

Pakistan has adopted a Code of Conduct for Gender Justice in the Workplace that will deal with cases of sexual harassment. The Alliance Against Sexual Harassment At workplace (AASHA) announced they would be working with the committee to establish guidelines for the proceedings. AASHA defines sexual harassment much the same as it is defined in the U.S. and other cultures.

Philippines

The Anti-Sexual Harassment Act of 1995 was enacted "primarily to protect and respect the dignity of workers, employees, and applicants for employment as well as students in educational institutions or training centers. This law, consisting of ten sections, provides for a clear definition of work, education or training-related sexual harassment and specifies the acts constituting sexual harassment. It likewise provides for the duties and liabilities of the employer in cases of sexual harassment, and sets penalties for violations of its provisions. It is to be noted that a victim of sexual harassment is not barred from filing a separate and independent action for damages and other relief aside from filing the charge for sexual harassment."

Russia

In the Criminal Code, Russian Federation, (CC RF), there exists a law which prohibits utilization of an office position and material dependence for coercion of sexual interactions (Article 118, current CC RF). However, according to the Moscow Center for Gender Studies, in practice, the courts do not examine these issues. The Daily Telegraph quotes a survey in which "100 per cent of female professionals [in Russia] said they had been subjected to sexual harassment by their bosses, 32 per cent said they had had intercourse with them at least once and another seven per cent claimed to have been raped."

Switzerland

A ban on discrimination was included in the Federal Constitution (Article 4, Paragraph 2 of the old Federal Constitution) in 1981 and adopted in Article 8, paragraph 2 of the revised Constitution. The ban on sexual harassment in the workplace forms part of the Federal Act on Gender Equality (GEA) of 24 March 1995, where it is one of several provisions which prohibit discrimination in employment and which are intended to promote equality. Article 4 of the GEA defines the circumstances, Article 5 legal rights and Article 10 protection against dismissal during the complaints procedure. Article 328, paragraph 1 of the Code of Obligations (OR), Article 198 (2) of the Penal Code (StGB) and Article 6, paragraph 1 of the Employment Act (ArG) contain further statutory provisions on the ban on sexual harassment.

The ban on sexual harassment is intended exclusively for employers, within the scope of their responsibility for protection of legal personality, mental and physical well-being and health. Article 4 of the GEA of 1995 defines sexual harassment in the workplace as follows: "Any behaviour of a sexual nature or other behaviour attributable to gender which affronts the human dignity of males and females in the workplace. This expressly includes threats, the promise of advantages, the application of coercion and the exercise of pressure to achieve an accommodation of a sexual nature."

United Kingdom

The Discrimination Act of 1975, was modified to establish sexual harassment as a form of discrimination in 1986. It states that harassment occurs where there is unwanted conduct on the ground of a person's sex or unwanted conduct of a sexual nature and that conduct has the purpose or effect of violating a person's dignity, or of creating an intimidating, hostile, degrading, humiliating or offensive environment for them. If an employer treats someone less favourably because they have rejected, or submitted to, either form of harassment described above, this is also harassment.

United States

In the US, the Civil Rights Act of 1964 prohibits employment discrimination based on race, sex, colour, national origin or religion. Initially only intended to combat sexual harassment of women,{42 U.S.C. § 2000e-2} the prohibition of sex discrimination covers both females and males. This discrimination occurs when the sex of the worker is made as a condition of employment (i.e. all female waitpersons or male carpenters) or where this is a job requirement that does not mention sex but ends up barring many more persons of one sex than the other from the job (such as height and weight limits). Barnes v. Train (1974) is commonly viewed as the first sexual harassment case in America, even though the term "sexual harassment" was not used. In 1976, Williams v. Saxbe established sexual harassment as a form of sex discrimination when sexual advances by a male supervisor towards a female employee, if proven, would be deemed an artificial barrier to employment placed before one gender and not another. In 1980 the Equal Employment Opportunity Commission (EEOC) issued regulations defining sexual harassment and stating it was a form of sex discrimination prohibited by the Civil Rights Act of 1964.

In the 1986 case of Meritor Savings Bank v. Vinson, the Supreme Court first recognized "sexual harassment" as a violation of Title VII, established the standards for analyzing whether the conduct was welcome and levels of employer liability, and that speech or conduct in itself can create a "hostile environment". The Civil Rights Act of 1991 added provisions to Title VII protections including expanding the rights of women to sue and collect compensatory and punitive damages for sexual discrimination or harassment, and the case of Ellison v. Brady resulted in rejecting the reasonable person standard in favour of the "reasonable woman standard" which allowed for cases to be analyzed from the perspective of the complainant and not the defendant.

Also in 1991, Jenson v. Eveleth Taconite Co. became the first sexual harassment case to be given class action status, paving the way for others. Seven years later, in 1998, this case would establish new precedents for setting limits on the "discovery" process in sexual harassment cases, and allowing psychological injuries from the litigation process to be included in assessing damages awards. In the same year, the courts concluded in Faragher v. City of Boca Raton, Florida, and Burlington v. Ellerth, that employers are liable for harassment by their employees.

Moreover, Oncale v. Sundowner Offshore Services set the precedent for same-sex harassment, and sexual harassment without motivation of "sexual desire", stating that any discrimination based on sex is actionable so long as it places the victim in an objectively disadvantageous working condition, regardless of the gender of either the victim, or the harasser.

In the 2006 case of Burlington Northern & Santa Fe Railway Co. v. White, the standard for retaliation against a sexual harassment complainant was revised to include any adverse employment decision or treatment that would be likely to dissuade a "reasonable worker" from making or supporting a charge of discrimination. During 2007 alone, the U.S. Equal Employment Opportunity Commission and related state agencies received 12,510 new charges of sexual harassment on the job.

Education: Title IX of the Education Amendments of 1972 (United States) states "No person in the United States shall, on the basis of sex, be excluded from participation in, be denied the benefits of, or be subjected to discrimination under any education program or activity receiving Federal financial assistance."

In Franklin v. Gwinnett County Public Schools (1992), the U.S. Supreme Court held that private citizens could collect damage awards when teachers sexually harassed their students. In Bethel School District No. 403 v. Fraser (1986) the courts ruled that schools have the power to discipline students if they use "obscene, profane language or gestures" which could be viewed as substantially interfering with the educational process, and inconsistent with the "fundamental values of public school education." Under regulations issued in 1997 by the U.S. Department of Education, which administers Title IX, school districts should be held responsible for harassment by educators if the harasser "was aided in carrying out the sexual harassment of students by his or her position of authority with the institution." In Davis v. Monroe County Board of Education, and Murrell v. School Dist. No. 1, 1999, schools were assigned liability for peer-to-peer sexual harassment if the plaintiff sufficiently demonstrated that the administration's response shows "deliberate indifference" to "actual knowledge" of discrimination.

There are a number of legal options for a complainant in the U.S.: mediation, filing with the EEOC or filing a claim under a state Fair Employment Practices (FEP) statute (both are for workplace sexual harassment), filing a common law tort, etc. Not all sexual harassment will be considered severe enough to form the basis for a legal claim.

However, most often there are several types of harassing behaviours present, and there is no minimum level for harassing conduct under the law.(Boland, 2002) *Many more experienced sexual harassment than have a solid legal case against the accused.* Because of this, and the common preference for settling, few cases ever make it to federal court. The section below "EEOC Definition" describes the legal definitions that have been created for sexual harassment in the workplace. Definitions similar to the EEOC defnition have been created for academic environments in the U.S. Department of Education Sexual Harassment Guidance.

EEOC Definition

The Equal Employment Opportunity Commission claims that it is unlawful to harass an applicant or employee of any sex in the work place. The harassment could include sexual harassment. The EEOC says that the victim and harasser could be any gender and that the other does not have to be of the opposite sex. The law does not ban offhand comments, simple teasing, or incidents that aren't very serious. If the harassment gets to the point where it creates a harsh work environment, it will be taken care of. In 1980, the Equal Employment Opportunity Commission produced a set of guidelines for defining and enforcing Title VII (in 1984 it was expanded to include educational institutions).

The EEOC defines sexual harassment as: Unwelcome sexual advances, requests for sexual favours, or other verbal or physical conduct of a sexual nature when:

1. Submission to such conduct was made either explicitly or implicitly a term or condition of an individual's employment,
2. Submission to or rejection of such conduct by an individual was used as the basis for employment decisions affecting such individual, or
3. Such conduct has the purpose or effect of unreasonably interfering with an individual's work performance or creating an intimidating, hostile, or offensive working environment.

1. and 2. are called "quid pro quo" (Latin for "this for that" or "something for something"). They are essentially "sexual bribery", or promising of benefits, and "sexual coercion".

Type 3. known as "hostile work environment," is by far the most common form. This form is less clear cut and is more subjective.

Note: a workplace harassment complainant *must* file with the EEOC and receive a "right to sue" clearance, before they can file a lawsuit against a company in federal court. (Boland, 2002)

Sex discrimination discrimination can take two forms, either 1) "Hostile Work Environment Harassment" or 2) "Quid Pro Quo Harassment."

Quid Pro Quo Sexual Harassment

Quid pro quo means "this for that". In the workplace, this occurs when a job benefit is directly tied to an employee submitting to unwelcome sexual advances. For example, a supervisor promises an employee a raise if he or she will go out on a date with him or her, or tells an employee he or she will be fired if he or she doesn't sleep with him or her. Quid pro quo harassment also occurs when an employee makes an evaluative decision, or provides or withholds professional opportunities based on another employee's submission to verbal, nonverbal or physical conduct of a sexual nature. Quid pro quo harassment is equally unlawful whether the victim resists and suffers the threatened harm or submits and thus avoids the threatened harm.

Hostile Environment Sexual Harassment

This occurs when an employee is subjected to comments of a sexual nature, unwelcome physical contact, or offensive sexual materials as a regular part of the work environment. For the most part, a single isolated incident will not be enough to prove hostile environment harassment unless it involves extremely outrageous and egregious conduct. The courts will try to decide whether the conduct is both "serious" and "frequent." Supervisors, managers, co-workers and even customers can be responsible for creating a hostile environment. Probably the most famous hostile environment sexual harassment case to date is Jenson v. Eveleth Taconite Co. which inspired the movie *North Country (film)*.

The line between "quid pro quo" and "hostile environment" harassment is not always clear and the two forms of harassment often occur together. For example, an employee's job conditions are affected when a sexually hostile work environment results in a constructive discharge. At the same time, a supervisor who makes sexual advances toward a subordinate employee may communicate an implicit threat to retaliate against her if she does not comply. "Hostile environment" harassment may acquire characteristics of "quid pro quo" harassment if the offending supervisor abuses his authority over employment decisions to force the victim to endure or participate in the sexual conduct.

Sexual harassment may culminate in a retaliatory discharge if a victim tells the harasser or her employer she will no longer submit to the harassment, and is then fired in retaliation for this protest. Under these circumstances it would be appropriate to conclude that both harassment and retaliation in violation of section 704(a) of Title VII have occurred."

Gender discrimination: Gender discrimination is a subset of sex discrimination. It is often non-sexual but is nonetheless directed at a person because of that person's sex. Examples of discriminatory comments and behaviours include employers:

- Asking whether an employment candidate is married or plans on having children;
- Making reference to an employee "PMS"ing;
- Claiming that a woman should be more feminine and wear makeup; Claiming that a person isn't fulfilling certain gender role;
- Calling an effeminate male a "fairy," or "prissy" or stating that he should 'act more like a man;'
- Refusing to hire a man in a "woman's job" and vice versa;
- Retaliating against an employee for assisting in or cooperating with an investigation or lawsuit based upon gender discrimination.

Sexual Orientation Discrimination: There are no federal laws against discrimination against employees of a certain sexual orientation. However, Executive Order 13087, signed by President Bill Clinton, outlaws discrimination against workers of a different sexual orientation in federal government. If a small business owner owns his or her business in a state where there is a law against sexual orientation discrimination, the owner must abide to the law regardless of there not being a federal law. Twenty states and the District of Columbia have a law against this form of discrimination in the workplace.

These states include California, Connecticut, Colorado, Hawaii, Illinois, Iowa, Maine, Maryland, Massachusetts, Minnesota, Nevada, New Hampshire, New Jersey, New Mexico, New York, Oregon, Rhode Island, Vermont, Washington, and Wisconsin. For example, California has laws in place to protect employees who may have been discriminated against based upon sexual orientation or perceived sexual orientation. California law prohibits discrimination against those "with traits not stereotypically associated with their gender," such as mannerisms, appearance, speech, etc. Sexual orientation discrimination comes up, for instance, when employers enforce a dress code, permit women to wear makeup but not men, or require men and women to only use restrooms designated for their particular sex regardless of whether they are transgendered.

Retaliation: Retaliation has occurred when an employee suffers a *negative action* after he or she has made a report of sexual harassment, file a grievance, assist someone else with a complaint, or participate in discrimination prevention activities. Negative actions can include being fired, demotion, suspension, denial of promotion, poor evaluation, unfavourable job re-assignment—any adverse employment decision or treatment that would be likely to dissuade a "reasonable worker" from making or supporting a charge of discrimination. Retaliation is as illegal as the sexual harassment itself, but also as difficult to prove. Also, retaliation is illegal even if the original charge of sexual harassment was not proven.

A Critical Appraisal

It is pertinent to note that though the phrase "sexual harassment" is generally acknowledged to include clearly damaging and morally deplorable behaviour, its boundaries can be broad and controversial. Accordingly, misunderstandings can abound. Moreover, sexual harassment law has been highly criticized by experts, such as the criminal defense lawyer Alan Dershowitz and the legal writer and libertarian Eugene Volokh, for imposing on the right to free speech. Prof. in organizational studies Jana Raver from the Queen's School of Business criticized sexual harassment policy in the Ottawa Business Journal as helping maintain archaic stereotypes of women as "delicate, asexual creatures" who require special protection when at the same time complaints are lowering company profits. Camille Paglia says that young girls can end up acting in such ways as to make sexual harassment easier, such that for example, by acting "nice" they can become a target. Paglia commented in an interview with Playboy, "Realize the degree to which your niceness may invoke people to say lewd and pornographic things to you—sometimes to violate your niceness.

The more you blush, the more people want to do it." Other critics assert that sexual harassment is a very serious problem, but current views focus too heavily on sexuality rather than on the type of conduct that undermines the ability of women or men to work together effectively. Viki Shultz, a law professor at Yale University comments, "Many of the most prevalent forms of harassment are designed to maintain work-particularly the more highly rewarded lines of work-as bastions of male competence and authority." Feminist Jane Gallop sees this evolution of the definition of sexual harassment as coming from a "split" between what she calls "power feminists" who are pro-sex (like herself) and what she calls "victim feminists," who are not.

She argues that the split has helped lead to a *perversion* of the definition of sexual harassment, which used to be about sexism but has come to be about anything that's sexual. (Gallop, 1997). There is also concern over abuses of sexual harassment policy by individuals as well as by employers and administrators using false and/or frivolous accusations as a way of expelling employees they want to eliminate for other reasons. Plus these employees often have virtually no recourse thanks to the at-will law in most US states. (Westhues, 1998).

O'Donohue and Bowers outlined 14 possible pathways to false allegations of sexual harassment: "lying, borderline personality disorder, histrionic personality disorder, psychosis, gender prejudice, substance abuse, dementia, false memories, false interpretations, biased interviews, sociopathy, personality disorders not otherwise specified." There is also discussion of whether some recent trends towards more revealing clothing and permissive habits have created a more sexualized general environment, in which some forms of communication are unfairly labelled harassment, but are simply a reaction to greater sexualization in everyday environments. There are many debates about how organizations should deal with sexual harassment.

Some observers feel strongly that organizations should be held to a zero tolerance standard of "Must report - must investigate - must punish." Others write that those who feel harassed should in most circumstances have a choice of options.

REFERENCES

Bingham, Clara, Gansler, Laura Leedy. *Class Action: The Landmark Case that Changed Sexual Harassment Law*. New York, Anchor Books, 2002.

Boland, Mary L. *Sexual Harassment: Your Guide to Legal Action*. Naperville, Illinois: Sphinx Publishing, 2002.

Dziech, Billie Wright, Weiner, Linda. *The Lecherous Professor: Sexual Harassment on Campus*. Chicago Illinois: University of Illinois Press, 1990.

Gallop, Jane. *Feminist Accused of Sexual Harassment*. Duke University Press, 1997.

Harper, Colin. *My Uncontrollable Urges*. Bridge Publications, 1998.

Harper, Colin. *Why I can't take 'no' for an answer...* Bridge Publications, 2001.

Heyman, R. (1994). Why Didn't You Say That in the First Place? San Francisco: Jossey-Bass Publishers.

Kamir, Orit. "Israel's 1998 Sexual Harassment Law: Prohibiting Sexual Harassment, Sexual Stalking, and Degradation Based on Sexual Orientation in the Workplace and in all Social Settings." *International Journal of Discrimination and Law,* 2005, 7, 315-336.

Koss, Mary P. "Changed Lives: The Psychological Impact of Sexual Harassment." in Paludi, Michele A. ed. *Ivory Power: Sexual Harassment On Campus.* Albany, NY, State University of New York Press, 1987.

Langelan, Martha. *Back Off: How to Confront and Stop Sexual Harassment and Harassers*. Fireside, 1993.

Patai, Daphne. *Heterophobia: Sexual Harassment and the Future of Feminism*. Lanham: Rowman and Littlefield, 1999.

Roberts S., Barry Mann A., Richard- "Sexual Harassment In The Workplace: A PRIMER".

Rowe, Mary & Corinne Bendersky, "Workplace Justice, Zero Tolerance, and Zero Barriers," 2001, in Negotiations and Change, From the Workplace to Society, Thomas Kochan and Richard Locke (editors), Cornell University Press, 2002.

Rowe,Mary "People Who Feel Harassed Need a Complaint System with both Formal and Informal Options," in Negotiation Journal, April, 1990, Vol. 6, No. 2, pp. 161–172.

Rowe,Mary, "Dealing with Harassment: A Systems Approach," in Sexual Harassment: Perspectives, Frontiers, and Response Strategies, Women & Work, Vol. 5, Margaret Stockdale, editor, Sage Publications, 1996, pp. 241–271.

Watson, Helen. "Red herrings and mystifications: Conflicting perceptions of sexual harassment," in Brant, Clare, and Too, Yun Lee, eds., *Rethinking Sexual Harassment*. Boulder, Colorado, Pluto Press, 1994.

Westhues, Kenneth. *Eliminating Professors: A Guide to the Dismissal Process*. Lewiston, NY: The Edwin Mellen Press, 1998.

2

Introduction to Status and Attitude of Working Women

> "Courage means to keep working a relationship, to continue seeking solutions to difficult problems, and to stay focused during stressful periods."
>
> —*Denis Waitley*

It is pertinent to note that until modern industrialized times, legal and cultural practices, combined with the inertia of longstanding religious and educational traditions, had restricted women's entry and participation in the workforce. Economic dependency upon men, and consequently the poor socio-economic status of women had also restricted their entry into the workforce. Particularly as occupations have become professionalized over the 19th and 20th centuries, women's access to higher education had effectively excluded them from the practice of well-paid and high status occupations. Entry of women into the higher professions like law and medicine was delayed in most countries due to women being denied entry to universities and qualification for degrees. For example, Cambridge

University only fully validated degrees for women late in 1947, and even then only after much opposition and acrimonious debate.

Such factors had largely limited women to low-paid and poor status occupations for most of the 19th and 20th centuries. However, through the 20th century, public perceptions of paid work shifted as the workforce increasingly moved to office jobs that do not require heavy labour, and women increasingly acquired the higher education that led to better-compensated, longer-term careers rather than lower-skilled, shorter-term jobs. Restrictions on women's access to and participation in the workforce include the wage gap and the glass ceiling, inequities most identified with industrialized nations with nominal equal opportunity laws; legal and cultural restrictions on access to education and jobs, inequities most identified with developing nations; and unequal access to capital, variable but identified as a difficulty in both industrialized and developing nations.

Although access to paying occupations (the "workforce") has been and remains unequal in many occupations and places around the world, scholars sometimes distinguish between "work" and "paying work," including in their analysis a broader spectrum of labour such as uncompensated household work, childcare, eldercare, and family subsistence farming. It must be remembered that division of labour by gender has been particularly studied in women's studies (especially women's history, which has frequently examined the history and biography of women's participation in particular fields) and gender studies more broadly. Occupational studies, such as the history of medicine or studies of professionalization, also examine questions of gender, and the roles of women in the history of particular fields.

In addition, modern civil rights law has frequently examined gender restrictions of access to a field of occupation; gender discrimination within a field; and gender harassment in particular workplaces. This body of law is called employment discrimination law, and gender and race discrimination are the largest sub-sections within the area. Laws specifically aimed at preventing discrimination against women have been passed in many countries; see, e.g., the Pregnancy Discrimination Act in the United States.

Status of Working Women

It is pertinent to note that 1870 US Census was the first US Census to count "Females engaged in each occupation" and provides an intriguing snapshot of women's history. It reveals that, contrary to popular belief, not all American women of the Victorian period were either idle in their middle class homes or working in sweatshops. Women were 15% of the total work force (1.8 million out of 12.5). They made up one-third of factory "operatives," but teaching and the occupations of dressmaking, millinery, and tailoring played a larger role. Two-thirds of teachers were women. Women could also be found in such unexpected places as iron and steel works (495), mines (46), sawmills (35), oil wells and refineries (40), gas works (4), and charcoal kilns (5) and held such surprising jobs as ship rigger (16), teamster (196), turpentine labourer (185), brass founder/ worker (102), shingle and lathe maker (84), stock-herder (45), gun and locksmith (33), hunter and trapper (2).

In the beginning of the 20th century women were regarded as the guardians of morality; they were seen as made finer than men and were expected to act as such their role was not defined as workers or money makers. Women were expected to hold on to their innocence until the right man came along so that they can start a family and inculcate that morality they were in charge of preserving. Yet at the turn of the 20th century, a civil war changed America was now educating their women more and more. By 1900, four out of five colleges accepted women and a whole coed concept was becoming more and more accepted.

In the United States, it was World War I that made space for women in the workforce amongst other economical and social influences. Due to the rise in demand for production from Europe during the raging war, women found themselves working outside the home. In the first quarter of the century, women mostly occupied jobs in factory work or as domestic servants, as the war come to an end they were able to move on to such jobs as: salespeople in department stores as well as clerical, secretarial and other, what is called, "lace-collar" jobs. In July 1920, *The New York Times* ran a head line that read: "the American Woman ... has lifted her skirts far beyond any modest limitation" which could apply to more than just fashion; women were now rolling up their sleeves and skirts and making their way into the workforce. World War II allowed for millions of jobs for women.

Thousands of women actually joined the military: 140,000 in the Women's Army Corps (United States Army) WAC; 100,000 in the Navy (WAVE); 23,000 in the Marines; 14,000 in the Navy Nurse Corps and, 13,000 in the Coast Guard. Although almost none saw combat, they replaced men in non combative positions and got the same pay as the men would have on the same job. At the same time over 16 million men left their jobs to join the war in Europe and elsewhere, opening even more opportunities and places for women to take over in the job force. Remarkably, the increase of women in the labour force gained momentum in the late 19th century. At this point women married early on and were defined by their marriages. If they entered the workforce it was only out of necessity.

The first phase encompasses the time between the late 19th century to the 1930s. This era gave birth to the 'Independent female worker.' From 1890-1930, women in the workforce were typically young and unmarried. They had little or no learning on the job and typically held clerical and teaching positions. Many women also worked in textile manufacturing or as domestics. Women promptly exited the work force when they were married, unless the family needed two incomes. Towards the end of the 1920s, as we enter into the second phase, married women begin to exit the work force less and less. Labour force productivity for married women 35–44 years of age increase by 15.5 percentage points from 10% to 25%.

There was a greater demand for clerical positions and as the number of women graduating high school increased they began to hold more 'respectable', steady jobs. This phase has been appropriately labelled as the Transition Era referring to the time period between 1930-1950. During this time the discriminatory institution of marriage bars, which forced women out of the work force after marriage, were eliminated, allowing more participation in the work force of single and married women. Additionally, women's labour force participation increased because there was an increase in demand for office workers and women participated in the high school movement. However, still women's work was contingent upon their husband's income. Women did not normally work to fulfill a personal need to define ones career and social worth; they worked out of necessity.

In the third phase, labelled the "roots of the revolution" encompassing the time from 1950- mid-to-late 1970s, the movement began to approach the warning signs of a revolution. Women's expectations of future employment changed. Women began to see themselves going on to college and working through their marriages and even attending graduate school. Many however still had brief and intermittent work force participation, without necessarily having expectations for a 'career'. To illustrate, most women were secondary earners, and worked in "pink collar jobs" as secretaries, teachers, nurses, and librarians. Although more women attended college, it was often expected that they attended to find a spouse—the so-called "M.R.S. degree".

Nevertheless, Labour force participation by women still grew significantly. The fourth phase, known as The Quiet Revolution, began in the late 1970s and continues on today. Beginning in the 1970s women began to flood colleges and grad schools. They began to enter profession like medicine, law, dental and business. More women were going to college and expected to be employed at the age of 35, as opposed to past generations that only worked intermittently due to marriage and childbirth. This increase in expectations of long-term gainful employment is reflected in the change of majors adopted by women from the 1970s on. The percentage of women majoring in education declined beginning in the 1970s; education was once a popular major for women since it allowed them to step into and out of the labour force when they had children and when their children grew up to a reasonable age at which their mothers did not have to serve primarily as caretakers.

Instead, majors such as business and management were on the rise in the 1970s, as women ventured into other fields that were once predominated by men. They experienced an expansion of their horizons and an alteration of what it meant to define their own identity. Women worked before they got married, and since women were marrying younger they were able to define themselves prior to a serious relationship. The reasons for this big jump in the 1970s has been attributed by some scholars to widespread access to the birth control pill. While "the pill" was medically available in the 1960s, numerous laws restricted access to it. See, e.g., *Griswold v. Connecticut*, 381 U.S. 479 (1965) (overturning a Connecticut statute barring access to contraceptives) and *Eisenstadt v. Baird*, 405 U.S. 438 (1972) (establishing the right of unmarried people to access contraception). By the 1970s, the age of majority had been lowered from 21 to 18 in the United States, largely as a consequence of the Vietnam War; this also affected women's right to effect their own medical decisions.

Since it had now become socially acceptable to postpone pregnancy even while married women had the luxury of thinking about other things, like education and work. Also, due to electrification women's work around the house became easier leaving them with more time to be able to dedicate to school or work. Due to the multiplier effect, even if some women were not blessed with access to the pill or electrification, many followed by the example of the other women entering the work force for those reasons. The Quiet Revolution is called such because it was not a "big bang" revolution; rather, it happened and is continuing to happen gradually.

Women in Decision-making

It is significant to mention that female decision-makers from around Europe are organized in several national and European wide networks. The networks aim to promote women in decision-making positions in politics and the economy across Europe. These networks were founded in the 1980s and are often very different from the "service clubs" founded in the early days of the century, like Soroptimist and Zontas. "Women in Management" is about women in business in usually male-dominated areas. Their motivation, their ideas and leadership styles and their ability to enter into leadership positions is the subject of most of the different networks.

As of 2009, women represented 20.9% of parliament in Europe (both houses) and 18.4% world average. As of 2009, 90 women serve in the U.S. Congress: 18 women serve in the Senate, and 73 women serve in the House. In the private sector, men still represent 9 out of 10 board members in European blue-chip companies, The discrepancy is widest at the very top: only 3% of these companies have a woman presiding over the highest decision-making body. List of members of the European Network of Women in Decision-making in Politics and the Economy:

- Committee of Women Elected Representatives of Local and Regional Authorities (Council of European Municipalities and Regions)
- BPW Europe, Business and Professional Women – Europe
- Association of Organizations of Mediterranean Businesswomen
- Eurochambres Women's Network
- European Platform of Women Scientists
- Network of Parliamentary Committees for Equal Opportunities for Women and Men in the European Union
- European Network to Promote Women's Entrepreneurship
- European women's lobby
- European Women's Lawyers Association
- CEE Network for Gender Issues
- European Women Inventors and Innovators Network
- European Women's Management Development International Network, EWMD
- Femanet - Eurocadres
- European Professional Women's Network, EPWN
- Women's Forum for the Economy and the Society

The EU Commission has created a platform for all these networks. It also funded the Women to the Top program in 2003-2005 to bring more women into top management. Some organizations have been created to promote the presence of women in top responsibilities, in politics and business. One example is EWMD European women's Management

Development (cited above), a European and international network of individual and corporate members, drawn from professional organizations.

Members are from all areas of business, education, politics and culture. Women who are born into the upper class rather than the middle or lower class have a much better chance at holding higher positions of power in the work force if they choose to enter it.

Barriers to Equal Participation

As gender roles have followed the formation of agricultural and then industrial societies, newly developed professions and fields of occupation have been frequently inflected by gender. Some examples of the ways in which gender affects a field include:

- Prohibitions or restrictions on members of a particular gender entering a field or studying a field;
- Discrimination within a field, including wage, management, and prestige hierarchies;
- Expectation that mothers, rather than fathers, should be the primary childcare providers.

Note that these gender restrictions may not be universal in time and place, and that they operate to restrict both men and women. However, in practice, norms and laws have historically restricted women's access to particular occupations; civil rights laws and cases have thus primarily focused on equal access to and participation by *women* in the workforce. These barriers may also be manifested in hidden bias and by means of many microinequities.

Access to Capital

Women's access to occupations requiring capital outlays is also hindered by their unequal access (statistically) to capital; this affects occupations such as entrepreneur and small business owner, farm ownership, and investor. Numerous microloan programs attempt to redress this imbalance, targeting women for loans or grants to establish start-up businesses or farms, having determined that aid targeted to women can disproportionately benefit a nation's economy. While research has shown that women cultivate more than half the world's food — in sub-Saharan Africa and the Caribbean, women are responsible for up to 80% of food production — most such work is family subsistence labour, and often the family property is legally owned by the men in the family.

Access to Education

A number of occupations became "professionalized" through the 19th and 20th centuries, gaining regulatory bodies, and passing laws or regulations requiring particular higher educational requirements. As women's access to higher education was often limited, this effectively restricted women's participation in these professionalizing occupations. For instance, women were completely forbidden access to Cambridge University until 1868, and were encumbered with a variety of restrictions until 1987 when the university adopted an equal opportunity policy. Numerous other institutions in the United States and Western Europe began opening their doors to women over the same period of time, but access to higher education remains a significant barrier to women's full participation in the workforce in developing countries. Even where access to higher education is formally available, women's access to the full range of occupational choices is significantly limited where access to primary education is limited through social custom.

Discrimination Within Occupations

The idea that men and women are naturally suited for different occupations is known as horizontal segregation. Statistical discrimination in the workplace is unintentional discrimination based on the presumed probability that a worker will or will not remain with the company for a long period of time. Specific to women, since employers believe that women are more likely to drop out of the labour force to have kids, or work part time while they are raising kids, this tends to hurt their chances for job advancement.

They are passed up for promotions because of the possibility that they may leave, and are in some cases placed in positions with little opportunity for upward mobility to begin with based on these same stereotypes. Women earn less money than men, despite establishing equal pay laws.

Network Discrimination

Part of the problem keeping women out of the highest paying, most prestigious positions is that they have historically not held these positions. As a result, recruiters for these high-status jobs are predominantly white males, and tend to hire similar people in their networks. Their networks are made up of mostly white males from the same socio-economic status, which helps perpetuate their over-representation in the best jobs.

Actions and Inactions of Women Themselves

Through a process known as employee clustering, employees tend to be grouped throughout the workplace both spatially and socially with those of a similar status job. Women are no exception and tend to be grouped with other women making comparable amounts of money. They compare wages with the women around them and believe their salaries are fair because they are average. Some women are content with their lack of wage equality with men in the same positions because they are unaware of just how vast the inequality is. Furthermore, women as a whole tend to be less assertive and confrontational. One of the factors contributing to the higher proportion of raises going to men is the simple fact that men tend to ask for raises more often than women, and are more aggressive when doing so.

Gender and Women's History in Particular Occupations

Choice of occupation is considered to be one of the key factors contributing to the male-female wage differential. In other words, careers with a majority of female employees tend to pay less than careers that employ a majority of males. This is different from direct wage discrimination within occupations, as males in the female dominated professions will also make lower than average wages and the women in the male dominated occupations usually make higher than average wages. The occupational dissimilarity index is a measure from 0 to 100; it measures the percent of labourers that would need to be rearranged into a job typically done by the opposite sex in order for the wage differential to disappear. In 1960, the dissimilarity index in America was measured at 62. It has dropped since then, but at 47 in 2000, is still one of the highest of any developed nation.

Women's Participation in Different Occupations

below are a list of encyclopedia article links detailing women's historical involvement in various occupations.

- Sciences - See generally Women in science and List of female scientists
    - Women in computing
    - Women in engineering
    - Women in geology
    - List of female mathematicians
- Medical professions - See generally Women in medicine
- Legal professions - See generally Women in the United States judiciary

Though women comprise approximately half of the student body of American law schools, they represent only 17% of partners at major law firms and less than a quarter of tenured law professors. Similarly, on the national level, we have had only one female U.S. Attorney General, three female Secretaries of State, two women Supreme Court Justices, and one acting Solicitor General.

- Arts, writing, media, sports and entertainment
  - o Women artists (visual arts)
  - o Women Surrealists
  - o Performing arts
    - Vulcana Women's Circus (organization for women in the circus)
  - o Writing
    - Women's writing in English
    - Women in journalism and media professions
    - List of female rhetoricians
    - List of early-modern women playwrights (UK)
    - List of female poets
  - o Film
    - List of female film and television directors
    - Women's cinema (discusses women screenwriters & directors)
  - o Music
    - Female composers in the United States during the 20th century
    - Women composers of Catholic music
    - List of female composers
    - List of female composers by name
    - List of female film score composers
  - o Sports
    - Women's professional sports
    - Women's sports and browse the category
- Humanities:
  - o Women in philosophy and List of female philosophers
- Crime: Women in piracy
- Government: Women in politics
- Military:
  - o Women in the military
  - o Women in the military by country, in Europe, and in the Americas

- o History of women in the military; Timeline of women in ancient warfare; Timeline of Women in Medieval warfare
- o List of women warriors in folklore, literature, and popular culture
- o Category:Female military personnel;
- o Women's Land Army;
- o Category:Female wartime spies

Gender Inequality in the Different Social Classes

In the last 50 years we have experienced great changes toward gender equality in America. With the feminist movement of the 1960s, women began to enter the workforce in great numbers. Women had also had high labour market participation during World War II as so many male soldiers were away, women had to take up jobs to support their family and keep their local economy on track.

Many of these women dropped right back out of the labour force when the men returned home from war to raise children born in the generation of the baby boomers. In the late 1960s when women began entering the labour force in record numbers, they were entering in addition to all of the men, as opposed to substituting for men during the war. This dynamic shift from the one-earner household to the two-earner household dramatically changed the socioeconomic class system of this country. The addition of women into the workforce was one of the key factors that has decreased social mobility over the last 50 years. Female children of the middle and upper classes had increased access to higher education, and thanks to job equality, were able to attain higher-paying and higher-prestige jobs than ever before. Due to the dramatic increase in availability of birth control, these high status women were able to delay marriage and child-bearing until they had completed their education and advanced their careers to their desired positions. In 2001, the survey on sexual harassment at workplace conducted by women's nonprofit organization Sakshi among 2,410 respondents in government and non-government sectors, in five States recorded 53 per cent saying that both sexes don't get equal opportunities, 50 per cent women are treated unfairly by employers and co-workers, 59 per cent have heard sexist remarks or jokes, 32 per cent have been exposed to pornography or literature degrading women.

In comparison with other sectors, IT organizations may be offering equal salaries to women and the density of women in technology companies may be relatively high but this does not necessarily ensure a level playing field. For example Microsoft (U.S.) was sued because of the conduct of one of its supervisors over e-mail. The supervisor allegedly made sexually offensive comments via e-mail, such as referring to himself as “president of the amateur gynecology club.” He also allegedly referred to the plaintiff as the “Spandex Queen. E-harassment is not the sole form of harassment. In 1999, Juno Online faced two separate suits from former employees who alleged that they were told that they would be fired if they broke off their ongoing relationships with senior executives. Pseudo Programs, a Manhattan-based Internet TV network, was sued in January 2000 after male employees referred to female employees as “bimbos” and forced them to look at sexually explicit material on the Internet.

In India HR managers admit that women are discriminated against for senior Board positions and pregnant women are rarely given jobs but only in private. Recently a sexual harassment suit against a senior member shocked the Indian IT sector. Recognising the invisible nature of power structures that marginalise women at the workplace, the Supreme Court in the landmark Vaishaka versus High Court of Rajasthan (1997) identified sexual harassment as violative of the women’s right to equality in the workplace and enlarged the ambit of its definition. The judgment equates a hostile work environment on the same plane as a direct request for sexual favours. To quote: “Sexual harassment includes such unwelcome sexually determined behaviour (whether directly or by implication) as: physical contact and advances; a demand or request for sexual favours; sexually coloured remarks; showing pornography; any other unwelcome physical, verbal or non-verbal conduct of sexual nature”. The judgement mandates appropriate work conditions should be provided for work, leisure, health, and hygiene to further ensure that there is no hostile environment towards women at the workplace and no woman employee should have reasonable grounds to believe that she is disadvantaged in connection with her employment.

This law thus squarely shifts the onus onto the employer to ensure employee safety but most mid-sized Indian service technology companies are yet to enact sexual harassment policies. Admits K Chandan, an advocate from Chandan Associates, “I have a few IT clients. When I point to the need for a sexual harassment policy, most tend to overlook or ignore it. Its not high on the agenda.” An HR Manager of India’s premier technology companies rues: “I am going to use the recent case to push the policy through. Earlier the draft proposal was rejected by the company.” Yet another HR manager from a flagship company of India’s leading business house, oblivious to the irony of her statement, admitted that the company had a grievance redressal mechanism but no sexual harassment policy in place.

The lax attitudes transgress the Supreme Court judgment wherein the Court not only defined sexual harassment, but also laid down a code of conduct for workplaces to prevent and punish it, "Employers or other responsible authorities in public or private sectors must comply with the following guidelines: Express prohibition of sexual harassment should be notified and circulated; private employers should include prohibition of sexual harassment in the standing orders under the Industrial Employment (Standing Orders) Act, 1946." As for the complaint procedure, not less than half of its members should be women. The complaint committee should include an NGO or other organization that is familiar with the issue of sexual harassment. When the offence amounts to misconduct under service rules, appropriate disciplinary action should be initiated. When such conduct amounts to an offence under the Indian Penal Code, the employer shall initiate action by making a complaint with the appropriate authority.

However, the survey by Sakshi revealed 58 per cent of women were not aware of the Supreme Court guidelines on the subject. A random survey by AssureConsulting.com among hundred employees working in the IT industry revealed startling results: Less than 10 per cent were familiar with the law or the company's sexual harassment policy. Surprisingly, certain HR managers were also ignorant of the Supreme Court guidelines or the Draft Bill by the National Commission of Women against sexual harassment at the workplace. Not surprisingly many cases go unreported. However given the complexities involved, company policy is the first step and cannot wish away the problem. Says Savita HR Manager at Icelerate Technologies, "We have a sexual harassment policy that is circulated among employees.

Also the company will not tolerate any case that comes to its notice. But the man at home is no different from the person at the office," thus implying the social mindset that discriminates against women is responsible for the problem. Considering sexual censorship and conservative social attitudes emphasising " woman's purity," the victim dare not draw attention for fear of being branded a woman with "loose morals". Women would rather brush away the problem or leave jobs quietly rather than speak up, even in organizations that have a zero tolerance policy. Says Chandan, "I do not have exact statistics but from my experience as an advocate one in 1,500 cases are reported." The problem cannot be resolved till more women speak up but the social set-up browbeats women into silence.

The social stigma against the victim and the prolonged litigation process for justice thwarts most women from raising their voice. Purports K Chandan "It may take between three and five years to settle a case, and in a situation where the harassment is covert, evidence is hard to gather and there is no guarantee that the ruling would be in favour of the victim. In one of the rare cases I handled a Country Manager was accused and the plaintiff opted for an out of court settlement." The dice is, thus, heavily loaded against women. Claims of new age companies of creating liberal and egalitarian workplaces are under serious examination. Companies can come clear by adopting a zero tolerance policy against sexism of any form. Probably the recent publicised case may just about drive companies to do so.

Effects of Women in the Workforce on the Working and Lower Classes

While middle and upper class women benefited from entering the workforce and the feminism movement, working and lower class women suffered. Women in lower wage jobs are more likely to be subject to wage discrimination. They are more likely to bring home far less than their male counterparts with equal job status, and get far less help with housework from their husbands than the high-earning women. Women with low educational attainment entering the workforce in mass quantity lowered earnings for some men, as the women brought about a lot more job competition. The lowered relative earnings of the men and increase in birth control made marriage prospects harder for lower income women. For the first time in the history of this country, there were distinctive socioeconomic stratification among women as there has been among men for centuries.

This deepened the inequality between the upper/middle and lower/ working classes. Prior to the feminist movement, the socioeconomic status of a family was based almost solely on the husband/father's occupation. Women who were now attaining high status jobs were attractive partners to men with high status jobs, so the high earners married the high earners and the low earners married the low earners. In other words, the rich got richer and the poor stayed the same, and have had increased difficulty competing in the economy.

STATUS AND ATTITUDE OF WORKING WOMEN

> "Marriage is a self-service cafeteria. You pick what you like and then you see what the other chap's got and you wish you had that, too."

It is pertinent to note that the employment of women has brought mixed reaction both from professional and lay persons. It is common knowledge that social changes evoke sometimes more negative than positive emotions. In regard to the employment of women, even social scientists, for the most part, took a negative view. Psychatrists gave negative comments.

Lundberg and Farnham expressed a particularly pessimistic evaluation. Some sociologists also tended to lump the increased employment of women along with other trends, such as higher divorce rates, more crime and delinquency.

Others, such as Bossard took a strong negative position contending that such employment was gravely detrimental to children. Many a people alert for a simple explanation of the numerous and complex social problems, speculated that the employment of women was the principal cause of current social problems. It was proposed that women should be forced out of employment. A very small number of sociologists such as Komarovsky and Landis favoured changes. In the absence of sufficient empirical data, it is, however, difficult to say anything definitely.

Only recently there have been some serious efforts to examine empirically the attitude and related aspects about women's employment. The enquiry described in these pages is designed to elicit the opinion of working women about some aspects of their life, their attitude towards working and related matters and also to assess the attitudes of their family members, relatives and neighbours to their employment in terms of the perception of the working women themselves. The question that comes up is: what is, on the whole, women's reaction to their dual role? Do they feel harrassed or not? The study commences with the understanding of the position of working women in their families.

In this investigation, women respondents were asked about their position in two respects; namely, (a) their status in the family and (b) in matters of finance. The first question asked, therefore, was: "what would you say are the main differences your job has made to you in your family?" The answers to this questions are largely in favour of the status quo (fifty-seven per cent). A very large percentage (eighty-two per cent) of the semi-skilled working women felt that there was no change in their status, smallest being the percentage of the low-professionals (46.5%). It is presumably because of their low income that, on the whole, no change was perceived. Klein mentioned that in her study, only twenty-seven per cent of the women reported that job made no difference. A little more than two-fifths of them mentioned improvement in status in the family (42.5%).

In addition to the women employed in N.C.C., a relatively larger section of the low-professionals closely followed by professionals reported improvement in their status. Those who reported improvement in their status, frequently mentioned that they enjoyed more power in family decision-making than before and husbands paid more attention to them. In Klein's study fifty-nine per cent of the married working women mentioned advantages. A very negligible section (0.5% only) reported a decline in their status in the family. They were the semi-skilled workers. Both of them said that when they were not working, their husbands gave for expenses whatsoever they required but after their employment they refused to give a single penny and their requirements were not covered by the income they earned. That is why they felt that there was some decline in their status. Five per cent of them stated disadvantages in Klein's study.

Employment and Change in the Financial Position

Nest, it was to be examined if the employment brought any change in the family finances of the working women. Since most of the women were in employment because of economic pressures, it was worthwhile to elicit information about this aspect. On the basis of the responses. It was observed that only one-third of the working women were of the opinion that the employment made great change in their financial position (thirty three per cent) and almost the same number reported (32.5%) that it made only some change. In the British study, sixty-four per cent of the respondents mentioned that employment raised their standard of living.

Those reporting change in this study, frequently mentioned that they were in a position to fulfil their needs easily and that they were not to depend on others. They also mentioned that they were in a position now to provide better facilities to their family members. A little more than one third of them said that it did not make any difference in their economic condition (34.5%). They were still depending on their parents/husbands as usual. In order to make the study of working women regarding their employment adequate, it was necessary to ascertain from them as to what extent did they receive support from the members of their families. Did family members, on the whole, approve of their going to work? The working women were asked to indicate their assessment about the attitude of their family members and neighbours and relatives to their employment. These questions were asked since it was hoped that the attitude of the family, neighbours and relatives might operate as facilitators or barriers to their employment.

Attitude of Family Members

Since, women started entering a variety of occupations, the traditional notion of women's role as being exclusively concerned with house-keeping is likely to change. Considering the many objections that could be anticipated to the idea of women working out-side the home, it is surprising that the percentage of respondents whose family members had been reported by them to have objected to their employment is less than over one-tenth

(8.5%). As against this, there were as many as three-fourths of them who reported that the family members accepted the idea without qualification (seventy-five per cent). Slightly more than one-tenth remained netural (twelve per cent). Ross also found in her study that two-thirds of the men interviewed favoured the idea of women planning careers. Kapadia found that 44.2% of the teachers interviewed favoured the idea. Nye also found that husbands of working women generally approved women's employment. In Detroit sample, sixteen per cent of the working mothers reported that their husbands gave unqualified approval to their working and nineteen per cent reported that their husbands were opposed to the idea.

In Klein's study, sixty per cent of the working women reported that their husbands approved of it, six per cent approved conditionally and, five per cent were indifferent. In Gore's study of Delhi Aggarwal families, forty-three per cent of them totally rejected the idea, twenty-four per cent accepted it without qualification and thirty-three per cent conceded that women might work under special circumstances. An examination of data according to the occupations reveals that irrespective of their occupations, working women reported that their family members approved their working.

The highest number was that of petty traders, the lowest being that of the semi-skilled. Some of the women (16.9%) employed in clerical and low-professional jobs reported that their family members totally disliked their employment. Their percentage was the highest of all other working women whose family members did not like the idea of employment at all. Similarly, 15.4% of the semi-skilled workers said that their family members had some objections. Their percentage closely followed by that of the skilled workers (11.8%) was the highest in relation to working women of others occupations.

As many as 22.2% of the professionals said that their family members were neutral and this number was comparatively higher than that of other working women giving similar response.

Initial Opposition

The working women were also asked to indicate whether there was any initial opposition from the side of their family when they began earning. Most of the working women, seven-tenths of them, gave out that they did not face opposition from their family members (70.5%) whereas less than three-tenths of them said that they faced initial opposition (28.5%). The question was not applicable on one per cent of the working women. Responses enumerating the reasons of initial opposition to their employment by family members indicate that as many as 68.4% of the working women reported that their husbands/parents felt ashamed of the idea of women going to work; 21.9% of them said that in their opinion it would interfere with domestic work and according to 2.5% of them, it might have bad effect on children. Seven per cent of them were of the opinion that family members were afraid of the criticism likely to be made by other people.

Some of those working women who reported other reasons (twenty-one per cent) said that their parents wanted them to complete their study first and then get married. They did not prefer that their daughters would run after low paid jobs. About one-third of the working women engaged in skilled occupations mostly the nurses affirmed that their husbands/parents felt embarrassed and opposed their employment. Their family members were not favourably disposed to their job. In some cases the objection was partly because nurses violated caste rules by handling bed pans, and in other cases, partly because nurses went out for night work, or lived out-side the family premises which was considered indecent in many Indian families. Cormack also pointed out this fact. It may be noted here that prejudice against nursing prevailed in several other Asian countries. In Pakistan, as in India, there was the same feeling. Burmese girls avoided nursing leaving this profession to girls from Karen tribe.

In Malya too, nursing is frowned upon. One-tenth of those in semi-skilled occupations reported that their family members felt that it would interfere with the domestic chores, another 10.2% of them felt adverse effects on children; and 5.1% of them apprehended the adverse remarks of the neighbours, relatives and others. Thus, the initial objections varied widely and involved considerations of family status, concept of appropriateness of certain roles for women because of innate qualities and disabilities attributed to them, fear of neglect of home and children, and the fear of being unconventional. When the working women were asked to indicate the attitude of their relatives and neighbours towards their employment, 57.5% of them told that relatives and neighbours very much appreciated their working for they were making use of their training and talents and supporting their families instead of sitting idle at home and wasting their time and energy unnecessarily. Twenty-four per cent of the working women were of the view that relatives and neighbours were generally neutral in this regard.

Only 6.5% respondents mentioned about neighbour's and relatives criticism. Twelve per cents of the working women did not know as what were the attitudes of their neighbours and relatives towards their employment. Attitude of neigbours and relatives on the basis of occupation of working women reveals that in addition the N.C.C. instructor, the largest proportion of the semi-skilled working women reported that their relatives and neighbours appreciated their working and only 7.7% of them said that they were critical. Unmarried girls working in family planning and drama division of AIR reported that since their jobs involved touring for several days and they had to stay at different places at night, their relatives and neighbours criticised their parents for allowing their daughters to remain out-side home for many days. Similarly if some male colleagues came to their residence, neighbours started making adverse comments.

Women's Own Attitude towards Employment

According to the traditional notion, women are expected to perform household duties and it is for men to take care of other out-side work. It is just as undesirable for a woman to work out side home in other to earn money as it is for the man to do the domestic work. That this view is held by the women or not was examined. A comparison was made of the views of working as well as of non-working women. It is seen that the percentage of working women disapproving the idea was only 10.5% and that of non-working women is 20.3%.

Almost an equal percentage of both the working and the non-working women (34.5% and thirty-five per cent respectively) conceded that women could work under special circumstances. Frequent responses favouring women's employment conditionally were as follows:—Women should work if husband/father was unable to earn due to illness, unemployment and old age; the income of the husband/father was so meager that it was difficult to make two ends meet; children were adult and there was no adverse effect on them; she could work for a change; if a woman was widowed or separated and had to support her family. Gore found that forty-three per cent of women rejected the idea totally and twenty-three per cent of them accepted the idea of women's employment under special circumstances. It is significant to note that more than one-half of the working women responded favourably (53.5%). Some working women (1.3%) and non-working women (1.2%) were not sure about their own views in this regard.

The frequent responses of those who favoured the idea were. In the present days of spiralling prices a woman should work to contribute to her family income; it was necessary for a woman to make use of her talents and training; a women should work in order to compete with men in every field; women should work so that she might become economically independent. It would affect children adversely; community would be critical; working against the will of husband/parents lead to marital/ family tensions; one should not work if husband was well paid because it would otherwise amount to depriving an equally qualified male worker of the employment he needed to support the family as it sole bread winner.

Work Service as an Interim between Education and Marriage

It is a prevalent view that women do not take their employment seriously. They consider it as a temporary arrangement. In order to while away their time before marriage, they should do something and one way of filling the gap was to do gainful work readily available to them. For the educated girls, service was just a stop-gap measure between their education and marriage. This attitude towards employment was likely to affect employment opportunity for women and also their performance. It is, therefore, essential to study the views of woman whether they considered service as an interim between education and marriage. The opinion of the working women seemed to be sharply divided on the question of whether service for women was an interim between education and marriage.

They were almost equally divided, 42.2% of them reporting as an interim and 43.3% said it was not More than one-half of the non-working women considered employment of girls to be only an interim arrangement (fifty-three per cent) whereas this view was held by less than half of the working women. Among those who did not consider it as an interim arrangement the percentage of the working and the non-working women. Among those who did not consider it as an interim arrangement the percentage of the working and the non-working women was almost equal (42.8%).

Some 14.5% of working women and 4.2% of non-working women did not know whether service was an interim between education and marriage. In fact, there is a tendency among some employed girls not to marry and lead an independent life. The respondents were asked to give their opinion whether they approved of their attitude of young girls who did not wish to marry but continued in employment because they thought that after marriage they might not be in a position to lead a free and independent life. The question asked was: "A tendency is observed among some employed girls that they want to live an independent life and that they do not want to marry. An overwhelming majority of both the working (74.3%) and the non-working women (74.0%) did not like the idea of young working girls remaining unmarried. Only a small number of women approved the idea, 16.5% of working and 20.5% non-working Some 9.2%) working women and 5.5% non-working women were not sure about their views.

The main objections stated by both the working and the non-working women against this view of remaining unmarried are as follows:

> Marriage is a necessity of life. One needs life partner; unmarried girl is a burden on parents; one must marry because times are bad; community will raise an accusing finger; girl would lose her character; in old age who would help if the girl does not marry? Parents can not live for ever. Those who approved the idea were generally of the view that if a girl did not want to marry, parents should not insist on her getting married. After all she has to lead her own life. Some considered marriage as a gamble. Some considered it an unnecessary hurdle in the way of free and independent life of a woman. In the light of these remarks, it seemed worthwhile to enquire about the attitude of the unmarried working women regarding their future plan.

There were eighty-one unmarried working women and their responses were analysed to show the inclination of the unmarried working women towards their future career, *i.e.* whether they wished to continue their work even after they were married. A question was asked. "Supposing you were married, do you think you would want to continue in a job?" Slightly more than one-fourth of the unmarried working women expressed their desire to continue work (twenty-six per cent). Slightly more than one-fifth of the unmarried working women said outright that they wished to give up employment on marriage (twenty-one per cent). In Klein's study twenty-eight per cent of the single women were for giving-up employment and only fifteen per cent of them said that they proposed to continue indefinitely. A relatively larger proportion of the working women of this study, seemed to have an open mind on the question. Whether or not to continue in employment after marriage would depend on their husbands or family members' consent (thirty-seven per cent).

In Klein's study only four per cent of them mentioned that it depended on their future husbands' financial position. As many as 11.1% of the working women of Jodhpur said that they were not certain as to what they would do in future and 4.9% of them stated that they had decided not to marry in future but to continue in their job. It has been remarked that work place is the best possible marriage market because there the unmarried working women will meet a high concentration of her mental equals. To ascertain the views of women about this, the respondents were asked to tell whether in their view working girls were able to get more chances for mate selection.

More than one-half of the working women and only two-fifths of the non-working women were of the opinion that it was not necessary that working girls would get more chances to select mate at their work-place. Compared to working women, relatively a large section of the non-working women felt that working girls got more chances for mate selection. A very small number of both the working and the non-working women considered that working girls did not get more chances for mate selection.

Balance of Domestic Work and Employment

One of the problems for the employed home makers was the difficulty of combining the two roles-home making and employment. In order to sind out reaction of the working women about the question whether it was possible to carry on two roles. Over one-half of the working women felt that employment and domestic work both could be carried simultaneously. But non-working women did not feel so sure. As against working women, a relatively small section of them said that home making and employment could be balanced. Only 44.8% of working women thought that it would be difficult to do both home and outside work and one-half of the non-working women observed that it was not possible to do so. In Japan also sixty-five per cent of the wives reported incompatibility between occupational work and home. It is possible that those working women who held that it was possible to do both might have approached the domestic work differently.

They must have re-scheduled their domestic chores. They also expressed the view that a woman could do both if she got the co-operation of husband, adult children and other family members and also by getting-up early in the morning, she could finish her household duties easily. Working woman cannot look after her family and children properly; the husband gets annoyed if the wife does not pay due attention to him; one does not get time for leisure; leaving home under the supervision of servant means double expenditure and less gain; work-load on children increases. The information were gathered whether the married working women should be given lesser burden of work than the unmarried working women in the same occupation. Only a small percentage of the working (39.8%) and the non-working women (37.5%) said that married women should be given less burdensome work whereas a little more than half of working (52.5% and non-working women (51.5%) did not consider it proper to do so. Some working women (7.7%) and non-working women (eleven per cent) did not give their opinion. Those who were in favour, frequently mentioned that married women had also to bear the burden of household tasks and the care of children. In their comparison, unmarried girls had to shoulder less responsibilities, so less work should be taken from married working women.

Those who did not favour the idea, their most frequent responses were that one should be ready to do everything that was required to be done at work place and there should be no discrimination. If married women had responsibilities, the unmarried working women were not devoid of home responsibilities; that only the nature of responsibility might be different which did not call for discrimination. Surprisingly, some women maintained that unmarried girls should be given less burdensome work as they were inexperienced, immature and less attentive than the married working women. It is clear from the emphatic way in which many informants replied that it would be wrong to differentiate between the married and single woman. Some social scientists, more particularly economists have pointed out the need for higher participation of women in economic activities specially in developing countries. But an equally strong opinion has been expressed against this view. It is argued that the advantages to some families by employment of women would be offset by a corresponding loss for other families whose bread-winner would lose his job if more women were given employment.

This question became part of serious consideration in many international gatherings of ILO since 1964. A delegate to ILO Conference of 1964 described a draft resolution from the women's committee as "the result of excited and often stormy verbal exchanges in the Committee." He continued by saying: "I firmly believe that it is a serious error of judgment for developing countries to ascribe high action priority to plan for encouraging women to enter the market, especially women with family responsibilities, when those same countries do not have or cannot create sufficient jobs for their male populations" The discussions at various other meetings showed considerable disagreement.

They recommended that women's employment should be very carefully considered, and suggested that there might be need for giving priority to men in employment market, while other delegates thought that development in all spheres required the contribution of its women power as well as it men power. With this debate in view, an attempt is made here to understand the attitude of women towards this issue and hence a question was asked whether employment of women lead to unemployment among men.

The data indicate that more than one-half of the working women considered that their employment would not create unemployment for men whereas similar view was expressed by less than one-half of the non-working women (forty-seven per cent) Approximately three-tenths of the working women reported that their employment would create unemployment among men and as against this opinion about one-third of non-working women said that women's employment created unemployment among men. One-third of them were unaware of the consequences.

Rights to Women

The constitution of free India guarantees all its citizens equal rights and it goes a step further and makes a special provision for safeguarding the interest of women. Women enjoy the same right of franchise as men, they get equal pay and equal opportunities for selection and appointment in various services of the country. They also enjoy the right to inherit property and the right to divorce. Legally speaking they enjoy equal rights in all aspects of the social, economic and political set-up of the country. It is maintain that they are in a very favourable position. In some cases they enjoy greater freedom than even those enjoyed by their counter-parts in some of the Western countries, hence, it was considered appropriate to assess the views of women about the extent of the right they have been constitutionally provided.

Whether they are adequate for them. A large percentage of both the working women (fifty-nine per cent) and the non-working women (69.8%) felt that it was almost adequate, but compared to working women (6.8%) a larger section of non-working women (nine per cent) considered it more than needed, and the percentage of the working women was more (13.2%) than that of the non-working women (7.5%) among those who considered it less than required.

Independence or Over-Burdened

After having examined the various factors of opinion and attitude of working women, an attempt is made to present in the end, their own assessment about the fact whether in the name of giving freedom to women, the men-folk had actually over-burdened them with variety of tasks and responsibilities such as making household purchases, arranging admission and education of children, going to banks and post offices when required and doing other odd jobs. The were asked to give their own assessment about this question. As is obvious, in this chapter an attempt has been made to show if employment had brought any change in the life of the working women and also to assess their attitude towards employment and some related issues. In the case of majority of working women there was no change in their status in family, but their had taken place some change in their financial position.

An overwhelming majority of working women reported that the members of their families approved their employment. But there was some initial opposition in some of the cases. The main reason of the initial opposition in some of the cases. The main reasons of the initial opposition was the feeling of embarrassment among parents. Neighbours and relatives generally appreciated their employment. With regard to the attitude of women towards employment, it was found that both the working and the non-working women approved the idea of women's employment and the percentage of working women in this category was more than that of the non-working women.

A majority of the non-working women considered employment as an interim arrangement between education and marriage but most of the working women did not think so. However, a large selection of both the working and the non-working women were of the opinion that the unmarried young girls must also marry and they should not remain unmarried even if they were in employment. More than one-fourth of the unmarried working women expressed their desire to continue work after marriage. A large number of working women did not consider that working girl necessarily got more chances for mate selection whereas most of the non-working women were of the opinion that they did get more chances for marriage. Contrary to the view expressed by non-working women, a majority of the working women held that it was possible to carry on domestic work and employment simultaneously.

There was no difference of opinion among the employed and the non-employed women with regard to the differential treatment to be accorded to women on the basis of marital status. An equal percentage of both the working and the non-working women was of the view that the married women should not be given any special treatment. A relatively large number of working women considered that unemployment among men was not created on account of the employment of women.

A majority of both the working and the non-working women was of the view that adequate rights had been given to women and the percentage of the non-working women was higher than that of the working women. A very large number of both the working and the non-working women felt that in the name of giving freedom to women, men had over-burdened them with various types of work.

EMPHASIS ON REASONS FOR WOMENS' SEEKING EMPLOYMENT

Here in this chapter an attempt is made to delineate the causes for seeking employment by the women. The inferences are based on a case study. It is pertinent to note that causes that prompt women to enter into employment are as complex as those influencing other choices that affect their way of life. It is generally believe that socio-cultural changes play a very important role in creating a situation in which women would like to seek employment.

While one would not deny the importance of socio-cultural changes, there are several other factors which lead one to take individual decision to work or not to work. It might be that in a particular cultural context, one was in a position to get employment but her desire might not be translated into action, if she was not in a position to go out of home. Examples can be multiplied and we could see that actual decision involved several underlying consideration requiring careful examination in any study dealing with motivating factors that impel women to seek employment.

It is possible that one may have one's own reasons but scrutiny of data collected is likely to show some pattern which might throw light on these underlying considerations. It is, therefore, appropriate to know those factors which pull and push women to enter the working force. The analysis of individual's decision to work give insight about the processes inducing women to take to employment. Such an analysis also helps in making prediction abut the future impact of the employment of women, i.e., whether it would increase or decrease? This is why the study of the factors inducing women to join the working force deserves serious consideration.

The present chapter therefore, deals with the factors that explain as to why women go to work. In one of the ILO studies dealing with women's employment it was presumed that motives *differed* with marital status both objectively and subjectively. Not only the economic needs but the motivational reasons also vary with marital status. They broadly mentioned two reasons: (a) Women's economic need, and (b) national necessity for increased production. Some other studies have brought to light the fact that loneliness is a powerful motive for women to seek employment outside their homes.

The Ministry of Labour, Government of India has pointed out that whatsoever the stage of economic or social development of a country, four factors prevail which lead women to join working force. They are: (a) the inadequate income of the principal earner which forces a women to work and supplement the income; (b) mishaps, such as incapacity of the bread winner; (c) death of the bread-winner; and (d) a women's desire for economic independence or for securing higher standard of living.

There is also the desire on the part of the women to give expression to their own talents and skills. The percentage distribution of responses given by the employed women stating reasons of employment shows that women, essentially worked for financial motives. Like Klein's study, where she found that seventy-three per cent women worked for money, more than three-fourths of the working women of this study mentioned financial reasons while less than one-fourth of them reported non-financial reasons. Delhi and Bombay studies also mentioned that a large proportion of working women worked for economic reasons (sixty-nine per cent and sixty-five per cent respectively).

Financial Reasons

Among various reasons which have been termed as financial, three sub categories are noted: (a) economic pressures which pertain to the fulfilment of basic minimum needs of life, (b) other economic needs—money required to help relatives, (c) higher standard of living some of the women reported that they worked for financial reasons. They desired to have better education of children and a supply of objects of comfort. On the basis of the criteria used to identify financial reasons, it was found that economic pressures accounted for 58.5%. Of these, some women were working so as to satisfy the basic minimum (27.8%), to support dependents (25.7%) because of the death of the principal bread-winner in the family, and 4.5% of them reported that rapid increase in the cost of living had brought the family income to a difficult situation and it was imperative for them to work to provide for the family requirements.

Two of them (0.5%) reported that they were working to repay the debts incurred due to necessities such as prolonged illness in the family and marriage of sons and daughters. Besides economic pressures, they mentioned other economic needs. 14.3% of them said that they worked to support their relative while 0.5% worked to bear the expenses of medicines that they required to keep them fit. Higher standard of living was mentioned by a very small number of women. Only 1.5% of working women reported that they wanted to make provisions for higher education of their children as well as for their own education and 2.7% of them maintained that they worked to live decently.

Non-Financial Reasons

The non-financial reasons for working have been classified into three categories.

(a) Personality Traits

There are several personality factors which are involved in the motivation for employment. For instance, in this study 10.8% working women who had deliberately chosen careers reported that they wanted to fill a need for accomplishment and 1.8% of them said that they worked because they wanted to attain recognition by proving themselves able to compete successfully with men in activities for which they were once debarred. Some (1.8%) considered it as a national duty, 1.2% of them worked for personal independence and only one women said that she was working because of the uncertainty of the future. On the whole, 15.8% of working women have mentioned one or the other type of personality traits to be the factor inducting them to work.

(b) To Occupy Time

3.7% of working women reported that they felt boredom with the continuous routine of household tasks and felt lonely and isolated in the home. They want an escape into the work day world to utilise time meaningfully.

(c) Traditional Occupation

Three per cent of working women reported that they worked because of the tradition of the family in a specific occupation. It also helped them to earn their living. The financial reasons, thus, seem to be the most important reasons for women's seeking employment. However, it is possible that reasons for work differ among women themselves. Possibly, easily measurable demographic characteristics such as age, education etc. might be useful to explain the variations. To understand this, we shall compare these demographic variables to reasons for work.

Age

It is pertinent to note that the percentage distribution of the response indicates that irrespective of their age, the working women reported that financial reasons were more important for them than the non-financial reasons. Though the percentage of working women seemed to be increasing with the increase in age, it was found that there were no significant differences in the percentage accounted for by financial reasons. The old as well as the middle and the young working women were pressed almost equally by financial factors. But within the broad group of financial reasons, there were significant differences in the number of those working on account of one particular financial reason. Thus, more than three-fourths of the old aged working women (78.2%), more than three-fifths of the middle aged working women (63.8% and even less than one-half of the young working women (48.8%) worked due to economic pressures.

There was, however, a decrease in the percentage of the working women accounting for other economic needs with increase in age. The young and the middle aged were almost equally distributed (15.9% and 15.2% respectively) while the working women of old age in this category were only 4.4%. Young working women's percentage accounting for standard of living is much higher than that of middle aged working women. Of those who worked because of personality traits or to avoid domestic responsibilities the number of young working women was more than that of the women of other age groups. Old working women 8.8%) who stated non-financial reasons as factors in their employment held to traditional occupations. In short, it may be inferred that though economic pressures accounted for a sizable number of young working women, they were less than even one-half of all the working women of young age group.

Some of them would like to live a life which gave them some compensation. For middle and old aged working women, and especially for the latter economic pressures were the most dominant factors. Economic pressures, therefore, were the dominating factors with the working women irrespective of age. They became much pressing as the age. Increased. The old working women were continuing largely in the working force not to rise their standard of living or to occupy their surplus time, or for some self-compensation. They worked to provide for the necessities of life. The middle aged working women were working on account of economic pressures.

Though young working women also worked largely on account of economic pressures yet some of them were motivated by self-expression and actualisation. Therefore, with the increase in age, the continuance in the working force was mainly determined by economic considerations and self-expression as determinant lost its significance. Standard of living was not found to be a motivating factor in this study.

Caste

It is significant to mention that with the rise in the status of the caste, the number of those working women reporting financial reasons declined whereas the number of those reporting non financial reasons increased. It is to be noted that economic pressures accounted for the largest number of lower and Scheduled Castes/Tribes. Three-fourths of them reported this whereas only one-half of the working women of middle castes and less than half of the upper caste women stated that they worked because of economic pressures. Though the number of working women reporting other reasons was small, there was a reverse trend with the rise in the status of caste.

There was a decline in the number of working women reporting other economic needs, higher standard of living or personality traits. Only a very negligible section of working women of lower and Scheduled Castes/ Tribes mentioned standard of living and personality trait as reason for employment. The number of upper caste working women was higher than that of lower and Scheduled Castes/Tribes and middle castes. Thus, economic pressure was the compelling reason for employment irrespective of caste differentiation. But it is also evident that it was comparatively more dominant among lower and Scheduled Castes/Tribes. Standard of living and personality traits were not dominant. However, motive of actualisation accounted for more than one-fourth of the upper caste working women and some of them had also the desire for higher standard of living. Somewhat more than one-fourth of other-castes-working women also reported personality traits as factor in their employment.

Marital Status

The data with respect to marital status and reasons of employment indicate that a substantially large number of the working women irrespective of their marital status were in employment due to financial reasons. But a difference in response was perceptible among those reporting economic pressures. Only one-third of the unmarried working women (33.3%) reported that they were in working force because of economic pressures and almost the same number of them (34.6%) asserted that they worked because they wanted to attain recognition in the community. Only a small percentage of them (11.1%) talked of higher standard of living, but their percentage was higher than that of other respondents in this study. Contrary to this findings, Ferdinand Zweig who has made a study into the attitudes and habits of Lancashire working women, estimates that "among married wives no more than about one in three goes out to work under economic pressure...".

In this study slightly more than half of the married working women worked due to economic pressures. It is the widowed and the separated women whose largest number, slightly more than nine-tenths of them (92.6%), reported their being in labour force because of economic pressures. It is in conformity with the findings of a study by the Women's Bureau, U.S.A. Of 8,300 women workers in 100 Trade Union Locals which showed that ninety-eight per cent of those without husbands (widowed, separated and divorced) were working to support themselves and others. None of them has said that they worked to raise standard of living and only 2.1% of them attributed this working to personality traits. It can be inferred that though the economic pressures was dominant as a factor of employment of the women, it was not much dominant among the unmarried.

Their main consideration was to live a life which might give them compensation. Standard of living was not a motivating factors. Was perceptible only in some of the unmarried working women (11.1%). Among married women its percentage was negligible (3.6%). Almost all the widowed and the separated women were working because of economic pressures. It was clear then that marital status played an important role in creating difference in the responses related to reasons for work. The working women lived in various types of families. The composition of the family in which a working woman lived helped or hindered her entrance into employment.

However, it may be seen that the percentage of working women with joint families is the highest (80.3%) when compared to the working women belonging to a single member family or nuclear family. But the differences are not much. Economic pressures have been most important for 72.2% of the single member family and 60.1% of the nuclear family working women. Other economic needs were mentioned by 15.6% of working women of the joint families, 14.8% of nuclear and only 5.6% of single member families. Higher standard of living was mentioned by working women of joint and nuclear families (4.6% and 4.3% respectively).

The working women of nuclear and joint families went to work to occupy Their time. Their percentage distribution is 4.8% and 2.9% respectively. A large number of the working women irrespective of the size of their families mentioned that they worked for financial reason. The percentage of those with larger families is the highest and of those with small-size families is the lowest. Single member family working women worked for economic Pressures wheres the number of those belonging to large families, where others are to support is the lowest in this respect. The percentage of working women with large families mentioning other economic needs and higher standards of living was more than that of others. Some (8.1%) of the working women with small families mentioned that they worked to while away time and 16.4% of large family women reported that they worked to carry on the traditional occupation. As many as 16.7% single member of 16.1% small families' women mentioned personality traits as cause for their taking to work.

Number of Children

A very large number of working women, irrespective of the number of children worked because of financial reasons; the highest being the percentage of working women with medium number of children. Though the percentage of working women who worked to occupy time was very small yet of those working women who had no children (9.8%) worked to avoid boredom. Their percentage was three times more than that of working women with small and medium number of children giving boredom as reason for their employment.

Number of Dependents

The data show that those working women on whom depended larger number of persons, were more likely to work because of financial reasons than those who had no dependents or small or medium number of dependents.

Earners

With the increase in the number of earners in the working women's families, the percentage of those who mentioned financial reasons decreased; the highest being only when one was earning i.e. working woman herself. A reverse trend was noted among those who mentioned non-financial reasons. The percentage was also decreasing with increase in number of earners in the category of those who worked under economic pressures.

There was only one working woman with more than six earning members and she said that she worked to avoid boredom. It is also seen that with the increase in number of earners upto six, there was an increase in the percentage of working women who were in employment because of personality traits or of those who wanted to carry on their family occupation.

Educational

An analysis of the cause of employment by the educational standard of the employed women brings out the fact that with the increase in the level of education, the number of the working women reporting financial reasons was declining and increasing where non-financial reasons were in operation. More than three-fourths of the unlettered working women and slightly more than a half of low educated and also a little more than one-third of the highly educated working women reported that they worked due to economic pressures. Contrary to this, the number of working women who reported higher standard of living or non-financial reasons increased with the increase in education. It may be noted that more than three-fourths of non-lettered working women (78.0%) mentioned economic pressures whereas only one of them reported higher standard of living, and only two mentioned personality traits to be the cause of their going to work.

Contrary to this only slightly more than one-third of highly educated working women reported economic pressures, one-third of them reported personality traits and eight per cent mentioned higher standard of living. In short, non-lettered women worked mainly because of economic pressures. Among highly educated, slightly more than one-third worked on account of economic pressures and one-third worked because they preferred attainment and recognition. One-tenth of them reported higher standard of living as the main cause of their work. The finding of this study in regard to educated women is more or less comparable to that of Kapoor who has reported that educate women take up jobs not only out of sheer economic necessity but also out of various other socio-psycho situational reasons.

Occupation

In fact, a very large section of the working women employed in unskilled occupations described their work to financial reasons. Their percentage was the highest (94.2%) compared to that of the working women employed in various occupations. The lowest was the percentage in this category of the working women engaged in professions (29.6%). Similarly, the percentage of unskilled working women mentioning economic pressures as cause was the highest. They formed 82.8% of all the unskilled working women closely followed by those employed in petty trades. In this response category, the lowest percentage was again of the professionals (7.0%). Those who mention other economic needs, the percentage of working women engaged in semi-skilled occupations is the highest (30.8%) compared to women employed elsewhere; the lowest being that of the professionals (3.7%).

The higher standard of living accounted for 18.5% of the professionals which was the highest percentage of the other categories of working women; the lowest being that of the unskilled. The percentage of the professionals is the highest (11.1%) who take to work to occupy time. The Semi-skilled workers (20.5%) banked upon traditional occupation. Only one working women was engaged in N.C.C. and she considered it as a national duty. Like her, 59.3% of the professionals and fifty per cent of the skilled workers reported personality trait as cause of employment. The occupationwise distribution shows that economic pressures were dominant among unskilled and petty-traders, whereas among those employed in N.C.C., professionals and skilled workers, personality traits seemed to be dominating. It was apparent then that the occupation of working women distinguished the factors making for employment. It may, thus, be inferred that working women of prestigeous occupations were not working because of economic pressures but mostly because of the desire of attainment and recongition; and those in non-prestigeous occupations worked because of economic pressures.

Family Income

In fact, the number of working women reporting financial reasons went on declining with the increase in the average income of their family whereas a reverse trend was perceptible among those mentioning non-financial reasons. Three-fourths of the working women of the Family of the lower income group, less than half of the working women of lower middle income family and even less than one-fifth of the upper middle income family relied on economic pressure compelling them to work. None of the upper-income family working women considered economic pressures as imperative for employment. However, one-third of the working women of the family of the upper income group said that they worked to raise their standard of living.

The working women of the lower income families did not consider personality trait as any major cause of their employment. Slightly less than half of the working women of the families of the upper-middle and upper income group considered that they worked because of personality traits. It is apparent that the family income and the reasons of employment were very significantly related to each other. As the family income increased the percentage of the women working because of economic pressures declined to the extent that no working women belonging to the family of the upper income groups reported that she worked because of economic pressures. Instead, one-third of them reported higher standard of living, approximately one half of them and also slightly less than half of the upper-middle income group families mentioned personality traits, attainment and recognition as cause of employment. From the responses one could note that with the increase in the income of husbands there was likelihood of substantial decrease in the number of working women who worked because of economic pressures.

However, they would work for recognition and higher standard of living. This is also the finding of a study conducted by Kapoor of Delhi educated working women. Similar results were obtained by Durand also. It is pertinent to note that here we emphasised the importance of studying the factors involved in women's decision to work. The flow of women into the labour market can be considered as directly related to their general economic conditions. Financial reasons, especially the economic pressures, were the major factors to draw women into the working force. This was more than evident from the responses given by approximately three-fifths of them.

There were others who did not work just to keep the wolf away from the door but because of the desire for achievement and self-compensation. Some of these were professionally trained and considered it a duty to utilise their capacities in the interest of the community. A few of them felt social isolation because they had nothing to do in their homes and therefore, they went to work to avoid the boredom. It may, however, be kept in view that the number of women who stated non-financial reasons was small, less than one-fourth of all the working women. It has been found that with the increase in the age of working women, there was an increase in the percentage of those stating financial reasons and there was a corresponding decrease among those stating non-financial reasons.

With the increase in age the continuity in employment seemed to be determined by economic pressures and considerations such as actualisation and self-expression lost their significance. Higher standard of living was not an important motivational force. Irrespective of caste status, financial reasons were stated as the most important; but with the increase in the status of caste there was a decline in the percentage of those stating these reasons. The working women of lower, Scheduled Castes and Tribes worked mostly because of economic pressures whereas it was not so with the majority of upper caste working women. Practically all the widowed and the separated women worked on account of financial reasons, under economic pressures; married working women took to work for the same reasons.

A larger section of unmarried working women worked on account of personality traits. Economic pressures had been the main reasons for employment irrespective of the nature of the family, (the percentage of single member family being the highest). The working women with single member family were mostly in employment because of economic pressures. The working women with medium number of children, a large number of dependents and less number of earners were mostly working on account of dire economic needs economic pressure was most felt by non-lettered working women. A sizable section of highly educated women worked to eke out their personality traits.

Unskilled working women closely followed by petty traders joined the working force due to economic pressures, but a large majority of the professionals worked to give out personality traits. It was observed that the larger the income of the family, the lesser was the chance of women joining the labour force on account of financial reasons and economic pressures, so much so that not a single working woman of upper income group was found in the working force because of economic pressures. Approximately one-half of them worked because of personality traits and one-third of them took to work for higher standard of living.

Remarkably, there existed an inverse relation between the percentage of wives in employment and the income of their husbands. The working women whose husbands had no earnings of their own or had low earnings, worked mainly on account of economic pressures whereas a small percentage of working women whose husband's income was higher, worked because of this reason. Not a single working woman whose husband's earnings is very high worked due to economic pressures.

REFERENCES

Audrus, J. Russel, *Burmese Economic Life,* Stanford, 1948, p. 291.

Barbara J. Harris, *Beyond Her Sphere: Women and the Professions in American History*.

Bossard, James H.S., *The Sociology of Child Development,* New York: Harper, 1954, pp. 282-86.

Carroll Wetzel Wilkinson, *Women Working in Nontraditional Fields References and Resources 1963-1988* (Women's Studies Series).

Challenging Professions: Historical and Contemporary Perspectives on Women's Professional Work by Elizabeth Smyth, Sandra Acker, Paula Bourne, and Alison Prentice.

Cormack, Margaret, *The Hindu Women*, London pp. 5,160.

Durand, John D., "Married Women in Labour Force," *American Journal of Sociology,* 26 (November, 1946), pp. 217-74.

Gore, M.S., *Urbanisation and Family Change,* Bombay: Popular Prakashan, 1968, p. 159.

Government of India, "International Trends," *Women in Employment,* Labour Bureau, Ministry of Labour and Employment, 1964, pp. 58-59.

Hoffman, L.W., 'The Decision to Work," in *The Employed Mother,* p. 36.

Husain, A.F.A., *Employment of Middle Class Muslim Women in Dacca.* Dacca, 1958, pp. 60, 65.

Kapadia, K.M., "Changing Pattern of Hindu Marriage and Family," Part II, *Sociological Bulletin,* 3 (September, 1954), p. 153.

Kapoor, Promilla, *Marriage and the Working Woman In India,* Delhi: Vikas Publications, 1970. p. 395.

Klein, Viola, *Britain's Married Women Workers,* London, Routledge and Kegan Paul, 1965, pp. 36-37.

Klein, Viola, *Britain's Married Women Workers,* p. 59.

Komarovsky, Mirra, *Women in the Modern World,* Boston: Little Brown, 1953, as quoted in *The Employed Mother,* p. 7.

Landis, Paul, H., *Making the Most of Marriages,* New York: Appleton-Century-Crofts, 1955, as quoted in *The Employed Mother* p. 273.

Leaflet, 11, "Why Do Women Work?" 1951, as quoted in Ray E. Barber, *Marriage and the Family,* New York, McGraw Hill, 1953, P. 348.

Lewis, W.A., *The Theory of Economic Growth,* London, 1957, pp. 16-17; Nath, Kamla, "Urban Women Workers—A Preliminary Study," *The Economic Weekly,* 37 (September 11, 1965), p. 1412.

Lundberg, Ferdinand, and Farnham, Marynia F., *Modern Women: The Lost Sex,* New York: Harper, 1947 as quoted in *The Employed Mother,* p. 7.

Mary Kinnear, *In Subordination: Professional Women, 1870-1970.*

N. Sokoloff (1992). *Black Women and White Women in the Professions: Occupational Segregation by Race and Gender, 1960-1980* (Perspectives on Gender).

Nellie Alden Franz (1965). *English women enter the professions.*

Nye, F. Ivan, *The Employed Mothers,* p. 279.

Penina Migdal Glazer and Miriam Slater, *Unequal Colleagues: The Entrance of Women into the Professions, 1890-1940* (Douglass Series on Women's Lives and the Meaning of Gender).

Ross, Aileen D., *The Hindu Family in its Urban Setting,* 1961, p. 201.

Stephanie J. Shaw, *What a Woman Ought to Be and to Do: Black Professional Women Workers during the Jim Crow Era* (Women in Culture and Society Series).

Wanda F. Neff, Victorian Working Women: A historical and literary study of women in British industries and professions 1832-1850 (Economic History (Routledge)).

Wee, Ann, E., "Some Aspects of the Status of Chinese Women in Malya," In Appadorai, A. ed., *The Status of Women in South Asia,* Bombay, 1954, p. 162.

Zweig, F., *Women's Life and Labour,* London: Victor Gallanz 1952, p. 74.

3

Social Characteristics of Working Women

"Women don't want to hear what you think. Women want to hear what they think - in a deeper voice."

—*Bill Cosby*

Generally, it is seen that in a large number of studies, social characteristics such as age, marital status, occupation, income, employer-employee relation, motivation and social background have been found to have significant influence on the employment structure. Many researchers, in their studies have tried to assess the significance of these variables. In India, the study of working women has been conducted mainly by economists with emphasis on occupation wage-structure, economic status, unemployment, under-employment, standing of living and indebtedness. Some casual references have been made to household features also. A proper understanding of the working women is, however, not possible without a consideration of all the related factors.

Age

It is pertinent to note that the study of the working women necessitates an enquiry into their age distribution. For, age acquires a special significance as far as efficiency is concerned. It influences the capacity for work. The age of the working women ranges from a low fifteen to a high of seventy five years. For the purpose of analysis the different age groups have been classified into three broad categories, i.e., Young (below thirty years), Middle (thirty years and below fifty-five years) and Old (Fifty-five years and above). The percentage of working women in various age groups shows an increasing trend reaching the maximum in middle age group after which it shows a falling trend.

It may be seen that while 42.5% of the working women are young, a little more than one-half of the working women fall in middle age group

(51.3%). As we go to higher age-group, the percentage of working women declines drastically. As a matter of fact a very small percentage of working women belongs to old age-group (5.7%). Age was not specified by 0.5% working women. A convenient summary index of age composition is the mean age. The mean age of the working women is 34.3 years. In Mumbai and Delhi, most of the working women are of young age group (77.3%) and 81.9% respectively). In Japan also, the vast majority of the working women are young under the age of twenty-five years.

Religion

Remarkably, religion is an important basis of social organization in India. In this study there is not even a single working women who does not affiliate herself with one of the other religious category. The two major religious groups Hindus and Muslims account for 81.8% and 8.2% respectively of all the working woman of this study. Hindus form the majority and Muslims the most substantial minority. Other religious groups such as Christians (6.7%), Sikhs (2.0%) and Jains (1.3%) form only insignificant minority. In Bombay, Christians form the majority of the working women (88.1%) and in Delhi 86.36%) are Hindus.

Caste

Caste has become so significant in Indian social structure that a meaningful study is not possible without its being taken into account. The working women represent various castes. They belong to more than thirty-six different castes. The Brahmins constitute the single largest group among all the working women. For purpose of convenience, various castes were grouped into four main ordinal groups: (1) Upper, (2) Middle, (3) Lower and Scheduled Castes and Tribes, and (4) Others. Brahmins represent the highest caste as per he traditional caste system. They constitute the upper caste which accounts for fifteen per cent of all the working women, the middle castes for twenty-six per cent lower Scheduled Castes and Tribes for 43.2% and others fifty per cent. It appears that relatively large number of working women come from lower, Scheduled Castes and Tribes. A survey of working women in Delhi reports that Khatris formed the majority i.e. 53.6% and Brahmins only 10.9%.

Number of Earners

The number of earners in working women's families ranged from 1-8. A majority of them (71.3%) belonged to such families as had 2-3 earning members. In one working woman's family we found eight earning members whereas in the families of 16.7% working women there was only one earner, i.e., the respondent herself. The mean earners in working women's families were 2.3.

Marital Status

To determine the marital status of the working women, we attemnted to find out the number of those that were unmarried, married and widowed or separated at the time of enquiry. It is found that more than a half of the working women are married (56.3%). Widowed and separated constitute 23.5%. Only 20.2% are unmarried. This distribution is similar to the one given in a Survey Report of Government of India. Nature Delhi and Bombay fifty-two per cent and forty-three per cent of working women respectively were unmarried.

Nature of Family

The incidence of nuclear family was higher among working women of this study. Slightly more than half of the working women belonged to the nuclear family. They constituted 52.3% of all the working women; 43.2% come from joint-families and only 4.5% belong to single member families. The difference between the percentage of nuclear and joint families is not much.

Size of Family

The family size ranged from the extremes of a uni-member family to a family consisting of as many as seventeen members. Relatively larger percentage of the working women (44.7%) has medium-sized families, 35.3% large sized families and 15.5% small sized families. Only 4.5% of them belonged to single member family. The average size of the family of the working women was found to be of 5.8 persons per family which is slightly higher than the average size of Indian household which according to 1961 census is 4.16 per household.

Number of Dependents

The number of dependents in a working women's family ranged from

0 to 15. Ten per cent of working women did not have any dependent. This also included those women who were all alone in the family. The largest percentage of working women (42.3%) had 1-3 dependents. There was only one working women who had as many as fifteen dependents. The average number of dependents was 3.92.

Region to Which Working Women Belong

A little more than three-fourths of the working women belonged to Rajasthan (76.2%) whereas a little less than one-fourth were from outside Rajasthan (23.8%) of those who claim to be of Rajasthan only 16.1% belonged to rural Rajasthan whereas 83.9% belonged to urban areas of Rajasthan. Of those who were from regions outside Rajasthan only 1.2% were from rural areas whereas 96.8% from urban areas.

Having ascertained the region of the working women, we proceed to inspect by studying their local distribution how far they represented the city of Jodhpur. We note that as many as 64.2% of working women belonged to Jodhpur and the remaining 35.8% were from outside Jodhpur, but they were residents of Rajasthan. Out of the 196 working women belonging to Jodhpur, 96.8% were city born and only 3.2% were village born.

Distribution by locale indicates that the working women were mostly local and urban. As many as forty-eight per cent of the working women had been living in this city since their birth and fifty-two per cent of them for several years with a mean of 16.9 years.

Education

So far as formal education is concerned, slightly less than half of the working women were non-lettered (48%); 10.5% were educated up to junior basic or even less in some cases; 27% were under-graduates and 14.5% had received education upto graduate level and above. Of those who mentioned education upto graduate level and above, two reported that they were Ph.Ds, and some of those (37.4%) had been trained in education. For purposes of analysis, these educational categories have been grouped into three, (1) approximately one-half of the working women were *non-lettered;* (2) only one tenth of them were *low-educated;* and (3) slightly more than two fifths of them were *highly educated.* In Delhi forty-four per cent of the working women studied upto matric and forty-two per cent were graduates. In Bombay fifty per cent studied upto matric and forty-four per cent were graduates.

Occupation

In this study, the percentage of working women engaged in unskilled occupations was the highest (39.55) lowest being that of petty-traders (6.2%). The distribution indicates that women did not generally work in more skilled or professional occupations but were employed in unskilled jobs such as day-labour, domestic servants, sweepers etc. This finding is in conformity with that of Pune. But in delhi fifty-nine per cent working women were engaged in teaching, fifteen per cent in clerical jobs, thirteen per cent in professional and technical jobs and thirteen in miscellaneous occupation; and in Bombay, thirty-seven per cent in teaching and related jobs, thirty-nine per cent in clerical and twelve per cent in professional and twelve per cent in miscellaneous occupations.

Length of Service

Only one-third of the working women were in service for more than ten years and two-thirds, for about ten years or less. The average service period of the working women was 8.3 years. In Bombay study women were in their present job for an average period of 4.61 years and in Delhi only 27.84% of them were employed in their present job for a period of more than five years.

Nature of Employment

As many as 82.8% of the women were employed full-time, and only 17.2% part-time. In Delhi and Bombay only nine per cent of the working women were working as part-time workers.

Occupational Mobility

More than four-fifths of the working women (84.2%) reported no change in their occupations. They had been working throughout in the same occupation. The remaining 15.8% reported a change. In fact, there was only nominal occupational mobility. In Bombay study also 50.38% women were in their first job and the remaining 49.62% changed their jobs ranging upto six. In Delhi study 73.17% women had no previous employment experience, while 26.83% had the experience of working in two or more jobs. Of those working women who reported change in their occupations, a larger percentage (68.2%) changed from one occupation to another, i.e., from one household work to another but these occupations were of the same status; 19.1% reported upward mobility, i.e., when they started work they joined those occupations which were readily available to them but later on they moved to comparatively better occupations. For example, one peon became a teacher, four teachers became lecturers. 12.7% of working women however, reported downward mobility.

When such women started work, they found better occupations as lecturership, but these jobs were temporary and later on they had to leave them. Then they took up the job which was readily available to them, even if inferior. The lack of mobility might be explained in terms of the fact that most of the working women were unlettered and the job opportunity was not much. Besides, the women did not want to go elsewhere.

Income of Working Women

The distribution of the monthly income of he working women brings out the fact that the greatest proportion of them (45.@%) earned only up to Rs. 100/- per month; 32% earned between Rs. 101/- to 200/- and less than one per cent of them earned more than Rs. 700/- per month. On an average, the monthly earnings of a working women was Rs. 150.75. The average income of women workers was also low in Chandigarh. In Delhi, only sixteen percent carned less them Rs. 100/- per month, sixty eight per cent earned Rs. 101-300 per month, twelve per cent earned Rs. 301-400 and four per cent earned Rs. 401 and above.

In Bombay to five per cent earned less than Rs. 100/-, 78% earned Rs. 101-300, seven per cent earned Rs. 301—400 and three per cent earned Rs. 401 and above. By now with the increased price index monthly income of working women has risen to minimum Rs. 3000. In addition to the individual income earned by working women, there were also earnings by other members of the household. The total of these two sources of income has been termed as the family income. Only two working women belonged to families where the average income of the earners went beyond Rs. 1900 00 per month. Half of the employed women 50.2%) came from families of low income groups. Two fifths of the working women (40.5%) belonged to lower-middle income groups. A small proportion of them 7.8%) came from upper-middle income groups and only 1.5% were from higher income group.

The mean monthly income was Rs. 193.25. Delhi and Bombay studies also report that mostly working women belonged to lower income families. The data regarding the income of the working women have further been analysed in terms of the contribution they actually make to family income. Proportionate contribution by each working women suggested that more than seventy per cent of the working women contributed on an average fifty per cent or less per month, but on the other hand, 16.8% of the working women contributed more than ninety per cent o the family income.

These working women were the only wage earners in their household. They were mostly widowed and the separated having no other bread winner in their families to support. Working women contributed, on an average, Rs. 45.3 per month to the total income of the family. Nearly one-third of the women interviewed in Delhi were earning upto sixty per cent of their families' total income, and their contribution did not help to raise the standard of living. In many cases it was a matter of keeping the wolf away from the door. Low income and high prices were responsible for this situation.

Each of the following aspects is not related ot other for a better picture to emerge. It appears that proportion of illiteracy was higher in old age group, which was quite natural. Free educational facilities are available to women to-day in Rajasthan which were not available to them in the past.

This is evident from the proportion of young-age-group women in highly educated category which was much more than that of the working women of other age-groups. One-half of the working women of young age group were engaged in teaching and clerical occupations, whereas only 14.2% of middle aged working women were engaged in these occupations and none of the old aged were found in these occupations because the age of retirement was fifty-five years and most of them were not so educated as to be in these jobs.

One-half of the middle age working women were in unskilled occupations. As many as 56.5% of old aged working women were engaged in unskilled occupations. Only 18.8% of working women of young age group were found in unskilled occupations. The decline in caste status, there was an increase in the mean age of the working women. The working women of upper caste were the youngest of all the working women. This is because of the fact that upper caste women took no part in any out-door activities in the past and many observed purdah. They never left the house without purdah.

Thus, the question of their serving outside did not arise. In a caste-ridden society we expect to find that the educational level of different caste-groups would be different and that educational level of caste-groups higher-in-order would be higher than that of caste-groups lower-in-order. The Working women of the upper and middle caste groups were highly educated in comparison to those of lower, Scheduled Castes/Tribes and other castes. A large number of upper and middle-caste working women had received education above the High School level.

The rate of illiteracy was very high in lower, Scheduled Castes/Tribes (83.8%), lowest being in the upper caste group (7.9%). It suggests that there was a sharp and significant difference in the educational standard of the working women belonging to upper, middle, lower and Scheduled Castes/Tribes and other castes. Recent studies have clearly shown that in communities which are stratified on the basis of caste-system, there tends to be a congruence between the social status of the caste-groups and the occupations followed by the members. Describing the emergence of caste system Nesfield maintains that castes have emerged out of occupations and that they are related.

In this study, caste and occupation seem to be distinctly related. Through the working women of upper and middle caste groups did not differ significantly in their occupation, yet they differed significantly from working women of lower, Scheduled Castes/Tribes. The latter were largely employed in unskilled occupations. They were either domestic servants, ayaas in hospitals or factory workers. Larger section of upper and middle castes working women were employed in prestigious occuaptions. The percentage distribution shows that unmarried working women were clustered heavily in young age group (88.9%), whereas the clustering of married working women was in middle age group (59.6%).

The number of the widowed and the separated was relatively more in the middle age group. There appeared to be a striking difference between married and unmarried working women's education. Whereas there was only one unmarried working woman who was non-lettered (she was a factory worker), there were slightly more than one half of the married working women who were non-lettered (53.8%). About, Three-fourth of the widowed and separated working women are non-lettered. Compared to the widowed, the separated and unmarried working women, the proportion off married working women with low education was slightly higher.

On the whole, the unmarried working women are more educated than all others. Slightly more than half of the married, the widowed and the separated working women had small number of children (1-3)children). One-third of married working women had medium number (4-6) of children, whereas only sixteen per cent of the widowed and the separated working women had medium number of children. The percentage of working women with larger number of children (7) and above) was more among the married than the widowed and the separated.

Only one-tenth of married working women had no children whereas slightly more than one-fourth of the widowed and the separated working women did not have any child. The data clearly shows that more than half of the married working women had children of pre-school age and one-third of them had school age children. Even less than one-fourth of the widowed and the separated working women had children of pre-school age. The number of the widowed and the separated with school age children was some what higher than owners.

Approximately one-third of the widowed and the separated working women had children of eighteen years or above, whereas only one-twentieth of all married working women with husbands had children of eighteen years or above. It reveals that women not only with children of school age but also of pre-school age entered the labour force in greater number. This finding is different from that of Nye and Hoffman who found that women with children of school age have entered the labour force in greater number than mothers of pre-school children. About three-fourths of the widowed and the separated working women belonged to low income group with reference to their own income, whereas more than one-half of the married working women and even less than one-fourth of unmarried working women, belonged to this income group.

More than half of the unmarried working women belonged to lower-middle income group whereas only there-tenths of married working women and only one-fourth of widowed and separated belonged to this. The percentage of unmarried and married who belong to upper-middle income group was almost equal (9.9% and 9.3% respectively). None of the working women earned so much as to place them into the upper income group. The education and occupation are also related. The highly educated women were engaged in professions such as Medicines, Teaching, Law etc.

Those who were non-lettered or low educated were employed in unskilled work. This shows relation of occupation and education. Since professional work like Medicines, Law, Teaching in Universities or Administration could not be taken up without higher education, it was natural that educated working women were found in such occupations and those who were not educated would go to such occupations where education was not a prerequisite. It has generally been demonstrated in various studies that occupation is highly correlated with income derived from occupations.

Of those working women who were engaged in professions, 81.5% belonged to the upper-middle income group. Clearly the income range skewed on the lower side. It is significant to mention that order to present a comprehensive picture of the social characteristics, a detailed socio-economic enquiry into the conditions of working women was conducted. The average age of the working women was 34.3 years and they are clustered in the middle age-group.

Only a small number o9f working women belonged told age group. Hindus formed the majority of the women in employment. Most of the working women came from low castes, Scheduled Castes/Tribes. But if each caste was taken separately, Brahmins constituted the single largest group. The married women were found in larger number in the working force. Majority of the employed women belonged to nuclear families and the size of their household was generally medium. Generally 1 to 3 persons depended on them and most of the working women belonged to the families where 2 to 3 persons earned. Mostly they were local and urban. Nearly half of the women were non-lettered and engaged mostly in unskilled occupations.

The overwhelming majority was full-time workers. On an average, they had been working for about 8.3 years mobility was only nominal. Earning of most of them was low and they generally belonged to lower or lower-middle income group families. The working women contributed a sizeable proportion of their earnings to family income. Those of young age were more educated and were in prestigious occupations. Upper caste working women were mostly young and those of lower, Scheduled Castes/Tribes were mostly old.

Those who belonged to the upper and middle castes were highly educated and lower, Scheduled Castes/Tribes were generally non-lettered. Upper castes working women were engaged in prestigious occupations whereas lower, Scheduled Castes/Tribes were engaged in lower occupations. The unmarried working women were highly educated and even mothers of pre-school are children went to work. Earning of unmarried working women was more than that of others. Education and occupation seemed to be related. Those with high education were employed in prestigious occupations and with lower education in low occupations.

GENDER JUSTICE AND EMPLOYMENT DISCRIMINATION

It is significant to note that employment discrimination (or workplace discrimination) is discrimination in hiring, promotion, job assignment, termination, and compensation. It includes various types of harassment. Many jurisdictions prohibit some types of employment discrimination, often by forbidding discrimination based on certain traits ("protected categories"). In other cases, the law may require discrimination against certain groups.

In places where it is illegal, discrimination often takes subtler forms, such as wage discrimination and requirements with disparate impact on certain groups. In addition, employees sometimes suffer retaliation for opposing workplace discrimination or for reporting violations to the authorities.

Like most discrimination, employment discrimination may occur intentionally or unintentionally, because of prejudice or ignorance. Laws often prohibit discrimination on the basis of:

- Race or colour
- Ethnicity or national origin
- Sex or gender
- Pregnancy
- Religion or creed
- Political affiliation
- Language abilities
- Citizenship
- Disability or medical condition
- Age
- Sexual orientation
- Gender identity
- Marital status

Some jurisdictions prohibit employment discrimination against other social groups that have legal protections. They include discrimination or harassment based on socioeconomic class, height or weight if not relevant to employment, and provincial/regional origin.

Effects of Discrimination

Markets Punish the Discriminator

The Nobel prize-winning economist Gary Becker showed in his book *The Economics of Discrimination* (University of Chicago Press, 1957) how the markets automatically punish the companies that discriminate. The profitability of the company that discriminates is decreased, and the loss is "directly proportional to how much the employer's decision was based on prejudice, rather than on merit." Indeed, choosing a worker with lower performance (in comparison to salary) causes losses proportional to the difference in performance.

Similarly, the customers who discriminate against certain kinds of workers in favour of less effective have to pay more for their services, in the average. If a company discriminates, it typically losses profitability and market share to the companies that do not discriminate, unless the state limits free competition protecting the discriminators. There is also a view that "discrimination to satisfy customers' preference can increase profits".

Discrimination by the Government

In politics, the dominating part of the population rules. Therefore, the worst discrimination in the history has been committed by states. For example, the anti-semitic practices of the Nazi-Germany would not have happened on free markets, because they would have caused losses. Government officials and politicians need not care about losses as much as companies, which decreases their incentive not to discriminate. For example, around 1900 the afro-Americans started to compete of jobs that had previously been all-white jobs. Because whites had more voting power, they enacted a law that made photographs of the applicants obligatory in civil service job applications.

The number of blacks in federal employment plummeted for decades. In early 20th century South Africa mine owners preferred hiring black workers because they were cheaper. Then the whites successfully persuaded the government to enact laws that highly restricted the black' rights to work. Similarly, to make more profits, producers secretly hired screenwriters who were on Senator Joseph McCarthy's blacklist, which mitigated the effects of the list. Minimum wages enacted by the governments or unions decrease the loss caused by discrimination. Thus they weaken the markets' natural incentives not to discriminate. They also decrease the number of people whom the companies may profitably hire and thus make it unprofitable for the companies to hire people who have little expertise.

Effects of Discrimination in the Workplace

Discrimination in the workplace negatively affects businesses in that discriminatory policies can hurt a company's reputation. A business self-limits itself when it restricts advancement to certain groups or types of employees. Speaking negatively about a former employee can be damaging for a potential client. There is also a direct correlation between loyalty, retention, and discrimination. Employees are more likely to be looking for new jobs when they feel they have been wronged. According to a report on discrimination at the workplace by the International Labour Organization, "workplace discrimination remains a persistent global problem, with new, more subtle forms emerging." Sending wrong signals to potential clients can also cause conflict because customers can sense when employees aren't enthusiastic or don't believe in their company.

This is one reason that it is important for a job applicant to observe the attitudes of people they wish to work with. Sending positive signals to employees attracts future potential employees. Inequalities suffered by discriminated groups spreads. Due to affirmative action policies, a new middle class has been created that consists of formerly discriminated people in some countries but in others, people who are from discriminated groups are frequently involved in the worst jobs, denied benefits, capital, land, social protection, training, or credit.

Discrimination at a workplace can lead to poverty. "Discrimination creates a web of poverty, forced and child labour and social exclusion." In December 2005, a Gallup poll showed that job satisfaction was lowest when employees experienced discrimination.

Gender Discrimination and the Workplace

Even though there are regulations that are used to promote equality within the workplace, discrimination is still rampant. Women still do not measure up to men when it comes to income, employment rates and occupational range. Women's average salary is 72 to 88 percent of men's, even when variables such as education, age, position level and job tenure are considered. In most countries, the glass ceiling is ever present for women and the wage differences are significant compared to men. Based on a report by Catalyst in 2005, only "one in eight woman were CEO's in the Fortune 500; an additional nine were CEO's in Fortune 501-1000 companies."

Women are also more likely to be stuck in low-paid but more secure positions (i.e. education and healthcare). Historically the rate of employment for women was lower; however, due to the late 2000s recession the participation of women in the workforce has surpassed that of men. "Discrimination can occur at every stage of employment, from recruitment to education and remuneration, occupational segregation, and at time of layoffs."

Unintentional Discrimination

Unintentional discrimination (often termed "statistical discrimination") occurs when neutral selection practices produce a substantial disparity of outcomes between one group and another. Such practices include the use of standardized tests (which may disadvantage certain groups) and/or height or weight (which may disadvantage women and some ethnic groups) in the hiring process.

If the requirements are job-related and a "business necessity", the disparity is irrelevant. Some laws prohibit unintentional as well as intentional discrimination, but may have different standards for deciding what is acceptable. Substantial disparities in outcome are not necessarily illegal, if the practices that produce them are necessary.

Statistical Discrimination vs. Actual Discrimination

In some older studies, it has seemed as if the employers would discriminate for Far-Asians (15 to 25 percent more than for Caucasians) and against Afro-Americans (25 % less than for Caucasians) in pay and employment. When accounted for the amount and quality of the education and the geographic location, the differences disappeared. So it seems that the difference was not because of discrimination but because the Far-Asians usually had more and better education and worked in the North, where the salaries are higher also for Afro-Americans. Similarly, some other studies about wage discrimination often lacks several factors that account for the differences in productivity of different workers. For example, women more often choose low-wage careers or non-profit jobs and they have less working experience than men of same age.

In studies that sufficiently account for this kind of factors, remarkable wage differences are not found. Also the fact that some groups are underrepresented in some institutions and professions does not prove discrimination. For example, people born in cities are naturally underrepresented in farming. A company has the incentive to hire all people whose work produces more revenue than the cost of hiring them.

Legal Protection from Employment Discrimination

Many countries have laws prohibiting employment discrimination. Sometimes these are part of broader anti-discrimination laws.

- Employment discrimination law in the United States
- Employment discrimination law in the United Kingdom
- Employment discrimination law in the European Union

In the United States, Title VII of the Civil Rights Act of 1964 protects employees against various forms of employment discrimination. In addition to federal law safeguards, employees in California have broad protections under the Fair Employment and Housing Act (FEHA).

By Nation

Norway

In Norway, research indicates that 26 % of non-ethnic Norwegians (and 11 % of ethnic Norwegians) are overqualified for their work — Gro Mjeldheim Sandal (a professor) says employment discrimination is only one of the factors to account for differences in overqualification between those groups.

REFERENCES

Baber, R.E. *Marriage and the Family,* New York: McGraw Hill, 1953, pp. 341-47.

D'Souza, Victor S., *Social Structure of a Planned City Chandigarh,* New Delhi: Orient Longmans Limited, 1968, p. 73.

Government of India, *Economic and Social Status of Women Workers in India.* Labour Bureau, Ministry of Labour, Publication No. 15.

Hauser, P.M., "The Labour Force as Field of Interest of the Sociologists", *American Sociological Review,* 16 (1951), pp. 530-38.

Koyama, Takashi, *The Changing Social Position of Women in Japan,* Unesco 1961, p. 109.

Kyrk, Hazel "Who Works and Why?" Ibid., pp. 44-52.

Miler, Freida S., "Women in the Labour Force," *The Annals of the American Academy of Political and Social Sciences,* 251 (1947), pp. 35-40.

Mukherji, R.K. *Indian Working Class,* Allahabad: Hinditabs, 1945, p. 216; Thorner, Daneil, and Thorner A., *Land and Labour In India,* Bombay: Asia Publishing House, 1962, pp. 72-73.

Mukherji, R.K., "Caste and Economic Structure in West Bengal in Present Times," *Sociology, Social Relations and Social Problems In India,* Saxena, R.N. (ed.,) Bombay: Asia Publishing House, 1961, p. 157.

Nye F. Ivan and Hoffman, Waldis, "The Socio-Cultural Setting," *The, Employed Mother in America,* Chicago: Rand McNally and Company 1963, p. 8.

Pager, Devah (2009). *Marked: Race, Crime, and Finding Work in an Era of Mass Incarceration*. University of Chicago Press.

Papa, Michael J.; Tom D. Daniels, Barry K. Spiker (2007). *Organizational Communication: Perspectives and Trends* (5 ed.). SAGE.

Ranade, S.N., and Ramchandran, P., *women and Employment,* Bombay: Tata Institute of Social Science, 71 AS, 1970, p. 7 and p. 3.

Trentham, Susan; Laurie Larwood (1998). "Gender Discrimination and the Workplace: An Examination of Rational Bias Theory". *Sex Roles* 38 (112): 1–28.

Wadhwa, Vivek (6 June 2006). "The True Cost of Discrimination". *BusinessWeek Online*. http://www.businessweek.com/smallbiz/content/jun2006/sb20060606_087038.htm. Retrieved 29 August 2009.

4

Status of Women Workers in the Unorganized Sector

"A woman is like a tea bag - you can't tell how strong she is until you put her in hot water."

—*Eleanor Roosevelt*

OVERVIEW OF WORKING WOMEN IN INDIA

It is pertinent to note that an assessment of the trends in the magnitude and structure of employment (and unemployment) of women is beset with conceptual and measurement problems. Women are mostly engaged in household activities which are not considered "economic" and therefore, do not get counted as workers under conventional measures of employment Market-oriented concepts of income and employment do not capture a large part of women's economic activities as these activities consist of production of goods and services for the use of their own households. Even women's work in the production of goods and services for the market often gets ignored because of its being intermitant and subsidiary to their non-market and "non-economic" household work. [Papola 1992].

Sample surveys of the National Sample Survey Organization (NSSO)

and Population Censuses have tried to devise ways to reduce underestimation of women's work and such attempts have to continue. Comprehensive information on trends in the structure and levels of women employment is available from two sources, namely, the 1981 and 1991 population censuses and the quinquennial surveys on employment and unemployment of the National Sample Survey Organization (NSSO) conducted from 1972-73.

The two censuses had broadly comparable concepts of workers, but during the 1991 census, additional probing questions were put to informants so as to identify workers among women so as to minimise underenumeration of women workers. Trends during the period 1981-91 revealed by the two censuses, therefore, need to be treated with caution. The three NSSO sample surveys conducted in 1977-78, 1983 and 1987-88 are based on comparable concepts and, therefore, enable an analysis of trends over the period 1987-88.

These surveys also provide comprehensive information on the trends in the levels and structure of unemployment making uses of concepts designed to suit the specific features of a predominantly agricultural economy. Data on trends in employment in the organized sector of the economy are available from the Employment Market Information (EMI) programme of the Ministry of Labour (Directorate General of Employment and Training).

Extent of Participation of Women in Economic Activity

The Labour Force Participation Rate (LFPR), namely, the percentage of labour force to population, is a measure of the extent of participation in economic activity. These rates for women show that a majority of women, even in the working age groups, are outside the labour force. LFPR for women in the age group (15-59) is only 26.5% compared to 87.6% for men according to the NSSO 43rd Round (1987-88) survey on employment and unemployment. The rural-urban differential in the extent of women's participation in economic activity is substantial, LFPR for rural women being twice that of urban women (41.2% and 20.2%). On the other hand, LFPR for men is much higher in both rural and urban areas and not much different form each other (89% and 83.3% in rural and urban areas respectively).

LFPRs for women in the age group 5+ are similarly quite low both in rural (29.3%) and urban areas (14.7%), the overall rate being 26%; and these are substantially lower than the corresponding rates for men. LFPR for women have also been stagnant over the eighties, according to the 38th and 43rd Round (1983 and 1987-88) NSSO surveys. The low level of participation rates for women has also meant a low and stagnant share of women in total workers (28.%) over this period.

Trends in Levels and Structure of Unemployment among Women

The conventional and the most commonly used concepts of unemployment measure involuntary idleness but not 'invisible' unemployment and underemployment, which is a problem of a much larger magnitude in India. Involuntary idleness is measured in NSSO surveys of employment and unemployment using three concepts—Usual Principal Status (UPS), Current Weekly Status (CWS) and Current Daily Status (CDS). A person is considered unemployed on UPS basis if he/she was not working but was seeking or available for work for a relatively longer time during the reference year. A person is considered unemployed on CWS basis if he/she had not worked for even one hour during the reference week. Unemployment on CDS basis measures unemployment by aggregating unemployed days of all persons in the labour force during the reference week. UPS and CWS concepts estimate open unemployment, while the CDS concept, which is the most inclusive one, provides a measure of visible underemployment.

An idea of invisible underemployment could be had by comparing these rates with poverty levels. Incidence of unemployment is higher among women than among men, according to the 43rd Round (1987-88) survey of NSSO. The rates for women are estimated to have been 4.19% (of the labour force) on UPS basis, 4.92% on CWS basis and 7.61% on CDS basis. In absolute terms, unemployment is estimated to have been 3.61 million women, 3.99 million women and 2084 million women-days respectively during 1987-88. These respectively accounted for 31.%, 28% and 32% of total unemployment on the basis of each of the three concepts. The rates for different groups in different years estimated on the basis of the three concepts show that underemployment is a much higher proportion of unemployment among women than among men.

There is also a shift in the structure of unemployment from a state of widespread underemployment towards greater open unemployment. This trend is stronger in rural areas and in the case of women (Planning Commission 1992). Greater attention has, therefore, to be paid to creation of regular employment opportunities for women than to temporary, off season public works employment. Incidence of unemployment among educated women is higher (27%) than that for men (10%). Among all the educated unemployed 27% are women. Incidence of unemployment among educated women has declined from 32% to 27%; and the share of women among all the educated unemployed has come down from 42% to 27% over the decade 1977-78 to 1987-88.

Trends in the Growth and Structure of Employment of Women

Overall women employment has grown at the average annual rate of 1.90% over the period 1977-78 to 1987-88 according to NSSO surveys. The rate of growth has been more or less the same (1.97%) as that of employment of men during the period and as a result, the share of women in total employment has remained at the level of 28% over the period. Women employment has grown much faster in urban areas (3.62%) than in rural areas (1.66%). The rate of growth of urban employment has been more or less the same for men (3.66%) and women but in rural areas women employment has grown faster than employment of men (1.48%). While the share of rural areas in total employment has declined from 82.% to 78.% the share of rural areas in total women employment declined less sharply from 89% to 87.%; and the share of rural women in total employment fell only slightly, from 24.9% to 24.2% (NSSO 1981-1990). Women employment thus continues to be predominantly rural.

Although the share of women in total employment has been stagnant at 28.%, and in agriculture at 32%, it has increased in construction (from 14% to 24%) and in finance, insurance and real estate (from 4.5% to 7.5%) and has declined in trade and commerce (14.%) to 13.%) during 1978-88. The average annual growth rate of employment of women has been higher than that of overall employment in agriculture (1.1% against 0.9), construction (16% against 10%), electricity gas and water supply (10% against 5%) and finance, insurance and business services (13% against 7.5%) (NSSO *ibid*). As the last two are small sectors in terms of employment shares, major gains in employment for women would appear to have occurred in sectors mostly offering insecure and unstable employment, namely, agriculture and construction.

Differential rates of growth of employment of women in different sectors have brought about some changes in the structure of women employment. The share of agricultural in women employment fell from 80% in 1977-78 to 75% in 1987-88 and the shares of each of the other sectors in women employment increased. Construction registered the most significant increases, from 0.93 to 3.33% but the shares of sectors like manufacturing, trade, transport and services in total women employment increased slightly.

On the other hand, the share of agriculture in employment of men fell more sharply, from 67% to 59%; and that of construction increased less significantly, from 2.18 to 4.17% (NSSO *ibid*). An analysis of trends in the structure of employment by category of employment, reveals a shift from self employment to casual work, with the proportion of regular wage/salary earners remaining unchanged, but in the case of women workers, the shift is more towards regular wage/ salaried work 54.8% of women workers were self employed, 6.6% regular wage/salaried workers and 38.6% casual workers in 1977-78, while the corresponding proportions were 53%, 8% and 39% respectively in 1987-88.

On the other hand, the share of the self employed in employed men declined from 58.% to 54%, and that of casual workers rose from 24% to 28% while the share of regular wage/salary earners remained at 18% during this period (Planning Commission 1992). Although a larger proportion regular wage/salary earners than male workers, on the margin, women have been able to secure regular jobs better than men and avoid increase in the degree of casualisation. Average annual rates of growth of overall employment as well as women employment are higher according to the 1981 and 1991 Census (2.4% and 3.4%) than those revealed by the 32nd and 43rd Round NSSO surveys (1.95% and 1.90%).

The same is the case in some sectors, namely, agriculture, trade and commerce and 'other services' (other than transport etc.) Census rates of growth for overall and women employment are lower than NSSO rates in other sectors, namely, construction, mining and quarrying and transport, storage and communications. In all sectors except construction and trade and commerce, however, employment growth rates for females are higher than those for overall employment during the period 1981-91. The share of females in total employment has, therefore, risen from 20.3% in 1981 to 22.5% in 1991, though the share according to Census data is smaller than that revealed by NSSO surveys. Census data also reveal, like NSSO data, a slower shift away form agriculture in the structure of female employment (81.3% to 80.8%) than is the case with the structure of male employment (65.6% to 62.7%) (Registrar General, India 1993).

The shift noticed from Census data is also much smaller than shown by NSSO data. The low growth of employment of females in construction and the fall in the share of construction in total female employment as well as in the share of females in construction employment during 1981 to 1991, is, however, contrary to the trends during 1977-78 to 1987-88 revealed by NSSO surveys. All these trends have to be examined in detail, taking note of the reasons mentioned earlier as also other relevant factors. Work in the unorganized sector is the more predominant mode of employment of women than of men. The share of the organized sector even in overall employment is only 10%; but the share in the case of women employment is much less, only 3.2%. Employment of women in the annum) than that of employment of men 91.5% per annum); and as a result, the share of women in organized sector employment has increased from 12% in 1979 to 13.6% in 1989. Employment of women has grown relatively faster in certain subsecotrs of the organized sector, like financial services (8.8% per annum), transport, communications (6.8%), electricity, gas and water services (7.7%) and community services (4.6%). It registered an absolute decline in manufacturing and mining and grew slower than employment of men in agriculture and construction. Such deferential growth rates have led to changes in employment shares of women in different subsectors of the organized sector and in the structure of organized sector employment during the period 1979-89. Employment shares of women have risen fast in financial services (8% to 11%) and community services (16% to 20%); and the share has declined in manufacturing.

In 1979, half of the women employed in the organized sector were in community services and a little over one-fifth in manufacturing; and in 1989, the corresponding shares were 57% and 16% (Ministry of Labour-successive Annual and Quarterly Employment Reviews). Public sector has been the main contributor to the growth of organized sector employment, with the public and private organized sector employment levels registering average annual growth rates of 2.35% and 0.36% respectively. Employment growth rates have been higher for women than men in both the public sector (4.8% against 2.1%) and the private sector (0.85% against 0.25%) (Ministry of Labour *ibid*).

Employment of Educated Women

Employment of educated women has grown faster (almost 10% per annum) than overall women employment and also faster than employment of the educated in general (7.5% per annum) during the period 1977-78 to 1987-88. The share of the educated in total women employment has consequently increased from 7.5% to 1.5% during this period, but the increase in the share of the educated in total women labour force has been sharper, from 19% to 33% (NSSO 1981, 1990). It has been seen that (i) women's employment is more predominantly rural than that of men's employment, (ii) the share of women workers has increased mostly in sectors offering only low paid, insecure and unstable employment (like agriculture and construction), (iii) the shift from agricultural to non-agricultural employment has been less marked and that to construction is more marked in the case of female workers than of male workers, and (iv) the proportion of casual workers among female works, though stagnant over the Eighties, is still higher than for male workers.

These show that the quality of women's employment is not only relatively much lower than that of men but also that it has not improved over time. Data on earnings of male and female workers from NSSO surveys on employment and unemployment confirm these trends. Notwithstanding the Equal Remuneration Act, average earnings of female workers continue to be less than those of male workers; and the disparity in earnings between male and female workers, regular or casual, has worsened over the Eighties in the agricultural sector except in rural public works.

The disparity has reduced somewhat in the non-agricultural sector, and more sharply in urban sectors than in the non-farm rural sector. Further, the disparity between average daily earnings of male and female casual workers even in 1987-88 is greater that in the case of regular wage/salaried male and female workers.

Summary

(i) the level of participation, of women in economic activities is low; and this has meant a low and stagnant share of women in total workers (28%) over the years.

(ii) unemployment rates are higher for women than men.

(iii) visible underemployment is a much higher proportion among, women than among men.

(iv) The trend towards an increase in the incidence of open unemployment and a decline in that of (visible) underemployment, has been stronger in the case of women than in the case of men.

(v) Incidence of unemployment among educated women is much higher (27.%) than that for men (10%). A little over one-fourth of the educated unemployed in 1987-88 are women, though this share has come down from 42% to 27% in the Eighties.

(vi) Employment of women is more predominantly rural than of men.

(vii) Work in the unorganized sector is the more predominant mode of employment of women than men.

(viii) The share of women in overall employment has increased mostly in sectors offering only low paid, insecure and unstable employment; but here is also a trend towards an increase in some smaller sectors characterised by stable employment (namely, financial services and electricity).

(ix) The shift in the structure of employment from agricultural to non-agricultural employment has been less marked, and that to construction has been more marked, in the case of female than of male workers.

(x) There has been an increase in the stability of women's employment, in terms of proportion of regular wage/ salary earners among workers; the proportion has slightly declined in case of men. On the other hand, while proportion of casual workers has significantly increased in the case of males, it has remained unchanged in the case of female workers.

(xi) Women have been able to secure an increase in the organized, particularly public sector jobs much faster than men. A major part of this increase is accounted for by community services and financial services.

(xii) Quality of employment of women is, as seen from the foregoing, not only relatively much lower than that of men but also that it has not improved much over time. However, (viii), (x) and (xi) above indicate a trend towards some improvement.

(xiii) Average daily earnings of female workers continue to be less than that of male workers, the disparity being greater in the case of casual workers then regular wage/salaried workers. The disparity has worsened over the Eighties in the agricultural sector except in rural public works. It has reduced somewhat in the non-agricultural sector, and more sharply in urban sectors than in the non-farm rural sector.

Ever since attention was drawn to the widespread prevalence of informal or unorganized activities in the developing countries, studies of this phenomenon in numerous situations have been undertaken, often under the sponsorship of the International Labour Organization. On the basis of the data obtained from such country-wide studies, several scholars have tried to make generalisations about the salient features of these groups of activities and workers. However, attempts to delineate the definitive characteristics of this sector, whether in terms of the character of the product or the technologies used (traditional or modern), the markets served (local or general) or the consumers of the product (poor or rich), have not been very successful because no such pattern appears to be universally valid.

The exact combination of activities that actually exist in any one region at a given time, seem to be an outcome of the interaction of various factors such as the complexity of the economy, the actual extent and distribution of control of investment resources and the technological choices available to that economy. Since the configuration of such factors is almost always specific to each situation, what is true of one country at one time, fails to apply to another. All that can be said is that the sector usually consists of productive activities with loosely formed groups bound by diverse types of informal working contracts. It includes a section of the self-employed, wage earners, family producers as also the household workers. While the concept 'unorganized sector' cannot be defined precisely, few would deny that in each of these countries there is distinct break in the economy separating the 'formal' activities from the other activities and it is possible to assign any activity or group of workers to either of the two sectors with a fair degree of general agreement.

The division between the two sectors in each country is marked by a distinct change in the wages and working conditions enjoyed by the workers as they move from one sector to the other. This difference is sufficiently marked so as to warrant a qualitatively different treatment. For some reason, workers in the organized sector can bargain effectively with their employers while other workers in the country cannot. The bargaining strength of the former may be due to their superior skills, though generally it is greatly reinforced by the political militancy of their trade unions. Other workers are not capable of building up such bargaining strength and therefore continue to work under deplorable working conditions. There are several reasons why the prevalence of such working conditions has become a matter of grave concern to social scientists and policy makers in India as elsewhere in the world.

In India, as in most developing countries, small pockets of formal (officially recorded) activities were seen by the middle of the last century and this formalisation was concentrated mainly in the urban areas and often in organizations with a large-scale production for the far-flung markets. Since this period, industries such as textiles, steel, tea, chemicals and engineering have flourished in several large-scale factory units following modern management styles and having trade unions of workers. The scope of such activities gradually increased and with it the difference between the organization and working of the two sectors became clear. However, this dichotomy was not as important in India at the time of independence, as it is today, from the point of view of social justice. Workers in some occupations had well-organized and highly politicalised unions since the second decade of the twentieth century. However, till independence they had not won any significant economic concessions from the employers mainly because of the absence of political power in the hands of the Indian political parties.

Therefore, the differences in the working conditions of the formal and the informal sectors were not so sharply marked, and the imbalance between the supplies of labour and the investible resources had not become so glaring. In India today, a fast growing labour force is confronted with a relatively slow growing and closely held stock of capital and the pressure of this uneven bargain is holding down the real wages in the free market, both in the rural and the urban areas. Trade unions with greater political importance have managed to maintain the actual earnings of their workers at a level at least above that required for a minimal living, but workers without such protection have lost steadily in the inflationary situation of the sixties and the seventies.

Thus, the difference in the earnings and expectations of the two groups of workers has been steadily increasing. In the absence of any systematic data about the working conditions in the informal sector of any region, it is difficult to give conclusive evidence about the extent of difference in the two sectors. The occupations and activities, as also the technologies used in each sector are not quite the same and it is not always possible to compare them. Nevertheless, the trends are unmistakable. For example, a study of the electrical fan industry in Calcutta showed that the average earnings per worker in the small units were less than those of the workers in the bigger units. Similarly, in the shoe industry the minimum salary of a worker in a registered large unit was over twice as much as that of any of the artisans working in the informal shoe industry. The same is true of the *biri* industry where a worker under the putting out system earns less than half the officially fixed minimum rates of pay for a *biri* factory worker. Apart from these differences in their earnings, the workers in the organized sector received other benefits such as paid holidays, medical or old age allowances and enjoyed a fairly high degree of job security.

It is the absence of these very benefits that separates the lot of the workers of the unorganized sector from the rest. The unorganized sector presents two knotty problems of social justice to policy markers. First, an increasingly large segment of the working population is being forced to live at the margin of survival. Second, given the availability of such cheap labour in the unorganized sector, employers are likely to divert more and more activities to such organizations. This would mean that the working class as a whole, will in future receive an ever declining share in the products of development. No popular government can afford to ignore these possibilities for long.

The recent attempts at intervention by the state have, however, been rather confused and misdirected because very little is known about the production processes and working conditions in the informal sector. The need for more information has led policy makers, particularly the Central Ministry of Labour and the Planning Commission, to sponsor research in the field. The present study forms a part of the series of research studies of the unorganized sector that have been sponsored by the Unemployment Committee of the Planning Commission through the ICSSR for this purpose.

Employment in the Unorganized Sector. At the beginning of these explorations of the nature of the unorganized sector several public documents and records have attempted to delimit its bounds and to give rough estimates of its size both by the kind of activities involved and the areas where they exist.

TABLE 1

All India Work Force 1973

	Organized sector		*Unorganized sector*		*Total*	
	Urban	*Rural*	*Urban*	*Rural*	*Urban*	*Rural*
Male	154.16	12.73	158.74	1258.97	312.90	1271.70
Female	15.30	6.05	56.40	700.25	71.70	706.30
Total	169.46	18.78	215.14	1959.22	384.60	1978.00

The employment figures in the organized sector are based on regular official records and are therefore, fairly accurate. The other figures are estimates based on nationwide sample surveys of employment and unemployment by the National Sample Survey authorities. In these surveys, the main problem is of definition of the term employment. Several alternatives defining this concept ranging from the most rigorous to the most permissive have been considered.

At the rigorous end is the measure of the size of the work force by the daily status of each person—strictly on the basis of whether or not a person had worked on the day of the interview. A less rigorous alternative considered a person's weekly status, in other words, to include all those in the work force who had worked at least sometime during the previous week. A still more accommodating definition takes into account seasonal or part-time employment, or even a person's usual status whether he considers himself a regular worker or not. These alternative specifications of the word 'employment' become necessary because of the amorphous character of the unorganized sector where the status of being employed does not, in itself, imply that a worker works for any standard number of hours a day or that he works regularly for a certain given number of days a year.

Moreover, in the unorganized sector, employment does not necessarily mean that the worker gets a regular wage payment for the work. The work may take the form of unpaid family labour, or be a combination of manual labour and risk bearing ability as in the case of a self-employed person, or a contractual obligation for repayment of an outstanding loan as in the case of bonded labour. The payment may be in cash or in kind or a combination of the two, and it may be a regular time rate wage, a piece rate wage, a share in the family consumption, or merely a guarantee from the employers of a minimal living for a specific period.

Women Workers

Measurement of women's employment presents some additional problems. Even if the majority of women can be described as engaged in household tasks, the category 'housework' is very much an extended one for poor women. If a woman using her own labour produces from freely available materials certain kinds of goods and services which the family otherwise, would have had to purchase at a price in the market, then she has, in principle, earned that amount of real income for the family. Even if one ignores the alternative costs of services such as washing or cooking, there are several additional tasks that poor women perform for which the decision as to whether they are economic activities or not is really difficult. For example, rural women collect fuel and edible roots, greens and fruits from the forest. Urban women of Calcutta collect half burnt coals from rubbish heaps, make cakes from cowdung in the streets and use the combination as a fuel for cooking.

In most areas and communities, women of artisan families participate in the family's production activities. They also look after the family's milch animals, poultry or vegetable plots—products which are partly sold in the market. Women's economic tasks in India can thus be divided into three categories (a) as an entrepreneur, a self-employed worker or a wage earning employee producing goods and services for the market; (b) as a participant, in return for a share in the living, in the family' production activities whose products are, at least partially, meant for the market; and (c) as a contributor to the family's real income by processing some goods which are available free (at the expense of some labour in collection) in order to supplement or replace its market purchases.

There is no uniform official policy as to whether or not all these three categories of tasks are to be taken into account for measuring women's employment. Nor is there any standard requirement about the number of days per year or hours per day a woman has to work on such tasks in order to be considered employed. This has led to frequent controversies about official estimates of women's employment. Controversies about measurement have obscured another equally important issue, a large part of women's work tends to fall in the second and third categories mentioned above. Changes over time have, if anything, reinforced this tendency. Work in the second category is slightly better than bonded labour—even if a particular person has some special aptitude or has acquired a skill with experience and age, there is no way that these extra qualifications can be rewarded at work by an increment or promotion. Work in the third category can only be an anachronism in present Indian society, where the supply of freely available goods is fast shrinking.

The people still following this practice are doing so, not by choice, but only because they are the rejects of the market mechanism. Work in either of these categories does not give the woman any control over family's disposable income, including the share she has earned, and also denies her the status of a socially productive worker. For the purpose of this survey, the universe studied included all women who, at the time of listing and interview, were engaged in the delimited activities for a money return. This does not exclude the possibility that they also received some additional benefits in kind. To qualify as a worker in this investigation, there was no stipulation that a woman had to work at these jobs for a minimal number of days per year or hours per week because the intention was precisely to bring out the variations in the labour contracts that exist in the unorganized sector.

Sexual Discrimination. Even as an entrepreneur, the work experience of women is distinctly worse than that of men with equal qualifications. The available data clearly supports this contention. First, the overwhelming majority of women work in the unorganized sector even in urban areas. This is in sharp contrast to the experience of the male workers, whose numbers are almost evenly divided between the two sectors. It may be possible that the activities in which women form a significant section of the workers do not get organized. Second, for women, work is relatively less regular and steady.

As the definition of the term employment becomes more rigorous the number of unemployed increase for both males and females. Unemployment figures are highest following the daily status concept where a person is unemployed even if only on the day of the interview. It is somewhat lower if a person is considered unemployed only if he has not worked on any day during the previous week. Unemployment is lowest, when confined only to people who are usually unemployed that is, those who have not found work for a fairly long period. As the table shows, the relative rates of unemployment are increasingly higher for women than for men as the definition of the term employment becomes more rigorous both in the rural and urban areas.

Even when they are employed, women on an average, get less work per period of time and also a lower rate for the same work as compared to men holding the same qualifications. Generally, for each category, the number of days per week for which women get employment is somewhat lower and the ratio of the weekly earnings of females to males is even lower, thus indicating that even for the days worked, women get a lower rate of payment.

Recent History of Women's Work. During the first half of the twentieth century, opportunities for Indian women to participate in economic activities increased at a much slower rate as compared to the rate of increase in female population. As a result, in the case of women, work force as percentage of the population (WFPR) decreased rapidly during the period between 1911 to 1951. In the 1961 and 1971 Census reports, the definitions of the term employment have been somewhat different but Mitra concluded that there was no marked change in the earlier trend of falling female WFPR. The decline in women's employment was a part of the general process of loss of industrial employment that affected the entire Indian population during the nineteenth and the early twentieth century. The once flourishing cottage industries in India suffered a severe set-back through the loss of both foreign and domestic markets because of stiff competition from British manufactured goods. The process was further accelerated in the early part of this century by competition from goods manufactured in Indian factories.

The traditional textile industry of India was one of the worst affected by this process. Women textile workers suffered relatively more because the spinning yarn industry where they worked was almost entirely wiped out by competition from imported and mill-made yarn. This process of shrinking industrial employment was further speeded up by the secular demise of the *yajamani* system during this period. The *yajamani* system was a traditional one whereby in each village, families belonging to particular service and trade castes such as barbers, blacksmiths and potters used to provide these services to the entire village in return for a traditionally fixed supply of grain or land from each family.

As the pressure on land increased following an increase in population (especially agrarian population) and agriculture became more commercialised, this bargain became non-viable for the other residents of the village. As a result, the custom of maintaining entire castes by such occupation became obsolete and was replaced by isolated workers providing these services in return for monetary payment. A few economic historians have argued that the decline of court life in towns led to the disappearance of some of the finer arts and crafts existing there (Naquvi). The decline of industries such as textiles and metal products, and of crude services rendered by potters and blacksmiths affected not only women but also men in large numbers. Surprisingly women's overall non-agricultural employment till 1961 never regained the absolute level it had reached in 1911, while for men, it only a meant a temporary set-back.

After 1921, non-agricultural male employment rose both in absolute numbers and in proportion to total male employment. Of the non-agricultural jobs that women lost during the period 1911 to 1961, only eight per cent could be accounted for by specific female tasks becoming obsolete, and in the remaining 92 per cent cases, women were simply replaced by men in their past occupations. This was particularly seen in food processing and textiles industries and in construction. As a consequence of this loss of opportunities in non-agricultural occupations, more and more women workers joined the ranks of agricultural labourers if their communities permitted it. Not only did women not retain their share in their traditional occupations, but they also took little part in the newly developing industries in India. During this period male employment in engineering, metallurgical and chemical industries increased.

However, only two industries, textiles and food processing, accounted for the employment of three-fourths of the female manufacturing group both in 1911 and in 1961. The remaining female manufacturing group was employed in wood, rubber and ceramics industries. It may be added here that even in industries like textiles or food processing, over four-fifths of the female workers were confined to the household sector and the expansion in the factory sector of these industries meant little or no increase in women's employment opportunities.

Another interesting fact was that though a few women had earlier gained entry into the factory sector of the textile industry, as soon as the factory sector wages and working conditions began to improve substantially after independence, a majority of women workers lost their jobs in these factories in the name of rationalisation. Only 16 per cent of the men in non-agricultural occupations worked in the household sector, as compared to 38 per cent of the women who worked in that sector. Till 1961, the census reports did not give separate employment figures for urban and rural population. However, they did give the employment figures for the four major cities of India which reiterate the general conclusion that non-agricultural employment of women was falling very sharply throughout this period.

Female Employment and Urbanisation. The downward trend in female WFPR in urban areas in India was all the more remarkable because during this period, female migration to urban areas was exceptionally slow. The general pattern of Indian urbanisation between 1911 to 1961 can be summed up as follows (a) a growing concentration of population in the larger cities; (b) a lower and, for sometime, a falling sex ratio in towns, especially in large cities; and (c) a marked decline over time in work opportunities for women in the larger cities resulting in a clear trend showing that the larger the city, the lower the female WFPR. In view of these facts, the Committee of Experts on Unemployment Estimates concluded that if economic development meant greater urbanisation, it would lead to a fall in work participation rates, particularly in the case of women.

Recent Trends

Although the changed definitions of the terms worker and employment in the 1971 Census make it difficult to compare its results with those of the previous census reports, there is little reason to believe that the secular trends vis-a-vis women's work force participation have altered materially during the period following 1961. Subsequent to the 1971 Census, attempts were made to reconstruct the employment position in that year to make it comparable to the 1961 Census reports. On the basis of the results of these exercises the Planning Commission in its Draft Plan for 1978-83 claimed that for 1971, the female work force participation rates have not fallen any further from the 1961 level. However, a survey of employment and unemployment conducted in 1976-77 by the National Sample Survey Organization seems to indicate that the 1971 WFPR for women may have been at par with the 1961 figures because the 1971 estimates included in the work force at least a section of the persons who gathered free materials strictly for the use of their own families.

The 1961 Census definition on the other hand had specifically excluded them. The fact that even in 1976-77 over 20 per cent of the adult rural women of India had to depend on such work for helping their families reflects badly on India's planned economy. Nevertheless, there are some minor but significant changes noticeable in the pattern of women's economic participation which may assume importance over the passage of time. For the first time, the proportion of agricultural and allied pursuits in the female work force did not increase but it actually registered a slight fall.

The WFPR of urban women increased slightly from 11 per cent in 1961 to 14 per cent in 1971. This was seen in spite of the acceleration in the rate of urbanisation of women during this period. A contributing factor here was the fairly rapid increase in women's employment in the organized, mainly public, sector. Since such employment is largely concentrated in the larger cities, it would not be wrong to conclude that metropolitan cities are no longer as hostile to women's work as before.

Nevertheless, as noted elsewhere, organized employment still accounts for less than 33 per cent of the urban female employment. Not all such changes need necessarily be indicative of an improvement in women's position. For instance, after a decline in its absolute level between 1961 and 1971, women's factory employment figures have recently registered an increase. In spite of this, women continue to lose their jobs in traditional areas like large-scale textile manufacturing and mines. They have not made any headway in the better paying metal or chemical industries and are mainly concentrated in poorly paid industries like food processing or tobacco. Further, women are gaining ground mainly in occupations where the majority of workers are women. Of the total non-agricultural women's employment in 1971, nearly 40 per cent were engaged in occupations where at least 70 per cent of the workers were women.

Such high concentration of women in an occupation is usually indicative of very poor wages and working conditions. The slight increase in the urban female work force is the outcome of not only an increase in the number of adult women in the work force but also of children and old people. In any society this is a bad omen reflecting a state of acute crisis in various sections of the population. It seems plausible that the increased work effort of women in the cities, at least partly reflects the increasing poverty in urban areas during the sixties.

Case Study: Kolkata

Since independence Calcutta and the State of West Bengal where the city is situated have witnessed a pattern of development which is somewhat distinct from that of the rest of the country. On the eve of independence, West Bengal was the most industrialised of the Indian states and the major share of the foreign industrial investment in India was located in this region, mainly around Calcutta's industrial belt. After independence, the growth of new industrial investment in this region was somewhat slower as compared to the other industrialised regions of India. This was partly because a large part of the new investment funds of the region were used for buying out foreign interests in the existing industry. On the other hand its initial lead in the industrial field meant that public sector investments which aimed at a more balanced inter-regional growth tended to by-pass Calcutta and its surrounding areas. During the Second and Third Plans, there was considerable new private industrial investment in this region, but not at rates comparable with those of Bombay, Pune, Ahmedabad, Baroda or Delhi.

Since then that channel has also dried up. All these factors have produced a situation where among the more advanced states of India, the growth of organized employment has been one of the slowest in West Bengal. During the period 1947 to 1961, Calcutta received wave after wave of refugees from Bangladesh, so that by 1971 this immigration had increased the population by almost 18 to 20 lakhs. This number accounted for about 25 per cent of the total population of the Calcutta metropolitan district in 1971. Unlike the other migrants to Calcutta, these refugees came with their families. For these migrants there was no possibility of any source of rural income to supplement their earnings in the city.

While it is true that the entire country is experiencing an imbalance between the supplies of capital and labour, the situation is particularly difficult in Calcutta with a large unwarranted increase in the labour force coupled with a stagnant investment picture. The traditions of women's economic participation have been particularly weak in West Bengal in comparison with the rest of India. The table above indicates that for all censuses during the twentieth century, whatever the definition of the term worker, West Bengal female WFPR was always one of the lowest in the country. Table 11 indicates that even in 1961 the women workers in West Bengal were from the scheduled castes or tribes, and there was little or no tradition of women from the upper castes or class taking up economic activities.

In spite of these facts it is worth nothing that the downward trend in women's WFPR in West Bengal between 1911 to 1961 was no less dramatic—it fell from 12.5 per cent to 6.1 per cent. The strength of the social bias against female work in Bengal was highlighted by a Survey of Earners in the Calcutta Municipal Corporation area conducted by the NSSO in 1953. According to the findings only about five per cent of women in Calcutta formed a part of the work force and almost all of them were from the scheduled castes. A large majority were widows or deserted women, and were from outside Bengal, speaking languages other than Bengali. There was no tradition of caste Hindu Bengali women working unless under crisis. Nearly all these women were paid to work in personal services.

A similar pattern was observed in the 1958 survey of Calcutta by S.N. Sen. There have been some marked changes in the last few years. A noticeable increase in women's participation in economic activities has been observed which is supported by available statistics. For urban West Bengal, Women's WFPR according to the 1961 Census was 5.12 per cent, and the NSSO in its 27th round Survey of Employment and Unemployment in 1972-73 gave an estimate of about 11 per cent. This increase of over 100 per cent is partly due to increased opportunities of work for women in the public sector and the professions, though it must be borne in mind that over 60 per cent of the women workers of Calcutta Metropolitan District in 1977 were in the unorganized sector. The brief review presented here cites some of the facts that establish the relevance of the study.

The unorganized sector employs a large section of the work force even in the urban areas of India and especially in calcutta. Although it is difficult to estimate the contribution of this part of the urban economy to the national product, there are signs that its span of activities and products is increasing. If the difference between labour costs in the formal and informal sectors continues to increase as it has in recent years, then it is likely that more activities would be switched over to the informal sector. In a labour surplus situation this will ultimately weaken the position of the working class as a whole, because the areas where the labour can bargain collectively will remain restricted. Women's work patterns have been more or less complementary to that of the other workers.

In the past, in the labour markets where they had participated, their employment acted as a balancing factor adjusted to changes in the overall labour demand so that male employment suffered relatively less from such vissisitudes. Within the family, they were expected to supplement male labour and perform the more tedious and less killed jobs in return for a share in the family living. Their enterprise and labour contributed to the family's product and income without giving them an unambiguous claim to either. Recent trends show that in the urban areas, women's employment is increasing at a significant rate in an otherwise stagnant labour market.

It is evident that women as a group, accept wage rates and working conditions inferior to those of other workers. These two facts taken together imply that women's employment is increasing at the cost of male employment and the relation between male and female employment is no longer complementary but competitive. Women in the urban economy are working largely outside their household occupations and their wages form an important part of the total family income.

However, it remains to be seen whether or not this gives them an added status in the family. One conclusion about he tradition of women's employment in India does not seem to be unwarranted on the basis of the facts outlined earlier. Women workers here have always formed a separate category in the labour market, concentrated in certain specific occupations and under particular types of organizations and working conditions. This category has shown wide variations from time to time in the size of the total employment vis-a-vis the population. Changes in the occupational structure of the group have often failed to match those warranted by the direction and speed of development in the economy as a whole.

Not only have these changes lagged behind the general trend but have often been in a contrary direction. This tendency appears to have been more pronounced in the case of women in Calcutta. Although there have been some improvements in women's work force participation since the seventies, it has not led to a complete integration of women with the rest of the labour force. Even in 1972-73 not more than 15 per cent of the women in Calcutta were in the labour force and the majority of them were in the informal sector. On the whole, women's work experience at each level was distinctly inferior to that of men. This continued segregation of women workers could be partly explained in terms of their social backgrounds and characteristics which have been briefly reviewed in this chapter.

Personal Characteristics

Age. For working in the unorganized sector there is no upper or lower age limit for a worker. Therefore, age limit was not stipulated in drawing this sample. The sample showed a surprisingly wide distribution of ages ranging from below 15 years to 60 years and above. The modal age of the workers was over 30 years though their distribution between age groups was about even with a gentle taper at the two ends. Children below 15 years formed seven per cent of the total sample. This figure was significantly higher than the figure reported in the 1961 Census—below two per cent among West Bengal urban women workers. Compared to the average educational level of all women in Calcutta of whom less than 40 per cent are illiterate, the overall educational records of women in the sample were very poor, possibly because they were from very poor backgrounds—women's education is closely correlated with the level of family income.

The younger women fared somewhat better which confirms the general impression that educational opportunities for children are improving with the passage of time. But literacy level was very low among the child workers, thereby implying that even if opportunities for education were expanding, children from poor families who had to earn a living could not take advantage of them. On the whole, the low literacy level of this group probably worked as a barrier to their access to information about the labour market and tended to isolate them from other workers. The education level of the head of the household had a significant influence on the education level of the respondents—higher the education level of the head of the household, the better the chances of a woman receiving higher education.

Only 13 per cent of these women came from households where the head was less educated than themselves. On the whole, only about 32.5 per cent of the women could read and write, but in households where the head was educated, about 61 per cent of the women could read and write.

Language, Marital and Religious Status. The overwhelming majority of women in the sample were Bengali speaking. Only 15 women workers had come from outside the Bengali speaking areas. Of these two Oriya women spoke Bengali fairly fluently in addition to their own language. The others were from Hindi speaking areas except for one who was from Gujarat, but most of them understood Bengali. The high percentage of married and unmarried Bengali women in this sample indicated that there had been a fairly radical change in the social attitudes of the people of Calcutta regarding female work force participation.

As already indicated elsewhere, a study of female earners in Calcutta had shown that Bengali women constituted only about 33 per cent of the total female earners. This was observed even though these studies had considered female earners in all occupations, including the professions and the organized sector where the overwhelming majority is Bengali. It was striking to observe that in this sample where all these occupations had been excluded, married and unmarried Bengali women still constituted nearly 70 per cent of the total workers. Evidence relating to social conventions such as early marriages, and multiple and early child-bearing which tend to restrict women in their performance as workers is very significant. Although marriage was an universal feature seen among all females above 25 years of age, there was a slight increase in the average age of marriage for women below 25 years.

This improvement was confined to women with some level of education. If a woman was to remain unmarried after the age of 16, it was expected that she be from a social class where women's education was an accepted value. The older a woman, the more important was her class in determining whether she remained unmarried or not. On the other hand in social groups where women's education was not an accepted feature, the age at marriage or at the birth of the first child as well as the average number of children was not significantly different for older and younger women. The younger women were still able to bear children and there was no apparent reason why their average number of children were much below that of the older group. In fact, the average age of 16 years of women in the sample at the birth of the first child was well below the average for all females of urban West Bengal for the period 1971 to 1975. There was a sharp difference vis-a-vis the conventions regarding marriage between women with and without educational achievements.

This was not due to the fact that educated women were more emancipated on account of their higher education level, but because in some social groups, women's position was somewhat better and this was reflected both in their access to education and in the relaxation of the practice of early marriage. Nevertheless, access to education did appear to help in the formation of maturer attitudes among women. Among the better educated, the chief reason for not practising family planning was lack of easy access to facilities, while in the case of others it was because of religious or family taboos.

Family Income and Standard of Living

According to the official policy of the Government of India as stated in the fifth Five Year Plan all persons with a per capita monthly income of Rs. 22.50 at 1960-61 prices were considered to be living below the poverty line. Allowing for a rise in the cost of living since then, the poverty level of incomes in 1976-77 would be approximately rs. 65 for Calcutta city. By these standards, nearly 70 per cent of these women and their families in the sample could be regarded as poor. Moreover, the percentage of families living below the poverty line of Rs. 65 per capita per month is especially high for the two groups namely, child workers and married women with young children. In other words, these two groups were particularly desperate when they entered the labour market. Surprisingly, the widows and divorcees were better off than the others in terms of their mean and modal incomes.

Unmarried women above 15 years of age generally belonged to higher social groups and their education levels were better. Married women had the support of their husband. Even then the per capita family incomes of both these groups were not comparable with that of the last group. In spite of these interesting variations, the overall family income of these women was meagre compared to the liabilities of the family. Their main strategy of survival was to send out more and more workers. Nearly half of the families sent out not less than three workers. Among those to be sent out first were unqualified and illiterate women, followed by children and old people.

The average income per earner was inversely related to the number of earners in the family, it can therefore be assumed that families sent out more workers not because of the abundance in skills but because the income of none of the workers was adequate. The difference between the mean incomes of families with and without one worker in the formal sector was significant no matter how many workers there were. Less than ten per cent of the families (37) had one person working in the formal sector, and among these, even families with only two earners were better off than others with as many as five earners. It may be noted that none of these 37 families had more than one worker in the formal sector.

In other words, having a relative working in the formal sector does not appear to make it any easier for other members of a family to get a similar job. Incidentally, the findings indicate that secondary or even higher level of education was neither a necessary nor a sufficient condition for getting a job in the formal sector. Of the 37 formal sector workers in these families, only 22 had such qualifications, the rest were either illiterate or barely literate. As compared to this, in the other 262 families, there were more than 100 people (apart from the interviewed women themselves) who had such qualifications but were either unemployed or employed in the informal sector.

Better education could have improved their chances of getting such a job but had not ensured it. In spite of the large number of earners in the family, only one-fourth of these women lived in joint families. The remaining two thirds lived in nuclear families and the rest, a small minority, lived singly. The ratio of earners to family members was 49.6 to 100 in nuclear families as against 44.96 to 100 in joint families. This clear shows that nuclear families were sending out more children as workers, though not all these children were minors, but they were all still unmarried. This was another indication of the desperate situation of these families. Although the survey was not necessarily confined to slum areas, the generally low income level of these families ensured that their housing standards would be about the poorest in the city.

Of the entire sample population, only 36 families had two or more rooms. The others lived in one room with a small verandah or partially covered space for cooking. For all families which had only one room, the average number of persons per room was 5.18 a figure significantly higher than the average of 3.41 persons per room for Calcutta city as a whole in 1971. Apart from being overcrowded, the housing structures were of a very poor quality. The residents there enjoyed very few of the urban civic services. Only 60 families lived in structures with *pucca* floors, walls and roof. Of these half the houses were in official slums. Another 107 families lived in houses which were completely made of *kuccha* material. There was no unambiguous information about the rest.

In Calcutta, only the relatively better off segment of society enjoys the exclusively use of a tap or a sanitary latrine or a service privy. The exclusive enjoyment of such facilities was rarely experienced by the families in the sample. Although half the area of the city is sewered, this was generally not seen in areas where these families lived. The population of Calcutta comprises of people born in the city, refugees who have migrated from Bangladesh after partition and those who have migrated either from other districts of west Bengal or from other states of India. The pattern of refugee migration differs from that of the other migrants quite significantly. According to earlier surveys, refugees coming to Calcutta generally travelled with their entire families; the heads of the refugee households were relatively better educated and, they were generally from urban or semi-urban centres and not from rural areas of East Bengal.

Compared to this, the other migrants were often single adult males who had come in search of a job or in case of women, after marriage. They had migrated from rural areas either of West Bengal or of the other states and the two types of migrants were treated separately. About 40 per cent of Indian women migrate at least once in their life time usually after marriage or to join the earning members of the family at their place of work. In this study, of the total sample population, 174 women that is, approximately 40 per cent were immigrants to the city. Of these one-third (58) migrated as refugees from East Bengal, 14 were from the other states of India and the rest from other districts of West Bengal—usually rural areas.

This kind of migration was particularly important in Calcutta as compared to the rest of India. At least 40 migrants had come individually to seek work in the city which was quite unusual compared to the All India pattern and more so because nearly all of them were Bengali speaking. 25 of them were not destitutes or widows but had families. Six of them had children below five years of age whom they had left behind with the rest of the family. This was probably an entirely new development in India. The migration of ten young unmarried women alone to he city was also very unusual considering the traditions of this region. A common factor underlying migration was the poverty of the family in their original place of residence and both single migrants as well as those moving in with their families had come to the city to look for work; though the difference in their expected incomes at home and in the city would probably be quite high, but that alone was not a sufficient cause for migration.

In all these migrant non-refugee families the incidence of unemployment was very low as these migrant women revealed that the decision to migrate was taken only when there were definite prospects of sufficient work and initially, only those members with such prospects migrated to the city. The others joined later when their own prospects of work improved, this implied that if there were jobs only for women or girls, then they migrated alone. In case of women who had come to the city for economic reasons, a study of the occupation of the head of the household indicated that the majority were from agricultural households and of these, about two-thirds including 37 single migrants came from landless families.

The other three came from homes where the head of the family was unemployed. The caste-wise distribution of these women was not clear as they did not usually specify their caste. They were classified on the basis of their family names which sometimes indicated the upper castes and scheduled castes but a large majority of women were grouped into the middle castes because their actual castes could not be accurately identified. Given that almost all the women in the sample belonged to very poor families, it was rather surprising that 12 per cent of them could be clearly identified as belonging to the upper castes. Only 32 women could be clearly identified as belonging to the scheduled castes. Surprisingly, the average family income of the upper caste women was not higher than the average for the entire group, though there was a slightly greater incidence of women belonging to families with one member working in the formal sector.

Upper caste women did have an edge over the others in educational performance since nearly one-fourth of this group had received secondary education or more, and only one-fourth were totally illiterate. This meant that their average age at the time of marriage was somewhat higher. Without going into a debate about the close coincidence between class and caste, it appears that upper caste families had more liberal views about a woman's position. Among the younger women, there was a sizeable group who had enjoyed some opportunity for education and faced less constraints in terms of early marriages and child-bearing. However, this liberalisation of traditional constraints was not universal nor was it progressive for all the young workers. Most of the child workers, that is, workers below the age of 15 years had been denied access to thee growing educational opportunities.

The results point to some radical changes in the social traditions vis-a-vis women's economic activities. As compared to the situation revealed by earlier surveys, there was a much higher incidence of married and unmarried Bengali women as opposed to widows or divorcees in the work force. Another striking change was the significant number of women who migrated singly to the city for work, a phenomenon hitherto unknown in this region.

The majority of workers were no longer from the scheduled castes or tribes and a significant proportion belonged to upper caste families. Two types of processes account for these changes. On the one hand there could be a general social movement towards women's emancipation which would be reflected in a shift in women's attitudes towards self-reliance. On the other hand it could be that the growing poverty of their families had forced them to join the ranks of workers. Although one would like to believe that the first explanation is valid, the weight of the evidence favoured the second explanation.

The family income of this group of women put the majority of them firmly below the official poverty line. Even for their meagre earnings, the families had to send out several, sometimes as many as five or six earners. The marginal contribution to the total income of a family from an additional workers usually declined as the number of earners increased indicating how unprepared these additional workers were for entering the labour force. The poor dwellings and the lack of access to civic facilities in the majority of the cases lent support to the hypothesis that extreme poverty and desperation led to the changes described above.

Surprisingly, though there was a significant percentage of women from upper castes or from social groups with more modern traditions, the poverty level was almost unvarying. The relatively better off families were those with at least one member working in the formal sector. However, there were only a few such families in the sample and of these few not one had more than one such worker. This does not augur well for ideas regarding mobility and connections between the formal and the informal sectors. A casual acquaintance with the existing state of affairs in the informal sector indicates that there are fairly stable traditions about the division of workers between occupations.

Apart from the division between sexes, there are long standing conventions in Calcutta about particular social groups undertaking specific tasks. For instance, the hand-*riksha*-pullers are usually Biharis, a large percentage of the tailors are either Hindu speaking Muslims or Hindu refugees from East Bengal, and the *biri* workers are usually Muslims. One does not know anything about the barriers which work to maintain these divisions nor how rigid they are in the context of the rapidly changing conditions of workers and residents. It has to be examined whether the barriers are raised mainly by social conventions or are based on more rational grounds such as the distribution of skills and access to training between workers. Nor is it clear whether these barriers are raised by employers who have definite preferences between groups of workers or by the which are not based on their respective working conditions alone. In other words, it remains to be seen whether the concentration of certain categories of workers in specific occupations is the result of differentials in the price offered by employers to these groups in specific occupations or in the demand price acceptable to each group in that kind of work. In contrast to the impression that the informal sector is divided into several imperfectly competitive groups, a few authors have commented on the high degree of competition between workers in the informal sector which stems from the mobility of workers between occupations.

According to them, the distinctive characteristics of the informal sector are the ease of entry of the new workers into these type of occupations and the non-formal methods of skill training available. In addition to these opportunities for accumulation of human capital in the form of skills and knowledge of markets and occupations, employment in the informal activities is also said to provide workers with opportunities for collecting some financial or physical capital for investing in small enterprises of their own. In a low employment, labour surplus economy, it is not unexpected that there should exist a high degree of competition between workers. Nor is it unexpected that despite their desperation in search for employment, workers still accept certain conventional taboos about the type of work they do. This could be explained in terms of the high degree of ignorance and illiteracy which is characteristics of this group.

Another widespread belief about the informal sector is that the employers in this sector are mainly small entrepreneurs who, either as self-employed workers or as petty producers, employ only a small number of workers. Therefore, it is believed that no one employer is in a position to influence the wage rates and there is no collusion between them. As a result, the market on the whole, is a competitive one where neither the workers nor the employers indulge in collective bargaining or use any kind of preemptive powers, instead they let the wage rates be determined by market forces alone. These hypotheses have not been adequately verified by studies in any region or period of the country so far.

Nevertheless, they form the basis of several policy measures relating to this section of the economy. In this study the occupational structure and its flexibility in the segment of Calcutta's informal sector and the process of organization as well as wage determination in it has been analysed with a view to shed some light on these questions. Although in the sample there were workers engaged in as many as 31 different occupations, they have been divided into four (or five when relevant) broad categories for the purpose of analysis. These categories differ significantly from each other in terms of the contents of the jobs and the attitudes of the people working there.

1. The 912 Code Workers were domestic servants who did cleaning and washing. The occupation code of this category as per the Indian National Code 1971 is 912; but in Calcutta they are generally known as *jhee*. If a worker lives at home but works for one or more employers she is known as *thika jhee*. Less than one-fifth of this '912' category lived in an employer's house and worked exclusively for one family. The rest were *thika jhees* working for more than one employer.

2. Other Domestic Workers were domestic workers who had some special skills. This group included cooks, housekeepers, *ayahs* and nurses. They often combined one type of job with another. A few of them lived in the employer's house while the others lived either with their own families or in a women workers' boarding house. While most domestic workers worked on monthly contracts, a few worked as casual workers on daily wages.
3. Skilled Workers included workers in either manufacturing or service occupations and they had some degree of formal or non-formal training.
4. Other Unskilled Workers included workers who performed non-domestic tasks requiring no initiation or training.

In fact, without going into the question whether the skills required in these categories were distinctly different or not, the grouping here was in harmony with the standard social attitudes towards such employment. Domestic service was an accepted 'woman's job', and the 1955-58 survey of Calcutta by Professor S.N. Sen showed that over 70 per cent of the women workers from a universe comparable to this sample were in domestic service. Among the domestic servants, workers of the second category belonged to a somewhat distinct group, for example, cooks were usually from the upper castes and midwives in urban areas were usually better educated. The two groups of domestic servants could be meaningfully separated.

The other two categories—skilled workers and unskilled workers, were not so clearly defined as they included many occupations which were new to women. However, there was an objective requirement of skill training for some of these occupations which made categorisation easier. The skilled worker category included conventional women's jobs such as embroidery, tailoring or *papad* making. Previously, workers in these traditional occupations came from certain specific groups. For example, embroidery was mainly done by Muslim women and *papad* making was confined to the Gujarati areas of the city.

There had been some liberalisation of these conventions when women of different social groups entered these traditional occupations and irrespective of social groups, they ventured into novel activities. The unskilled jobs included both a number of standard women's occupations such as making cowdung cakes, paper bags or garlands and new jobs like cutting rubber tyres for cheap shoes and fixing plastic parts. For such jobs there was literally no skill training required and no period of apprenticeship. The table below gives the distribution of the 400 workers by the major occupational category, they were employed in at least four categories at the time of the enquiry. In order to check the degree to which the sample was representative of the population, a random sub-sample of 200 workers was drawn from it.

This provided two sub-samples of 200 each. For testing the major conclusions, results for the two sub-samples are given separately. The distribution between occupational categories was similar in the two sub-samples and in the population, and it was concluded that this sample was fairly representative of the population in Calcutta. Domestic service was no longer the only avenue open to women as had been the case at the time of the previous survey in 1953. Even then, at the time of the survey, about 56 per cent of the women worked as domestic servants. The rest were engaged in a variety of tasks in manufacturing and the services. The most common skilled jobs were tailoring and embroidery and as many as 59 women were engaged full-time or part-time in these activities.

Some of the other skilled occupations were *biri* making or leather work, electrical fitting or glass blowing Although the total number of non-domestic workers in the sample was only 175, they held 191 jobs between them because 16 workers were engaged in more than one non-domestic job. This practice was most common in East. Calcutta where ten workers worked on two jobs simultaneously. They were mainly tailors who were frequently unable to find sufficient work to keep busy throughout the week and they sought other work like cutting and fitting plastic parts or electrical connections. Domestic workers also took up additional work like making paper bags or cowdung cakes for sale. Some of them were engaged in plastic or leather cutting, and sewing, and one even made toys. The area-wise spread of workers over occupations highlighted some between domestic and non-domestic categories was quite different.

The proportion of domestic workers to the total number of workers was much higher in South and South Central Calcutta. In Central and North Calcutta, the distribution of domestic and non-domestic occupations was almost even and in East Calcutta, the weightage was overwhelmingly in favour of non-domestic jobs. This pattern closely follows the distribution of activities in Calcutta. South and South Central Calcutta are mostly middle and upper middle class residential areas interspaced by huge *bustees* and some large industries. In these areas there are not many small workshops and industries (with the exception of a few engineering units) that are frequently seen in other parts of Calcutta.

In East Calcutta especially, there are numerous workshops for producing an ever-changing range of products from divorce materials. In South and South Central Calcutta therefore, the majority of workers were engaged in domestic service and there were relatively few non-domestic workers. The latter were confined to traditional activities like tailoring, making cowdung cakes or paper bags. A few were engaged in clay-modeling around the Kalighat area. In North Calcutta, there were two very large slums housing a sizeable population of East Bengal refugee tailors. Moreover, there was a huge industry of readymade garments which was earlier limited to family units with male tailors but had rapidly passed into the hands of large commercial operators who increasingly employed the services of women from these families for executing the orders.

The population studied here included many such women. North and Central Calcutta, apart from being thickly populated residential settlements, also house traditional small industries such as *biri* rolling, printing, book binding, and food processing. At the time of this study, these occupations were being passed from male of female workers and the latter were largely represented in the sample. It was observed that in East Calcutta women ventured into an array of newly developing occupations, some of which were thrown open to women for the first time. The latter included pottery, glass blowing, paper products, garlands, as well as electrical fittings, plastic goods and rubber and leather products. Making cowdung cakes or paper bags was commonly observed in all areas. Since there was no skill or capital required for these tasks, the work could be done in their spare time and there was always a ready market for these products everywhere. It would not be unwarranted to conclude that women were willing to participate in a wide variety of jobs and the particular occupational structure that existed in any region was largely determined by the availability of jobs.

There was little to indicate that women themselves were reluctant to take up non-traditional jobs or that there were barriers to their entry into these fields. In fact, there is a possibility that women had taken over some of the standard male occupations during this period. It is important to note that where such a choice of alternative occupations was given to them, domestic jobs (which were available everywhere) definitely got a lower rating. It still remains to be seen why. In expanding their occupational variety, women had broken several of the more obvious traditional taboos, for example, caste Hindu women worked on leather garments and bags. A woman with a high school certificate used to grind *dal* for a sweet shop and at the same time tutor students as well. Changes in this occupational structure over the seven years covered by this study offer further evidence about these tendencies in this labour market.

The total number of entries was 450 because this include 50 secondary jobs held by workers whose primary job was in another category. For each entry, the second figure is the frequency of secondary jobs in that category. Over time a clear trend emerged, more and more workers tended to opt for non-domestic jobs. The weightage of domestic workers, especially of the '912' code variety was much higher among workers who had worked before 1973. 1973 onwards, the pattern shifted in favour of non-domestic jobs and this was especially true in the case of secondary jobs. Before 1973 two-thirds of the secondary jobs entered were in non-domestic categories. Since 1973, this proportion increased to 84 per cent or even more, and jobs of the skilled variety were particularly rapidly increasing.

If non-domestic jobs were categorised by the type of product and the year of joining, it appeared that after 1973, the entrants overwhelmingly opted for jobs which were non-traditional. For example, though tailoring, food processing or tobacco still remained important jobs for women, the post-1972 jobs were largely concentrated around electrical fittings, plastic and rubber products, engineering and glass works. Therefore, even during this brief span of seven years there was a distinct shift in women's occupational pattern in this region. Not only did new workers enter into new occupations, but the older workers appeared to have acquired new skills and opted for different types of jobs, usually on a part-time basis though occasionally as a full-time occupation.

Thus, the hypothesis that there was some scope for training in skills in the unorganized sector and of mobility from one type of job to another could be accepted. The question arises how did this shift in occupational structure come about? The most obvious explanation appears to be that the younger workers as compared to the older workers preferred non-domestic work. 33 per cent of the workers in 25 years or less age group, opted for domestic work as against 60 per cent in the age group 26-35 years or 70 per cent in the age group 36-45 years. In the oldest age group nearly 90 per cent were in domestic jobs.

The variety in non-domestic jobs was a later development and therefore, it was not surprising that there was a lower incidence of such occupations among the older workers. However, for the younger workers the choice of domestic jobs was still open. Also, data regarding wage rates and working conditions shows that this was not on grounds of relative returns from such work. Wages and working conditions in domestic jobs were marginally better than in the other jobs. The likely explanation seemed to be that the younger women with their relatively better educational qualifications, had come from specific social groups where domestic service a priori got a lower rating.

As further evidence in support of this hypothesis it may be mentioned that in the case of domestic workers, either they themselves were the heads of their families or the heads were unskilled workers in casual employment. On the other hand, in the case of skilled workers in more than half the families the heads were white-collar or skilled workers. For a long time, domestic work had been the only employment open to women in Calcutta. The scale of employment was limited and workers came from a few specific groups.

Even at the end of the study, it was observed that the backgrounds of women who engaged in domestic service had not changed materially, but the entire group of women workers expanded to include many new groups who opted for work other than domestic service. Additional evidence was available which lends support to this idea that in the later half of the period under consideration, a new group of workers had entered the labour market—a group having even weaker traditions of women's work. Each interviewee was asked whether her mother or mother-in-law had ever worked for money.

Those who replied in the affirmative were said to have had a family traditional of women's work. Taking this as a criterion, women who joined work before and since 1973 appeared to fall into two distinct groups. 1973 onwards, women with a family tradition of work appeared to have opted for domestic service. Background data regarding women's work force participation in West Bengal indicated that working women largely belonged to the lower social strata. On the basis of this information regarding work tradition, one could conclude that before 1973 when opportunities for non-domestic work were relatively scarce, women from all social groups, if forced to work, had to take up domestic jobs.

Since then a wide range of jobs and avenues have opened for women and those with better backgrounds opted for non-domestic tasks. It was largely women from inferior social backgrounds who continued to man the domestic services. It is obvious that, given a choice, social taboo did work against women on the whole, with the exception of those belonging to specific social groups engaged in domestic service. It is not clear whether the new social groups who had entered the labour market during the mid-seventies would actually have done so had not the non-domestic jobs become available.

The Self-employed

Of the 400 workers, 34 skilled or unskilled workers were self-employed in the sense that they had their own business-selling the output (product directly to the consumers and had invested their own or borrowed capital in the business. Some of them were engaged in businesses ran by the family as a whole. A few also employed outside paid labour. It should be noted here that although 15 of these 34 self-employed workers had started their business after 1972, they had not been able to start making and selling any of the more sophisticated products such as electrical fittings, glass or pottery items. Although the self-employed were few in number, a definite pattern emerged from this group. There was a group of laundry workers who were *rajak* by caste, and had a family traditions of this business.

There were, at the other end, a few very poor and desperate women (either widows or with unemployed husbands) who earned their living by making cowdung cakes, paper bags or darned old clothes—anything they could do without any initial investment or training. There was yet another group of women from families which once belonged to the *Bhadralok* group—women with some education and training, and with access to capital, and they either singly or with their families, attempted to manage their enterprise. They usually took up tailoring or food processing—work which had no social stigma attached to it. All these groups differed from the others in terms of their background and expectations from the business but not necessarily in terms of the level of success they attained or the rate of return they earned from their labour.

Only the traditionally professional family workers like laundry workers did slightly better. In South East, south Central or Central Calcutta, areas which are relatively more affluent, there were very few self-employed women apart from the laundry owners or the occasional paper bag makers. The rest were from North or East Calcutta, areas having a tradition of small enterprises, especially among the Hindu Bengalis. It is worth noting that the *rajaks* or laundry workers were all Hindi speaking Hindus. One Urdu speaking Muslim family had a packing box business. The others merely sold a few cowdung cakes. One enterprise making leather *chappals* was run by a scheduled caste Hindu family.

The rest were Bengali speaking caste Hindus and a significant number were from the upper castes. A close study of the pattern of secondary jobs that these women engaged in provides an interesting sidelight. Over the years, there was a significant increase in the percentage of women holding more than one job. This could partly be due to the easy available of part-time work in this sector. Indeed, the extent to which workers experimented with new skills and occupations while maintaining their stake in their usual occupations showed that the employment contracts in this market were extremely flexible. This flexibility, no doubt, helped the workers who could find additional work to fit in with their existing commitments. It was particularly appealing to employers as it made the supply of labour continuously divisible.

In the organized sector, such divisibility in labour supply through part-time or over-time work is generally available at a greater than proportionate rate. For these workers the additional work was only rarely at a higher marginal rate of payment, and they offered this flexibility in employment contracts as an attempt to attract prospective.

For women working in Calcutta's informal sector, opportunities for work had increased and also diversified fairly rapidly during the period covered by this study. In each of the different areas of Calcutta, they had gained access to a number of occupations which were determined by the general character of the region and the overall pattern of activities in that region rather than by any kind of sex-wise taboos on the part of the employer. There were some significant reversals as well-occupations like *biri* rolling or glass blowing which were previously male strongholds became accessible to women. The workers themselves, appeared to entertain some reservations about the choice of occupation. While these reservations could partly be explained in terms of the relative rates of return from different occupation for the qualifications required in each, it was also possible that depending on their social background, they could have observed certain taboos in their choices.

An increasing number of new entrants to this labour market belonged to social groups which viewed domestic work as a less preferred alternative. Entry into these occupations in the informal sector was accompanied by a considerable degree of mobility of workers between occupations. There were instances of workers learning new skills while in a job and taking up some new type of work. However, it still remains to be seen how valuable were these skills to the workers in terms of an increase in their income earning capacity. A survey confined to workers in the informal sector alone cannot throw any light on whether this skill formation or waiting period in the informal sector helps the worker to move into the formal sector or not.

There is some information about a reversal in the process. In this study, there were several workers or other members of their families who had previously worked in the formal sector, but had lost their jobs and had moved into occupations in the informal sector. There is significant evidence supporting the hypothesis that additional skill formation takes place in the informal sector, but it does not support the contention that workers accumulate any physical or financial capital as a result of this work. The few self-employed workers in this study had obtained their capital either from the formal sector activities of some members of the family or had inherited it—several women tailors had inherited sewing machines from their husbands or fathers.

Other workers like those in food processing had bought the machines and paid for them from the retirement benefits of some family member. The laundry businesses were the only ones where families had built up their capital through generations of work. It should be remembered that except for the very rudimentary enterprises, the few workers who had made an effort in this direction were usually from higher social groups or had a background of such work experience. The question of the degree of competition in this labour market is not easy to settle.

The workers were not in any way practising collective bargaining. Each of them formed a small part of the total supply and they were constantly exposed to further competition from new workers because of the ease of entry and learning skills. This competition was further intensified by the fact that other workers could offer themselves for part-time or occasional work. Thus, a quick rise in the pressure of demand could be adjusted through the flexible employment contracts and gave no bargaining strength to the workers already in the labour market. Their lack of education and extreme poverty severely limited the mobility of these women between areas.

In the sample, none of the workers who had originally migrated from outside the city had moved from one area zone to another within the city. All the workers with the exception of those who lived in the employer's house, worked at jobs located within walking distance from their homes because they could not afford to spend time and money on travelling to work. Moreover, if there were social groups where certain prejudices inhibited the choices of workers, then the position of these women was highly vulnerable to market forces. Though the study provided no direct information about the employers, interviews with the workers highlighted several points. In case of domestic service, each employer was in search of only one or two part-time workers and there were numerous such employers in each area, but this did not put them on par with the employees.

Each employer had a much higher degree of staying power and could in the short run, keep his demand elastic by temporarily substituting his own labour and skills for that of the worker. The worker on the other hand, had nothing but her labour power to fall back on and was at a greater disadvantage for withholding her supply. In case of manufacturing in the unorganized sector, the employer could be in the market using the labour of several employees, but by the very nature of the unorganized sector, he did not want to build up a regular, steady contractual relationship with any particular group of workers at any one place.

Even if he had the same worker in his employ for several years, he was reluctant to enter into a lasting contract with the worker, and preferred to give the impression that at any time and price schedules, there were close substitutes available to him for the worker whose services he was using, and he was indifferent as to which worker actually worked for him. In this sector, the employer invested little on overhead of any kind—either in tools, buildings or amenities.

5

Case Study: Status of Working Women in Socialist Countries

It is pertinent to note that throughout history, the position of women has been crucial not only for social development, but also for the survival of society itself. In recent centuries, the changing role of women has been closely interrelated with other aspects of the development of society, such as industrialisation, urbanisation, demographic revolution, etc. The most characteristics feature of developed countries for roughly the past two centuries has been the growth and change of all social structures. It is necessary to see changes in the position, status and roles of women in society, together with changes in the levels of fertility, etc., in the context of this complex global revolution, as the position of women is deeply rooted in other social processes and has relatively little autonomy. The relationship between the status of women and fertility levels has been cogently expressed by a well-known demographer: "...Our past success at population replacement, throughout all of human history, has been conditional on the discriminatory treatment of women" (Ryder, 1979, p. 366). This relationship is, however, two-sided. It is difficult to answer even the simple question of whether women have fewer children than in the past as a consequence of their emancipation or whether they are emancipated because of fewer children. And yet the emancipation of women has often been mentioned in the past as an important cause of the decline in fertility levels, along with factors such as social mobility, rising standards of living, urbanisation, the rise of individuality, the curtailment of parental power, the decline of mortality (in particular that of infants), compulsory school attendance and changes in the economic importance of children to the family.

The decline in fertility levels during the past two centuries has been relatively well explained by the theory of demographic revolution. It is both a part and a consequence of the economic, social and socio-graphic changes which make up a global revolution. Changes in the position, status and roles of women are another aspect of this complex process. The period of increased birth rates lasted in the Czech regions until 1951, and in Slovakia for five years longer. This period is also marked by the start of socialist development which, with the introduction of a new social policy and population measures, influenced people's lives in many ways.

Although the Workers' Health Insurance Act had provided maternity benefits to insured women since 1888, and various financial measures designed to help mothers and families had been introduced after the First World War, the most important social policy measures were not implemented until after 1948. Family allowances for all employed persons, covering all children and increasing for every additional child until the fifth, were introduced in 1948. The National Insurance Act No. 99/1948 Sb. stipulated a uniform adjustment of all maternity benefits. Maternity leave was extended to 18 weeks, with maternity benefits to be paid for this period according to the wage or salary and the length of employment.

These measures were not expected to affect the level of fertility, as this was considered satisfactory after the World War II. However, they benefited employed women and families with children, as did the post-war rationing of goods and clothing. There was a renewed decline in the level of fertility, accompanied by a change in the age structure of mothers, in the 1950s. In the Czech regions, the proportion of children born to mothers under the age of 30 years was 65.6 per cent in 1947, 70.0 per cent in 1950 and 83.1 per cent in 1960, while in Slovakia the proportion rose from 61.9 per cent in 1947 to 67.6 per cent in 1956 and 72.2 per cent in 1962.

The reduction in the average age of mothers was no longer sufficient to compensate for the generally decreasing trend. However, in Slovakia, due to the postponement of the end of the demographic revolution, the level of fertility in 1962 was approximately the same as in the Czech regions ten years earlier. From 1958, the decrease in the birth rate was also affected by the new abortion law which permitted induced abortion on social grounds. It can be assumed that as a result of this law the number of higher-parity births and the birth rate as a whole declined slightly, but its adoption resulted in no marked step in the overall trend towards lower birth rates during that period. This suggests that, on the one hand, illegal abortions had been available before the adoption of the law and, on the other hand, the social causality of fertility development after the demographic revolution was so complex that the existence or non-existence of such legislation was of secondary importance.

In 1953, rationing was abolished and a currency reform was carried out. Although family allowances were increased simultaneously, incomes per head began to increase faster in childless households or in families with one child than in larger ones. From 1963 to 1972, both in the CSR and the SSR, the birth rate oscillated slightly, though on different levels for the two populations. After the low point in 1960, the fertility level rose slightly in the CSR until 1964, before falling again to reach the lowest post-war gross reproduction rate (GRR) of 0.09 in 1968. Fertility in the SSR wavered only in 1963 and 1964, and to a much lesser degree. After 1968, the fertility level increased again in the CSR and the GRR reached a peak of 1.20 in 1974.

A similar peak in the GRR occurred in the SSR in the same year at the level of 1.27, narrowing significantly the difference between the two parts of Czechoslovakia. Such an evolution has prompted a good deal of discussion. The population measures discussed in the following section no doubt had some effect but a closer analysis also demonstrates the limits of these effects. While the quantitative effect of the political and economic stabilisation after 1968 cannot be measured, it probably played a very significant role in the increase in fertility levels.

In large part, however, the upward trend seems to have been due to a change in the timing of birth (i.e. births delayed from an earlier period or those originally planned for the future). Such an evaluation is based on an analysis of the population climate, on the birth order of children born, and on generational fertility trends.

Population Policy Measures

The downward trend in fertility levels at the end of the demographic revolution and in the following decades gradually led to an increase in attention to population-development issues. Further measures to benefit mothers and larger families were adopted, and for the first time these measures clearly supported fertility. In 1956, maternity leave benefits were amended; leave remained at 18 weeks, but maternity benefit was made the same for manual and white-collar workers: for employees with less than two years' prior employment, 75 per cent of their wage; for those with two to five years' employment, 80 per cent; and for all other employees, 90 per cent. In addition, all women workers and employees as well as economically inactive women were to receive a birth grant of 650 koruna (Kcs) i.e. approximately 60 per cent of the average monthly wage of women at that time). Price reductions after the currency reform provided further help for families with children.

Moreover, with the price reduction of 1959, children's clothes and shoes were greatly reduced; this price subsidy was abolished as economically unjustifiable only in the 1980s. By the middle of the 1960s, population and population measures had become an important political issue. The 11th Congress of the Communist Party of Czechoslovakia, held in 1958, called for an increase in the personal spending capability of families, especially those in the lower income brackets with several children.

The 12th Party Congress in 1962 dealt with this problem in greater detail. In the resolution on the main lines for development, pre-school and out-of-school care for children was stressed, as well as school meals and the further establishment of nurseries and kindergartens. The following Congress held in 1966 spoke of further support for families and working women and the supply of nurseries, kindergartens and dwellings for young couples. Since the school year 1960-61, pupils in general educational schools up to high school level have received all textbooks and educational supplies free of charge. In 1959, family allowances were raised once more for third and subsequent children. In 1964, a differential pensionable age for women was introduced, dependent on the number of children raised.

At the same time, a special compensation allowance was introduced for women transferred to lower-paid jobs during pregnancy or motherhood. Since 1964, rent reductions have been granted in state-owned dwellings according to the number of children in a family. Act 58 of the same year introduced a significant increase in welfare during pregnancy and motherhood: maternity leave was extended to 22 weeks. For the first time, preference was given to single mothers; their paid maternity leave was extended to 26 weeks, provided that they dependent on their own earnings. Maternity leave and cash maternity benefits were also accorded to women who took into their care another woman's child for later adoption or because of the mother's death.

The Act also affords women legal claim to further leave, up to the end of the child's first year. The employer is obliged to re-employ the mother after this period has elapsed, in the same capacity and under the same financial and legal conditions as before the birth. Also in 1964, the co-operative farmers' social security scheme was improved: family allowances and birth grants were provided under the same conditions as for wage earners. Family allowances were increased again in 1968. Maternity leave was extended from 22 to 26 weeks and in 1970 the amended Labour Code increased unpaid maternity leave until the child reaches 2 years of age.

On 1 July 1970, a so-called maternity allowance came into force, amounting to Kcs500 per month, to be paid to employed mothers, with at least two children, who decide to stay at home after their paid maternity leave has elapsed in order to look after their children until the youngest child has reached 1 year of age. The 14th Congress of the Communist Party of Czechoslovakia, held in 1971, emphasised new population policy measures designed to increase family size and to support young married couples and families with young children. From 1 November 1971, the period of the maternal allowance increased to two years after the birth of the youngest child and was made universal for all mothers, including housewives.

From 1 January 1973, allowances for second, third and fourth children were increased and credits were established for young married couples to furnish their households after the birth of children. Apart from an increase in family allowances in connection with price regulations in 1982, there have been no other major changes in population policy. Contemporary population policy, which is made up of a series of social and economic measures, was formed gradually during the first stage of socialist development. It is aimed primarily at improving the economic situation of families with children and of young people after marriage and the birth of the first child, the living conditions of employed women, etc. Attention is also given to services available for families with children, to the working conditions of women, especially mothers, and to mother-and-child welfare.

It is pertinent to note that influence of the population policy measures can be seen both in the fertility levels and in change sin the population climate. The population climate may be divided into two components: the basic component, which changes very slowly and which is related to certain social norms as to the most suitable (ideal, planned, desirable) size of the family in a given population; and the secondary component, which concerns the most suitable timing or spacing of children. The secondary component, though it does not directly affect the total number of children desired, can have an important impact on the CBR and GRR over a period, by concentrating births into one year or by postponing them to a later date.

The first survey of the population climate was organized in Czechoslovakia in 1956 and several further surveys were carried out in the next 25 years. The number of desired children ranged from 2.1 to 2.4 in various years and was always considerably higher in the SSR. Apparently it was not affected by population policy measures. It can be concluded, therefore, that these measures influenced mainly the secondary component of the population climate which was not shown by the surveys (Pavlik, 1977). The oscillating fertility levels after the demographic revolution may be illustrated by an analysis of birth intervals. Parallel to falling proportions of childless families, there is a shortening of the interval between marriage and the birth of the first child, both in the CSR and the SSR. This is partly connected with increased proportions of premarital conceptions among first children.

On the other hand, the intervals between the first and second child, and the second and third child have been increasing, hence the oscillation of period rates. The main reason for the increase in the CBR around its peak in 1974; this increase was due primarily to first births, then to second births and much less to third births; higher parities did not significantly affect the increase. This was evident, in particular, in a fuller and perhaps even more rapid realization of the number of children planned but was not influenced by changes in the planned family size. The data were also affected by the age structure of population. But in spite of this their meaning is clear. Furthermore, the available analysis of cohort fertility has shown that generations with completed childbearing after the demographic revolution differ little in terms of completed fertility (Lesny, 1978, pp. 106-116).

Increase in Women's Economic Activity

The economic and social development of Czechoslovakia continued under socialist conditions after the demographic revolution. Changes in the structure of the economically active population between 1961 and 1970. In particular, notice that the share of agriculture has continued to decrease and that the economic structure of the SSR is approaching that of the CSR. The proportion of economically active women among all women of productive age (15-54) years) is very high: it reached 76.9 per cent in the CSR and 62.7 per cent in the SSR in 1970; comparable percentages for men were 86.4 and 83.7 (Statisticke a evidencni vyadavatesltvi tiskopisu (SEVT), 1975, p. 119). In spite of the high level of economic activity among women in 1961, the level increased even further in 1970 and 1980.

The largest increase was in the 25.34 year age group, when women up to the age of 30 years are still in the most intensive childbearing period or have young children. In 1980, the proportion of economically active women was high among married women, although it was slightly higher in the CSR than in the SSR. The decrease in economic activity in the 15-19 year age group was due mainly to the higher attendance of girls at secondary schools and at universities. There is no doubt that the increase in the level of women's economic activity in Czechoslovakia during the past two decades has been very striking. Women are becoming almost as important as men in the total labour force.

However, there are only two periods in women's lives when their situation is fully comparable with that of men: before the first child is born and after the youngest child leaves school. During the period when women are pregnant or looking after small children, they represent a specific kind of labour force as their economic activity in conflict with their maternal duties. The increase in the proportion of economically active women after 1961 can be explained by two contradictory factors: the fall in the fertility level in the 1960s and the population policy measures in the 1970s aimed at overcoming the conflict between maternal duties and economic activity (women on maternity leave are considered as economically active).

It is not easy to say which factor was more important. Hard evidence is difficult to obtain and various results from sample surveys can be interpreted in different ways; they depend very much on the methodology of the survey (for example, the formulation of questions, the self-censorship of respondents, not weighting the various factors which affect the respondent). The economic and social breakdown of economically active women in 1970. Differences between the CSR and the SSR can also be seen here. The far higher proportion of women working in industry in the CSR explains the higher proportion of the socio-occupational group "workers" (i.e. production workers) in the CSR in comparison with the SSR. However, the gradual economic equalisation between the republics is clearly shown by the similar proportion of women working in commerce, transport and communications, and by women who are "employees" (i.e. white-collar workers).

As a result of previous changes in the national economy, the age structure of these women in the SSR is considerably younger than that of the CSR. This holds for all branches of the economy, apart from agriculture and forestry where both republics are very similar. In spite of the fact that apprentices are not considered as economically active, the youngest age structure is found in industry. More than 41 per cent of women economically active in industry in the CSR and more than 52 per cent in the SSR were under the age of 30 years in 1970; the corresponding figures for agriculture and forestry were below 19 per cent for both republics. The oldest age structure is characteristic for co-operative farmers and independent farmers. The latter group will obviously become even less important in the future; almost 46 per cent of women in this group in the CSR and 29 per cent in the SSR were aged 55 years of above (i.e. of pensionable age) in 1970, and represented only 0.33 per cent of women in the CSR and 2.44 per cent in the SSR.

The age distribution of economically active women depends largely on the age distribution of the whole population; however, certain features already noted can be confirmed. The proportion of working women is often lower in the age group with the highest fertility, and when children are very small, than before and after, and this decline occurs more among workers than among employees and other groups. The small size of these differences suggests a rather quick return to work if the mother does not return immediately after maternity leave. As can be expected, the branches of the economy where the proportion of women is highest fall within the sphere of non-material activities—mainly in social care, health services and education, followed by commerce.

The lowest share of women is in construction and in transport and communications. The differences between the CSR and SSR are rather small. Czechoslovakia is one of the few countries in which population policy measures have been extensive. This might explain why the level of economic activity during the whole productive life of women is so high and is still rising. Although economic activity has always been high among unmarried increase among married women.

The increased proportion of women in the labour force has been a decisive factor in the increase in the total labour force in Czechoslovakia in the past decade. It is pertinent to note that the attitudes of women towards their economic activity can be characterised either objectively by their behaviour or by the opinions of women themselves. The most significant objective characteristic is the high economic activity rate and the relatively quick return to work after maternity leave. According to a survey carried out on, 6,176 women in 1962 (Srb, 1967, pp. 246-247), about one-third of women returned to work immediately after maternity leave; the remainder asked for unpaid leave or ceased working.

The situation changed dramatically after 1968 and 1971, when maternity leave was extended and the maternal allowance introduced. Although no similar survey has been carried out since 1962, the proportion of women staying at home after their maternity leave has been considerably reduced. This indicates that the most urgent demands were largely met by the last population policy measures. The kinds of reasons women gave in 1962 for not returning to work after their maternity leave were as follows.

Almost one-half of these women mentioned the lack of creches; they did not have anybody who could take care of the child. About 30 per cent of women clearly did not want to return and in 20 per cent of cases the husband did not wish it. The other reasons were much less significant in terms of percentages; about 10 per cent of women mentioned illness of the child and about the same percentage incapacity to cope with work and household duties. Further reasons given were the lack of working opportunities (7 per cent), health problems (5 per cent) and many children

(2 per cent). In another survey, carried out in 1977 (Srb, 1979, p. 308), women were asked what was of greatest help to a working mother.

In the first place they gave the understanding of their colleagues (30-49 per cent; more in the SSR than in the CSR); next was more places in creches (21-40 per cent; more in the cities and in the CSR). Other reasons were mentioned by smaller proportions of women—more time for children, a better financial situation, better services, etc. A fertility survey carried out in Czechoslovakia in 1981 (Dvorak, Srb and Ales, 1983) by and large confirmed the previous results. Problems of families and the position of women were the main topic of a survey which was carried out in Czechoslovakia in 1979 (Bauerova and Bartova, 1980, pp. 3, 11). A standard interview was held with 2,228 inhabitants of different ages, nationalities and socio-occupational groups.

The question which is of most interest here was formulated as follows: "Should a woman work outside the home or should she stay in the household and take care of the children?" The attitudes of the population towards the economic activity of women were generally positive. It is worth mentioning that women more often than men answered that women should work outside the home in any case. Older people preferred that women should stay at home. Workers and employees preferred that women should work, while the agricultural population declared the opposite.

People in small cities and with the lowest educational level were the most conservative. But how long should the woman stay at home with small children? The limit that was given most frequently was 3 years of age of the child (about 40 per cent); when the child is old enough to go to nursery school, the mother can go to work. Only about 30 per cent of the people interviewed put the limit at 6 years of age. This survey also gave an interesting picture of the use of time in the family.

Education

In fact, a significant increase in the number of female students at all educational levels has been characteristic of socialist development. Girls now form a definite majority at universities and at many kinds of high school. An especially high proportion of girls attend gymnasia, which mainly prepare students for university-level education. The increase in the educational level has also been significant among production workers. The proportion of skilled workers among all workers has risen considerably in recent generations, and the difference between the CSR and the SSR has practically disappeared among those below 30 years of age. Although the same process has occurred among women workers, they are still significantly behind men in terms of skills.

This should always be kept in mind if comparing, for instance, the level of wages. According to this micro-census, university-level education is still twice as frequent among men but all other levels, with the exception of apprenticeships, show a higher proportion of women. The vertical socio-occupational distribution indicates the high level of women's participation in professional activities. Men are slightly more frequent among higher professionals (leading positions, university teachers, scientific workers, physicians, etc.), but women predominate among middle-grade professionals. Men are more frequent among technicians and skilled workers, but women predominate among other employees. Such a distribution, which will change only slowly in the future, raises the following question: what degree of equality between men and women will be reached in the future under socialist conditions given the different roles and duties of each sex in reproduction and in social life?

Number of Children and Women's Economic Activity

In studying the relationship between the level of economic activity, education and fertility, we should start with the objective finding that economically active women have fewer children than inactive women. In 1961, economically active women in Czechoslovakia had on average 1.72 children below 14 years of age, while economically inactive women had 2.03 children. However, women with one or two children below the age of 14 (were more likely to be economically active than inactive; this proportion was reversed among women with more children. The differential fertility evident at the period of transition has been maintained until very recently. The differences have remained not only between the CSR and the SSR, but also among various socio-occupational groups.

The group of employees, which consists mainly of white-collar workers, had by far the lowest fertility level in 1970, while the highest number of children was still found among women in agriculture. (In the CSR in 1961, 42.4 per cent of women among workers were economically active, 50.2 per cent among employees and 52.4 per cent among co-operative farmers; the corresponding percentages for the SSR were 35.6, 49.4 and 45.3.) The level of economic activity, both among married and unmarried women, has increased significantly since 1961. The magnitude of this increase for married women; it rose by more than 20 percentage points among women below the age of 35 years with one or two children between 1961 and 1970, and only a little less among women with three or more children. As has been mentioned, the comparative significance of population policy measures and of the decrease in the fertility level cannot be measured from these data. Because of the fertility changes, a higher proportion women had children over 6 years of age in 1970 than in 1961, and most of these women would have gone to work anyway.

The extent to which the age of dependent children is important to the level of economic activity can be seen. In general, the significance of the relationship between the number of dependent children and women's economic activity decreased between 1970 and 1980, particularly for women whose youngest child was under 6 years of age. In 1970, mothers of young children were more likely to be inactive the more children they had. In 1980, this trend had almost disappeared except for those with three or more children. The increase in the level of women's economic activity between 1970 and 1980 occurred in all groups but was most marked for mothers of young children.

In 1980, women with children under 2 years old were benefiting from the 1970 measure which extended unpaid maternity leave until the child reaches this age. (In 1980, there were 265,763 women in the CSR and 114,027 women in the SSR on child-care leave, representing approximately 11 per cent of the active female labour force in each republic.) Since activity rates do not decline for mothers whose youngest child is 3-5 years of age, compared with those whose youngest child is 0-2 years of age, most women seem to return to work after the end of their maternity leave. It should be noted that the data concern only the CSR, where this process was the most pronounced. Here also one of the main findings is confirmed: economically active women have somewhat fewer children on average than inactive women, taking into account education and marital status.

Women with the highest educational level have fewer children than other women, and non-married women (mostly divorced) also have fewer children than married women; however, the proportion of single women plays a particular role here. Such factors as economic activity, socio-occupational group, education, fertility level, etc., are objective conditions of social development which are inter-related. Many more factors may be defined, but they are less often documented statistically; in other words, only soft data on them is available. Such data include women's attitudes towards their participation in the labour force, already mentioned above, and women's time use and the division of labour in households.

With the increasing level of female economic activity, the situation of women in households has not changed substantially in spite of the fact that after the demographic revolution the number of children decreased, usually to one or two. Even under socialist development, many traditional features of the division of labour between men and women in families still persisted. As early as 1959-60, a survey was carried out which aimed to describe the daily routines of women in one factory (Srb, 1967, pp. 232-233). The average daily work of a woman in the household (i.e. not at the factory) was very time-consuming (5-5.5 hours, including 1 hour for shopping and 2-3 hours for the preparation of meals; the rest was devoted to other work such as washing, sewing and looking after the children).

The results of this survey did not answer the question of whether women had enough time to cope with all their duties. The rest time of women was dependent on the number of children. Women without children rested 7.2 hours on average, with one child 6.6 hours and with two or more children 6.2 hours. The greater the time spent on caring for the children, the less the woman rested. These results are rather striking, but it should be kept in mind that one factory is not a very representative example. Another, survey was carried out in 1960; it covered 5,964 people from the whole of Czechoslovakia, 2,918 of whom were men and 3,046 women (Srb, 1967, pp. 238-241). The difference in time use was far greater between men and women than between various socio-occupational groups.

In particular, work in the household amounted to only a little less time than work outside the home (with the exception of women staying at home). Economically active women had a second shift at home and therefore had significantly less free time and rest time than men. Twenty years later, a similar survey showed comparable results. Differences can be explained mainly by the division of time use into working days and days off in the latter survey. In addition, a more detailed classification of activities was used.

The division of labour between men and women was much more pronounced than among men, women or various socio-occupational groups. The differences among workers, employees and members of the uniform agricultural co-operatives (UAC) were very small. As might be expected, women staying at home had the most different system of time use. However, they had almost as little free time as women workers and employees and they had even fewer days off. Apart from essential personal needs, they devoted a considerable amount of time to cooking, cleaning, sewing, shopping and caring for the children. The time they devoted to themselves was less than in all other groups.

It is interesting that the amount of household did not depend greatly on the number of dependent children (this amount rose only among women staying at home and among employees). Time spent in care of children did not depend on their number either. Some results were rather surprising and suggest a certain heterogeneity in the sample. Why do workers with three children have more free time than workers with one or two children? Why do workers and employees with five or more children devote less time to their care than all other women? Do these women perhaps belong to the gypsy (Romany) population or do older children help care for younger ones in these families? However, the main results correspond quite closely with the results of the previous survey. A recent survey (Bauerova and Bartova, 1980, pp. 3, 11) also confirmed that the greater part of the work in the household is done by the woman; only in younger families does the man participate more in work at home.

In many of these families, a grandmother provides considerable help to an economically active woman. All the persons questioned evaluated the time, and the physical and psychological demands on women related to their care of household and family, as great or very great. The women worked at home 25.5 hours a week, the men 14.5 hours; however, the amount of time for women was lower and for men higher than in the previous survey. Older people, people with lower education and those living in the country did more work at home than the others. Men considered work at home as somewhat demanding. The higher participation of men in work at home shown in this recent survey indicates the more democratic character of the family, and it is usually related to other attitudes and ideas. The persons questioned were more likely to think that the care of children should be divided equally between the man and the woman and that both partners should participate equally in family decisions. Only 7 per cent of men did not participate in work at home at all.

This recent survey showed one interesting feature which should not be overlooked. With the increased participation of men in home activities, the participation of children seems to be decreasing; it is higher in traditional families than in modern ones where the father shares the family duties. This could have negative consequences in the future when a new generation starts to build its own families. Standard of living and especially its material components are closely related to other social factors. In one survey carried out in 1961 (Srb, 1967, pp. 242-245), 7,955 women were asked why they worked. Such results are not surprising and confirm with other surveys that financial reasons are by far the most important. Such a conclusion can be made in spite of the significant increase in the standard of living in Czechoslovakia since the Second World War. According to selected indicators of increase in the standard of living, real wages rose from 100 to 255.8 between 1937 and 1980. Other indicators also show a considerable increase. National income per head rose more than 5 times between 1948 and 1980, while the yearly income per person rose 3.6 times between 1953 and 1980. The number of children in nursery schools and in creches also rose very markedly, as did the number of cars and other consumer goods.

6

Focus on Patterns of Women's Labour in Various Situations

> "Any woman who understands the problems of running a home will be nearer to understanding the problems of running a country."
>
> —*Margaret Thatcher*

The majority of the women had followed in their employment careers a pattern which has been well documented by sociologists and recognised by policy makers as the conventional one for married women. Broadly, it consists of entry into the labour force as a full-time employee on leaving school or college, and continuing this formal participation in economic life through the period of courtship and marriage, leaving the labour force only when the birth of the first child is expected. There then follows a shorter or longer spell devoted exclusively to household responsibilities, and above all to child rearing which is followed by a return to participation in the formal labour market, sometimes as a full-time, but very frequently as a part-time employee. A significant minority of the women in the study (25 per cent) broke with this more conventional pattern: their employment careers are discussed in detail later in this chapter.

PATTERN OF WOMEN'S EMPLOYMENT CAREERS

Employment Patterns before Birth of First Child

Most of the forty-eight women in this group left school at an early opportunity with no formal qualifications and immediately entered employment, although a few passed some examinations or went on to some form of higher education. A quarter of those who entered the labour force on leaving school stayed in their first job until they left employment several years later when expecting their first child. Only two of these had any educational qualifications, and all but one gave up her job when expecting her first child. (In most cases this first pregnancy was unplanned.) How did they feel about their fist jobs? Most claimed to have enjoyed them, although with the benefit of hindsight, some respondents were able to recognise the limitations of their jobs:

> *Heather (on clerical work):* 'I enjoyed it while I was there...looking back on it...it was completely unproductive with no room for initiative or anything like that.'

The majority had received some form of training in these initial jobs, with the exception of two factory workers (who had less positive memories of their jobs) and one of the clerical workers. Three-quarters of the direct entrants to employment, however, changed their jobs at least once before leaving the labour market to raise children. I have categorised the reasons given for changing or leaving jobs as follows: *instrumental* (for better pay and/or benefits), *family* (in order to fulfil obligations to parents or husbands, or to care for dependent children), *dissatisfaction* (because dissatisfied with working conditions, treatment at work or nature of duties), *travel* (to obtain more conveniently situated work), *social* (because dissatisfied with social contacts at work), *sexual harassment* (to escape unwanted sexual attentions at work), *redundancy, education* (to obtain further education or training), and *health* (of the woman concerned). For many (seventeen of the thirty), changing their job had also involved changing their occupation.

The case of Caroline, who began a hairdressing apprenticeship on leaving school, but was unhappy in her job and left, before completing her training, to become a sales assistant, illustrates this kind of job change. Those who changed jobs were mostly motivated by instrumental and family reasons, but other reasons were also important, as can be seen in *Table 6* and *22.7* overleaf. As already suggested, eight of the forty-eight women did not enter the labour force directly on leaving school, but engaged in some form of further education. Did their experience differ in any other important ways from the rest? The most striking differ in any other important ways from the rest? The most striking difference is that none of these eight women moved from one type of work to another during their first phase of participation in the labour force.

All but one, however, changed her job at least once over this period, during which time the eight women had between them a total of twenty-three jobs. The six who went to secretarial college all found employment in clerical and secretarial jobs, and Jenny, who went to teacher training college, worked as a teacher. Frances, who went to university, dropped out at the end of her first year, partly because she failed her examinations, and partly because she had married. Her two spells of employment following this, and prior to the birth of her first child, were both in sales jobs.

Another important difference between this group and the other women who had changed their employment during the first employment phase, is that *family* reasons were overwhelmingly the ones given for their job changes. These related primarily to marriage and husbands' job changes, but parents' job changes and health also played a part. Instrumental reasons, the most important explanation of job changes for the other thirty women, played a very significant part in shaping the early employment patterns of those who had gone on to further or higher education.

Leaving the Labour Market to Raise Children

If the process by which women leave the labour market in order to raise children is to be understood, it is important to know to what extent, if at all, their departure from paid employment has been a consciously planned event. Women in the study were therefore asked to disclose whether the birth of their first child had been 'planned' or not. Twenty-three of the women in this group said their pregnancies had been planned, while twenty said they had been 'unplanned'. All but four of those who had planned their pregnancies had conceived their first child at roughly the time they desired (The remainder all had some years to wait). On average, they had been in the labour force for about seven and a half years when they left to have their first baby.

The plans which these women had made (often jointly with their husbands) frequently took into account such factors as a desire to have children whilst they were still relatively young, and a recognition that they were 'settled' as a couple.

> *Christine:* 'We had decided about then—we had our own house as soon as we got married, and we gradually sort of spent the four years...getting it all together...and we had decided that the time had come to start a family.

Some of the women had mixed feelings about giving up their jobs to start a family, recognising the passing of a relatively carefree phase of their lives, whilst others had looked forward to motherhood without reservations.

> *Tessa:* 'I was really pleased—I couldn't wait to leave work. I think it was—at that particular time—it was really what I wanted. I wanted the home and the family and I wasn't interested in going out to work or earning a living or anything.'

> *Elizabeth:* 'I was a little bit reluctant to leave [my employers], but, you

know, it was just one of those things, I mean I wanted a family just as well, so I had to make the choice.'

Only Carol disclosed that at the time having a baby was more her husband's wish than her own.

Carol: 'We got to the stage that I was doing supervision and my husband could see the point that if I didn't soon leave, I wouldn't want to leave at all. There were people [at work] that were saying "You could go a long way...there's a lot you could do.... 'And he could see the point that I wouldn't want to leave—I would turn into a career person. He said, "I think we ought to start a family."'

Whilst their pregnancies and withdrawal from the labour force were thus in some sense 'planned', the idea of also planning for a return to employment had clearly not occurred to most of them.

Teresa: 'I didn't [think about it] at that time, no...I suppose I thought when my children were off hands I would go out to work.... But I didn't even think of it then.

Several had thought of returning to employment when their children started school or were old enough to look after themselves, and one or two seven said that they had definitely intended to seek a job at this stage. However, none had made any plans about how she would organize this. Nevertheless, the average length of time spent out of the labour force before the first return to paid work was just under three years, and almost a third had less than eighteen months out of employment. There were four women whose first child was 'planned' but who had to wait a number of years before conceiving. By the time these women left the labour force to raise children, they had been members of it for, on average, almost eleven years.

All had been very happy when, after what was often a rather distressing period in their lives, they finally became pregnant. Although one began doing seasonal farm work when her child was only a few months old, the other three all had a much longer break of between four and a half and six and a half years out of the labour force. Twenty of the women in this group had a first child as the result of an unplanned pregnancy. The average age of these respondents on the birth of their first child was just under 20 years, and the average length of time spent as members of the labour force before the child was born was just over four years.

Five of the women in this group disclosed that they had become pregnant before marrying, and of these, two did not marry until after the child was born. Despite the fact that their pregnancies had been unplanned, the women in this group expressed views about having a first child and giving up their jobs which were very similar to those expressed by the women whose first pregnancies had been planned. Many accepted their situation quite happily, and most either expected to be out of the labour force for some years, or had no thought about any future return to work.

> *BARBARA:* 'Well, I'd always wanted children.... I thought perhaps that eventually i might get another job, but I didn't intend to work when the children were small. It was a struggle, butt didn't intend to anyway...it was...just a matter of drifting along.'

> *Pru:* 'No, I didn't...it was purely accidental—I was quite shocked—it always happened to somebody else...quite honestly, I was on cloud nine—I thought I would never have to go to work again iii my life.'

The main difference between the women with unplanned pregnancies, and the women who had planned their first child was that a minority (four of the twenty) had experienced very negative feelings about their situation. In some cases the feelings stemmed from a sense of being unprepared to start on family life, in others from a reluctance to give up a job.

> *Margaret:* 'I felt terrible. I felt I was too young to have a child really. 1 liked my job so much and I wasn't really very happy about having a baby at all.'

> *Jenny:* 'Not very happy—we were living in a rented flat.., and it wasn't big enough to 'bring up a baby in...we wanted to own our own house.., it came a bit soon.... We didn't know what we were going to do...eventually, it got round that we could afford to buy a house.., and it just arose, really, that I was going to go back to work' (Jenny did not leave the labour force until the birth of her second child.)

Return to the Labour Force

By definition, the women whose employment careers had followed the 'dominant' pattern all moved from the first employment phase (described above) into a period outside the paid labour force. During the latter period, they were almost exclusively engaged in domestic labour,, principally the bearing and rearing of young children. In considering their subsequent return to the labour force, as mothers seeking employment, it becomes necessary to distinguish between three groups, each of which has a different set of experiences. The first consists of women who have only one child. Their return to paid employment is a relatively straightforward affair often a once-and-for-all event.

The return to paid work came sooner than many had originally anticipated, in most cases within three years. The initial return was usually prompted by either financial pressures or a perceived need for social contacts, or a combination of both. For many of these women, some unanticipated aspect of their lives as young, mothers prompted an early return. Gail was separated from her husband when her child was about a year old, and decided then to return to full-time employment.

> *Gail:* 'I decided that if I ever wanted to be as independent... I would have to go back to work and get some money together.'

Another young mother found to her surprise that she was not perfectly content with being at home all day with a small baby.

> *Shirley:* 'I don't like a lot of female company, so coffee mornings, tupperware parties—all of that—I just couldn't take, and basically that's the only thing you can do when you're at home with a baby...and nothing annoyed me more than somebody coming round and talking about how they washed their nappies, or something—it's just not me... I couldn't stand it...plus, I didn't like not being able to barn my own money.'

For others, the decision to take a paid job was prompted by both financial difficulties and a desire to escape the isolation of housework

> *Alison:* 'Mainly it was the money—we needed the extra money—and I was bored to tears at home.., although I had my daughter, it seemed I'd never, ever seen anybody, I was indoors with my daughter all day.'

One of the women, however, was prompted to return to paid work after only six months out of the labour force because of financial circumstances alone.

> *Marion:* 'The only reason I've come back out again is because (my husband's] overtime was cut... I didn't have any choice...we were on a tight budget anyway, so there was really no question—either he had to get another job, or I did. And it seemed better that I should, because he already works six days, and for tax reasons as well...it was better that I did.'

About a third of these women took temporary or seasonal jobs at first, but once the return to permanent jobs had been made, job changes tended to be prompted by a variety of factors: instrumental family, redundancy, personal health, and dissatisfaction. Wendy's account provides several illustrations of why women may change their jobs. She explained her move in 1971 from a part-time job as a shop assistant, to a full-time one in the school meals service.

> *Wendy:* 'Well, we'd had a lot done to the house, and we'd used up any money we'd had, and really more than £2 a week was needed then—so someone said, "Try school meals", and at that time they were very short of staff and they were glad of anybody.'

Wendy stayed in the school meals service for eight years, accepting promotion to assistant cook during this time. Why did she eventually leave to become a full-time sales assistant?

> *Wendy:* 'Well, school meals is really going down...and down...and down. When I first went in, the meals were—they had the best of everything and skimp.... I know school meals have always had a bad name, but it's not a case of how the meals were cooked. I mean, a lot of care and a lot of pride was taken in the meals themselves, especially where we were...and I enjoyed it like that.., it was excellent, and the money was good...but then the money didn't alter, and I mean the conditions got worse...staff left...they were not replaced, and so your conditions were worse...equipment wasn't replaced...and the pride.— I mean to them it didn't matter any more — you made do and mend...and now instant things are coming in...and what really made me decide to get [another] job was I was in charge, and I think we were really short of staff, and six came from...top level and walked into the kitchen, purely looking at how we were working, and not one single one spoke. They looked round the kitchen, noses in the air, and they were just standing there, and I thought "this is it, out!"—no way do you have to work under those conditions.'

Wendy's vivid description of her progressive disillusionment with this job demonstrates her active membership of the labour force. Pride in her work, the need for her skills to be recognised, unwillingness to put up with being treated as if she were a machine rather than a person, all suggest a commitment to her job which breaks with the more conventional image of female employees as very passive members of the labour force. This attitude was by no means uncharacteristic of the majority of my respondents.

Clare's account of her employment career illustrates the commitment felt by many of my respondents to both their families and their job responsibilities. She explained why she resigned her job as a sales assistant when she was finding it necessary to have frequent time off because of her daughter's health.

> *Clare:* 'I worked from May until...December, then again (my daughter] started having trouble, and I gave my notice in and said it wasn't fair—although [the Staff Manageress] did say to me that they would be prepared for me to have time off whenever she was ill, but I didn't think it was fair to the other girls. I mean.., it wasn't a long-term illness, but it used to spring up overnight and she'd be really ill for three or four days, and then be OK again.... I just didn't think it was fair to the company or to the girls I worked with to have to cover me.'

For almost all of those with one child, the kind of employment obtained after the break for childcare was of lower status and less well paid than that held beforehand. The post-childrearing phase typically included agricultural, domestic and catering, and sales employment, while the pre-childrearing phase had typically included clerical and secretarial, and sales employment.

The experience of women with larger families was different in several important respects, and these women form the second and third categories in the discussion here.

The second group consists of those who took paid jobs in between the births of at least two of their children (about two-thirds of those with two or more children). For them, the 'return' to employment was not a single event, but involved a series of moves in and out of the tabour market. The majority of them had two children, while others had three or four. For most of those with two children, there had been Only a short gap (of between eighteen months and three years) between the two births.

However, in a few cases the gap was longer, either because the second child was unplanned, or because there was a child from each of two marriages. For the women with three or four children, the longest gap between births was normally that preceding the last child—which in several cases represented an unexpected, and initially unwanted, addition to the family. Nearly all the women took paid employment between the births of each of their children. Most commonly this work was agricultural labour ('field-work'), often of a seasonal and casual nature, or domestic and catering work.

Factory jobs, and sales and clerical employment were also quite common. Most jobs were taken on a part-time or seasonal basis, and usually the first return to employment occurred within a year. Overwhelmingly, the motivation for taking a job at this stage was the need to supplement the family's income. At this point in their lives, most of the women were married to men in relatively poorly paid or insecure occupations—construction workers, semi-skilled manual workers, tradesmen, drivers, etc.

The few husbands who were in occupations with relatively good potential earning power (police officers, technicians, and a surveyor) were all at the outset of their careers, or in the process of moving into those jobs from less secure ones, and thus not earning high wages when their children were small. Most of the women were quite frank about their reasons for taking a paid job at this time.

> *Maria:* '[My son] must have been about three or four months...and then I went out to work again...it was a situation where we bought our own

> home, and financially he needed support, so I went out to work...a part-time job, to help towards the home.'
>
> *Cheryl:* 'I had an early morning job when I used to take my eldest one with me. That was cleaning in a pub.... She was about fourteen months.., we needed the money...my husband's wage was about £18 a week then (1968).'

Several women had been unsupported by a husband at this time, either because they were as yet unmarried, or because their marriages had broken down.

> *June:* 'I did a little cleaning job, which was three days a week...for about two hours, I suppose, every morning...and then from there I used to go on the strawberry fields. [My daughter was] about three, I would say.., she used to come with me.... At this time I was on my own.

Some acknowledged that for them there were other motivations besides purely instrumental ones:

> *Elizabeth:* 'She was ten months [when I went back to work] money got tight.., there wasn't that much to keep me occupied really, and she was a devil when she was a baby, so I was quite glad to leave her in some ways.'

For those women who had more than two children, the arrival of a third or final child sometimes disrupted what had been the mother's gradual return to full participation in the employed labour force. Dawn, for example, had only just returned to her career in hairdressing after a seven-year break, when she had to leave because of a third, unplanned, pregnancy. She has not since returned to this occupation, feeling that her skills have subsequently become 'rusty' and old-fashioned.

Pat's fourth pregnancy and temporary withdrawal from paid work came just as she had established herself in a permanent part-time job as a hospital bed-maker, following a number of years when she had only been able to undertake evening or seasonal work because of her family's needs. Thus for two-thirds of those with two or more children, raising a family had by no means meant a complete withdrawal from the employed labour force.

Much of the employment discussed above will not, of course, have been included in any official statistics on employment, but it is no less real or important for that, It should, however, serve as a reminder of the need to exercise great caution in interpreting official data about women's paid employment. For these women, finding a way of supplementing the family's income, by selling some of their labour power for wages, was an important part of what they saw as their family responsibilities.

Most were only too well aware that if they were not earning their families' standards of living would drop significantly and they might well sink into poverty. The third category contains women who remained out of paid employment until they had completed their families, just over a third of those with two or more children. The majority of those in this category had been in employment for over four years when they left the labour force to raise children, and on average had spent about eight-and-a-half years out of the labour force looking after their families. As one would expect, the women with larger families tended to stay out of the labour force for longer than those with only two children. When interviewed, all but two of the women were married and living with their first husband, In contrast to those in the second category, most of these women were married to men in white-collar occupations with relatively high earnings—technicians, managers, and administrators, for example. The fact that their husbands had been bringing home relatively good wages had obviously been important in enabling the women to stay out of the employed labour force whilst raising their young families, and in enabling them to adopt a particular ideology of family life.

> *Yvonne:* 'I believe that if you have children, then you should look after them, and I stopped at home until they went to school.'

I do not wish to suggest that economic considerations played no part in prompting these women's eventual return to employment. Indeed, for some, the need to earn an income was the decisive factor, placing them in a situation where they felt they had no choice but to get a job.

> *Tessa:* 'I didn't work at all until my second daughter was born My first marriage had broken up actually when I was still only six months pregnant...and it was necessity rather than anything else. Social Security wasn't very much and my husband's whereabouts were unknown. I took a part-time job in a local estate agents...purely and simply because I needed the money.'

> *Sandra:* 'I (still] had two [pre-school children]...the youngest one and the one I foster... I got a bit fed up with being at home...actually it was a case of having to (get a job], because my husband was out of work at the time.'

Sandra's remark, made apparently only in passing, almost conceals the importance which male unemployment may have for prompting wives to seek work. She was not alone among my respondents in having this motivation.

Christine, on the other Wand, took paid employment outside the home for slightly different reasons.

> *Christine:* We were going through a very dodgy time, you know, marriage-wise, and I was trying to consider what to do...and I thought perhaps if I could get some sort of job, it would make me more financially independent; and help me decide what I would do.'

Others saw employment as a means of achieving a limited, but specific, material objective.

> *Yvonne:* 'I started in September because I wanted to get two bikes for Christmas for them...and I thought I'll just go out to work and earn the money to get that.., and I got a job in a hotel, and I stopped there for five years.'

Several women-first began earning money again without needing to leave their homes, and in a few cases, husbands were active in providing their wives with income-generating work at home.

> *Christine:* 'I used to work sometimes for my husband('s firm) on a casual basis, doing their typing at home—he used to bring it home—and that all started when [the youngest one] was born...instead of getting a temp. in they'd send it home to me.

It would be misleading,, however, to concentrate on financial motives for returning to employment to the exclusion of the other important factors. For a number of women, obtaining a job was a constructive means of escaping their social isolation at home and of defeating their sense of lost identity once their children began to grow older.

> *Teresa:* 'I felt I needed something at that time. I was really getting into a rut at home and I felt I needed to be out. The children were both at school, and I needed... I felt I needed something different, it was really getting me down, so I thought, well, I'd have to do something...and that's when we decided that we'd go for the Christmas period, it would be a break—which several friends had done.... I stayed on there two years.'

How did their first employment on returning to the labour force compare with the jobs they had held prior to having children? Of the seven who had been clerical or secretarial workers before having their children, only one obtained such work when she first took a job afterwards. The rest went into sales jobs, factory work, and other manual jobs. Two other women had jobs with specific skills in their first employment phase: Anne had been a telephonist, and Yvonne a dressmaker. Both re-entered the labour force as domestic workers. The two other women who became domestic workers at this stage had previously been employed in sales and in factory work.

Thus for most, the break from employment resulted in a deterioration of their occupational status. Two women, however, were to find higher status occupations on their return to work. Tina, who had originally been a factory worker, found an opening in nursery nursing, while Frances decided to train to 'be a teacher. She explains how she finally reached this decision:

> *Frances:* 'I [had always] said that I wanted at some date, when we were in a suitable place, and knew far enough ahead etc., that I would hopefully go back and do some form of further education, but.., it's a very easy thing to put off unless you've got that extra bit of determination — and obviously [my husband's] leaving was the push I needed.'

The employment patterns of the women with two or more children are also of interest following their return to the labour force *and* the completion of their families. These patterns are best described in relation to the age of the youngest child, whether of pre-school, primary school, or secondary school age. All but two of the nine women who still had a pre-school child when interviewed had returned to formal, regular employment, most working part—time: only two were in full—time jobs (one as a the other as a hospital domestic) and both of these women had previously done a spell of part-time work. Five of the seven women had been employed in domestic and catering work, and other employment undertaken included clerical and secretarial jobs, sales jobs, agricultural jobs, and childminding.

Three of those in regular employment had been in clerical or secretarial jobs prior to having their families—however, when interviewed, only one had returned to using these skills, while the other two were engaged in domestic work. Seven of the eight women with a youngest child at primary school were in regular, paid employment, while the eighth was a full-time student at a teacher training college. Four were working full-time, and three part-time, and all but one of the full-timers had previously been a part-time employee.

Again, manual jobs had predominated in the post childbearing phase. Four of the seven were or had been engaged in domestic work, four in other manual work (in factories and warehouses), and two in agricultural work. However, when interviewed, the seven also included two sales workers, a clerical worker, and a telephonist Like those with preschool children, many of these women had also been unable to return to their former skills, especially in office work.

About half of those with two or more children (eighteen of the thirty-five) had a youngest child at senior school. Some had children in their late teens, or older ones who had left home. When interviewed, half were employed part-time, and half full-time, and all but one of the full-timers had worked part-time at some previous stage. Of the eight who had some kind of job-specific skills prior to having their children (clerical, hairdressing, dressmaking, telephonist), four had not obtained work using these skills after completing their families, and a fifth had only done so after taking a TOPS course.

Although a few of the women with two or more children were unsure of their future plans, the vast majority of them fell into one or other of two categories: those who expected to stay in the job they were doing when interviewed until retirement, and who did not intend to seek or accept any promotion or greater responsibility; and those who intended to remain in paid work until retirement, but who also planned to seek promotion, further training, or simply a better job.

How did the women who planned no changes in their employment careers understand their future? Just over half were employed part-time, the rest full-time. A third were in jobs where they had some responsibility, a supervisory role, or recognised seniority over more junior colleagues, while the remainder were in the basic grade in their various occupations—primarily hospital domestics and sales assistants. Many felt that they were happy in their current job, and desired no further changes.

Helen for example, a frill-time domestic supervisor in an NHS hospital, was quite clear that she did not want any further promotion. She enjoyed the close contact with staff which her job entailed and knew that any higher grade job would not have this characteristic. She expected to stay in her job 'until I retire'—a further seventeen years if she retired at 60. Nancy, also a domestic supervisor, had similar plans, but emphasised her lack of ambition in relation to her job.

> *Nancy:* '[Promotion] just sort of fell into my lap ye never been ambitious, to be quite honest with you, I mean, all I've lived for is my home and my children, but when you are here full-time, it's a long day, so you think...your opportunities are there, and I'm gonna take them m not one to keep changing my job—in my last job I was there eight years, I was made redundant, otherwise I expect I'd still be there I can't see me not working, quite frankly... I can't see that I'll ever be financially well enough [off]...to pack up work 'altogether.'

Teresa, a part-time deputy supervisor in a large retail store, also emphasised that her employment career had to fit into her family life.

> *Teresa:* 'I suppose really you can't be (promoted any further) because I am only a part-timer.... I think as I am now it suits my family commitments very well... I wouldn't want full-time work d be quite happy to continue as I am until, I suppose, retirement age.... I think if you have good working conditions, you adapt to them...that would be my only thing, if problems like that arose.'

Those who had basic grade jobs, and who were happy to stay in them, made similar comments.

> *Dawn:* 'I'm happy as I am...but, if they come and ask [if I'd like promotion]... I expect I'd say yes, I'd have a go at it.... I'd stay here, I should think [till retirement]—as I feel now, anyway.' (Dawn was a part-time sales assistant when interviewed.)

Mary would have been glad to have her experience as a part-time clerical assistant recognised by her employers, but was not ambitious in any other respects.

> *Mary:* 'Because I'm part-time, my grades don't go up—I mean, I'm doing a more responsible job within the department, than when I came—but my grades don't go up.... I know it's perhaps silly, but it would be nice for them to say "You've done well, you're now a clerk grade whatever".... I can't really see myself changing...basically, I feel that while the children are at home, you need extra money...but then, the way the situation is now, I think perhaps you'll continue to need extra money... I'll be fully happy to stay where I am.

Another respondent; a part-time domestic, put-it quite simply.

> *Olive:* 'I suppose [I'll stay] until I retire...yes, I shall be working until then, yes. I don't think I'd like promotion or anything m quite happy as I am.'

All but two of the women who had no plans to alter their jobs were married women, living with their husbands. The exceptions were Maria, divorced and living with her parents and one of her two small children, and Pru, who lived with her two late-teenage sons and her 'boyfriend'. Maria was not too certain about her future:

> *Maria:* 'I should think [I'll stay] until he goes to school—I can't see myself getting another job and changing it before then...and of course if anything comes of this supervisor [training] thing, then I would stay here and do it.'

Pru also anticipated possible changes in her personal life which might affect her employment career.

> *Pru:* 'The possibilities [for promotion] could be there, but I don't particularly want it.... I don't want any hassles.... I just want... [to stay'] as I am, because it suits home life.... If I could afford to, I'd leave because I prefer to be at home...possibly if I got married again, and finances were different, then I would probably try and leave.'

Nevertheless, many of the women wanted promotion, further training, or a better job. In other words, they were seeking further integration into the labour force. They fall into two categories: those who were already working for employers who made training opportunities readily available, and in jobs where there was an established career structure; and those, mostly in domestic and catering jobs, who recognised that their current jobs held little prospect of improved working conditions or employment opportunities, and who sought a future change of occupation as a result. Tessa, a full-time telephonist, was amongst those to whom job advancement was already available.

> *Tessa:* 'I'm waiting for a vacancy to arise...because I sat an exam and a Board for promotion to Clerical Officer. I mean I could stay here *ad infinitum* and just do the same job, which I'm not really prepared to do...but I could go there as a clerical officer, and Then do another exam perhaps and become an Executive Officer or a Higher Clerical Officer...really. I would like to...it's more of a challenge, and you're using a bit more of—your brainpower.... I like this job very much, but it doesn't require a lot of initiative, as long as you're polite and tactful and know your procedures, it doesn't require an awful lot more from you.'

Heather, a supervisor in a retail store, had set her sights relatively high. She had returned to full-time paid employment once her two children were both at school.

> *Heather:* 'I shall stay here till I retire...that's twenty-five years.... After I'd been here a while] I thought I'd like to make a career of it, I'd like to go into supervision, when I then did.... I was promoted quite quickly—I intend to go on further, too.'

Maureen, a full-time personal secretary employed by a large paper-making firm, also wanted more than 'just a job', as her discussion of future plans illustrates. She felt fairly confident of obtaining more rewarding work with her current employer.

> *Maureen:* 'I wouldn't mind staying with them (until I retire)... If I can alter my job slightly—[to one that's] a bit more interesting, a bit more involvement, then I wouldn't mind staying.'

Anne, like several other women, was currently in a 'dead-end' job at the bottom of the occupational status ladder, and hoped for better employment opportunities in the future.

> *Anne:* 'I only do what I do simply for the money, really, I don't really like the work, you know.... [I'll stay] really until I can find an alternative job that I liked...it's just a matter of if a job was available.... I should think two years would be the limit I'd stay here. It would be a different type of work altogether that I would look for. I'm going to night school in September.... I'm going to take biology—I'm very interested in nursing...that's probably what I will do.'

Pat worked full-time as a hospital domestic, and like Anne, hoped to gain access to employment in nursing at some future date.

> *Pat:* 'I love working here.., but I can't say I like doing what I'm doing. Because it's all mechanical, and, well, you just don't need a brain.... So later on I would like to change... I thought about going as a nursing assistant.'

Although plans for the future might not be achieved, many of these women nevertheless bore little resemblance to the passive members of the labour force which women are so often taken to be. Those who lacked am•bition for promotion mostly anticipated participation in the labour force until their retirement, and those who had become well integrated into their employment environment frequently demonstrated considerable determination to 'make something' of their jobs. Carol's and Cheryl's comments about their attitudes to future employment were illuminating.

Both lacked the kind of aggressive career ambition which characterises the 'male' stereotype, but neither was willing to accept a definition of their work as passive and non-assertive.

> *Carol:* 'I have been asked to do supervision, but up until now I've never had the confidence to do it But now I'm thinking about it, because my children are getting older and they're [shy] like me, and I want to show them that if you tell yourself you can do it, you can.... [I'll stay] probably until I retired quite like to, because they are a good firm as regards pensions. It would pay me to stay here... I'd be silly to leave really.'

> *Cheryl:* 'I always take it stage by stage... I was an assistant and knew I could do better, and I'm aiming at supervision. When I'm doing supervision I will then contemplate whether I am capable of doing better. But I never sort of say "Oh, I want to be a Departmental Manager"—I would love to, but I've got to take it in stages to see whether I am capable—just increase it gradually come back with the intention of working till I retire.'

Impact of Marital Breakdown

Fifteen of the forty-eight women whose employment careers had followed the 'dominant pattern' had experienced marital breakdown. Of these, nine had re-married following their divorce. All but two of the fifteen had at least one child when their first marriage ended, including in eight cases a child aged 5 years or younger. What effect, if any, did the break-up of their marriages have upon their employment patterns? For Angela and Elizabeth, neither of whom had children, the break-up of their first marriage had little effect upon their employment careers. Angela continued working full-time as a secretary, and did not change her job. Elizabeth gave up her job as an audio-typist partly because she could not cope with facing her colleagues at work, and partly because she decided to move back to her parents' home in a different town.

However, she only had a short break from employment before going back to work full-time as an office temp., and subsequently taking permanent secretarial employment. For the eight women who had-at least one child aged 5 years or under when their marriage broke down, the event either increased or prompted their participation in the paid labour force. Four had not been to paid employment: of these, two took part-time jobs, and one a full-time job when their marriages ended. The fourth began full-time training to become a teacher.

Of those already doing paid jobs, two changed from part-time to full-time hours (but staved with the same employer), one continued in her full-time job, and the remaining one took on additional casual and part-time work. The remaining five women (whose youngest children were of school age when their marriages ended) had all been in paid employment, three working part-time and two full-time. All remained with their employers, and one of the part-timers went on to full-time work, as she explained.

> *Pru:* 'I got promoted to a supervisor... I did that for about two and a half years...still 5 till 8.... Then, because of finances—I got divorced—I needed more money. I had to take demotion, to go on to the forty hours.'

Paula, a clerical worker and one of the full-timers, stayed full-time, and after her divorce went through (shortly before our interview) applied for promotion to a more senior position.

The evidence of these women suggests that the impact of marital breakdown upon employment careers is fairly straightforward. Existing participation in paid employment tends to be maintained, and is frequently increased from part-time to full-time. Where women have not been engaged in paid work, the break-up of their marriage may prompt them to seek employment Whilst instrumental motives are especially compelling at such a time, and the need to earn an income may appear to be paramount, women also recognise the social importance of their jobs at this stage, when self-esteem and confidence may be at a low ebb.

The 'poverty trap' into which women who have access only to low-paid employment or supplementary benefit may fallis one of which such women are well aware. But they may still choose to be at work One woman who worked part-time explained what had happened to her.

> *Brenda:* 'It wasn't enough to keep me and two children on... I was on Social Security, and I had a few bills that I had a job to pay, and I ended

up borrowing off my parents and getting deeper into debt. In fact I went up to Social Security one day, and they turned round and said, "Well, you'd be better off not working."'

S.Y.: 'How did you feel about that?'

Brenda: 'Oh, I couldn't have given the job up, I had to have something to keep me going.. I thought it was terrible...if 1 hadn't worked, the actual cash in hand would have been £4 less than what I was getting by working—and bus fares and other expenses were costing more than £4.... If I did extra hours at work, Social Security stopped the extra that I'd earned, so I was no better off by doing any, and I did feel a bit trapped, but there was nothing I could do to get out of it. Even if I was working full-time, I couldn't have—well, at the time, I wouldn't have left the children alone, not for too long anyway, because they were upset as well, and I think they needed me as much as I needed them at the time.'

Brenda's account, which refers to 1976, expresses many of the tensions and ambiguities affecting an unsupported lone parent. She recognises the need for time with her children, but also knows that her job is an important source of social contacts for her, and helps her to structure what at first appears as a shattered lifestyle. She wants to support herself, by earning what she can, but is caught by a bureaucratic social security system which lacks the flexibility to accommodate her particular needs.

A Note on Redundancy and Unfair Dismissal

In discussing patterns of women's labour, it is important to note that whilst many job changes made by women are (in the broadest sense) voluntary—women resign their jobs for personal, family, or instrumental reasons—this is not invariably the case. For the women in my sample, redundancy and dismissal (including various types of what may constitute constructive—and therefore unfair—dismissal) were also features of their employment careers. Almost a third of the forty-eight women in this group had experienced redundancy. Shops or restaurants where they had been working closed down, industrial firms cut back on staff or relocated, small companies went into liquidation. Most accepted their experience of redundancy as simply a fact of an employee's life. Rarely did women mention any kind of resistance to redundancies, and where they did, actions had been unsuccessful. I do not wish to suggest that women in general do not, and have not, put up determined and effective resistance to attempts to deprive them of employment.

There are, of course, numerous examples of such action, and the case of women workers at Lee Jeans in Greenock, Scotland, who occupied their factory when threatened with redundancy, provides a recent example (Ryan 1981). However, my respondents had not been involved in such struggles. Chapter 4 includes discussion of the women's trade union involvement, and their generally low level of union participation, indicating an individualistic approach to employment which is consistent with a failure to engage in collective action against proposed redundancies. In the interviews, women were not questioned closely or routinely about sexual harassment at work—unwanted or intimidating sexual attentions in the workplace—and it is entirely possible that some women had experienced problems of this type, but did not disclose them to me.

Nevertheless, three women described incidents leading to their resignation from a job which constituted clear sexual harassment. All had been in their teens at the time of the incident, two still unmarried, and one recently married. Sheila's interview illustrates the tendency for incidents of this type to go unobserved.

> *S.Y.: 'What happened to you when you left school—did you go straight into a job?'*
>
> *Sheila:* 'Yes, I worked at [the paper] Mill—my mother got me a job. The first job I had.., for four months—but it didn't work out.'
>
> *S.Y.: 'What were you actually doing there?'*
>
> *Sheila:* 'Making, well, no—sorting, paper.
>
> S.Y.: 'Why did you leave?'
>
> *Sheila:* 'I left there because—you know, they kept saying, "Oh, your Mum works here", and all this... I didn't like it...you know.'
>
> *S.Y.: 'So you think it was because of that you left, rather than because of the actual work?'*
>
> *Sheila:* 'I liked the work.... It was the foreman I didn't like...where I worked...he was dirty.'
>
> *S.Y.: 'So it was the people that you didn't really get on with?'*
>
> *Sheila:* 'Well, this particular bloke. He used to touch all the young [girls]...when the young ones used to start, they used to start in the cutter house; you know—they was all like fifteen-year-old girls, and he used to—you know—be rude to them. So... I told me mother, and she more or less smacked him in the mouth, and that was one of the reasons I left, you know.'

Barbara's experience was not dissimilar.

> S.Y.: 'What happened to you when you first left school?'.

> *Barbara:* 'I went to work in the dispensary at [a large chemist's store]...it wasn't what I wanted to do, so I was there a matter of three or four months I suppose.... I didn't settle in the job.... I felt that everything I did was wrong because I just didn't like what I was doing.... I was shut away in a little cubicle...plus, I didn't like the manager that was there, he was a creep.... I wouldn't have found (the work) difficult if I hadn't had this creepy manager behind me, so I think he was mainly [why I left]...you didn't have a proper office, you were just standing in this cubicle thing where they did the prescriptions, and I mean he was one of these people who'd come and smack your bottom, sort of, and in those days, you didn't turn round and tell him like they would today...he was I think the main reason why I left.'

Brenda was more direct than the other two.

> *Brenda:* 'I worked as a stock control clerk in a garage...up until I was married... I quite enjoyed it.'
>
> *S.Y.: 'You said you did that until you got married?'*
>
> *Brenda:* 'Until after I got married.'
>
> *S.Y.: 'Why did you leave the job?'*
>
> *Brenda:* 'The stores manager started getting a bit fresh...(laughs)

Thus in factory, shop, and office, these women had been subjected to intolerable pressure of an overtly sexual nature, from men in more senior positions than themselves; and this resulted in their resignation. The kinds of evidence now becoming available concerning sexual harassmentwould seem to suggest that these three women may represent the tip of the iceberg.

The optimism of Barbara's view, that 'nowadays' girls would not put up with the kind of treatment she left her job to escape in the early 1960s would appear to be unjustified by the emerging facts. Several women disclosed that their employers had offered them an impossible choice about their working hours and conditions, which in effect constituted 'unfair' dismissal. One had been taken on to work evenings as a catering assistant, but later found her employer insisting that she work weekends also. As she had a young family at the time this left her with no choice but to resign her job.

Another was forced to leave her job when her firm re-located about fifteen miles away. She was told she could travel daily to the new venue if she liked, and was prepared to work longer hours, but for a woman with both a pre-school and a school-age child, an extra burden of this kind was out of the question. A third woman, working part-time as a merchandiser; was faced with the choice of doubling her hours (to 40 hours per week) or giving up her job. Since full-time hours were impossible for her because of her family commitments, she too had no option but to lose the job. It may be that one or more of these women would have had a case for unfair dismissal under subsequent legislation.

However, it seems likely that they would not have brought a case, even if legally entitled and aware of their right to do so. One of the things employed mothers seek to avoid is 'hassle'. If they are to accommodate the demands of their families and go out to paid jobs; they must organize themselves in order to avoid spending time and effort in unnecessary ways. Most of the women I interviewed lacked the extra energy and determination which would be required to bring legal action for unfair dismissal, regardless of their chances of success.

CASE STUDY: WOMEN WHO HAD NOT LEFT THE LABOUR MARKET

Six of the women interviewed had not left the labour market since joining it on completing their school or college education. When interviewed, most were in their late thirties, and all were living with their (first) husbands. Since their continuous commitment to employment breaks with the more common pattern of at least a short period at home with very young children, it is worth examining their experiences in some detail.

Three had left school at 15 with no academic qualifications, two had left at 17 with four or five 'O' levels, but had not gone on to further education, whilst one had left school at 16 with several 'O' levels and 'CSEs', and had subsequently attended secretarial college for a year. When interviewed, most had been with their current employer for a number of years: three for over twenty years, one for thirteen years, one for five years, and one for just two and a half years. All were in white-collar jobs with established employers, five in clerical occupations (ranging from clerical assistant to accounts supervisor) and the sixth in an administrative grade which was considered to be an executive position.

Three had jobs which involved supervising other staff, whilst a fourth had responsibilities which included interviewing members of the public in connection with their requirements for personal financial loans. Interestingly, none of the six women was following an employment pattern set by her own mother. None of their mothers had been in permanent jobs whilst my respondents were children, and only two of these mothers had permanent occupations outside the home after her family had grown up. For most, there had been a delay of some years between marriage and the birth of their first child. Two had a first child within three and a half years of marriage, but for two others there was a five-year gap, and in the remaining cases the periods were seven and twelve years.

These longer than usual delays between marriage and the first child's birth were significant in explaining their employment patterns. In three cases, the respondents had planned their families so that they could continue in employment without leaving their jobs.

This involved not merely ensuring that the baby was born at a convenient point, but also making arrangements for the child to be cared for once it was born, and in one case, changing her job to one with less responsibility. I shall describe each of these cases in turn. Sara was born abroad but came to England in 1966 on marriage. Her husband has been in the nursing profession throughout their marriage, and at the time of the interview held a senior position. On arrival in England, Sara did manual work for a couple of years, before obtaining a job as a clerical assistant in a public sector company in 1968. She was subsequently promoted to clerical officer. Her first child was born three and a half years after she joined the company, and she took two months maternity leave.

> *Sara:* 'Well, we discussed it before we had children, and I've never liked the thought of staying at home, you know, I've always wanted children and wanted to work as well. So we discussed it then, you know, whether I would be able to do both. So we said, 'Well, we'll try—if we can't, then I'll pack up', you know. But as it is, we've managed.... He does his share of work, and I do my share.... We decided at first that my husband would go on night duty—we did that for a while.... He went to work at night when I got home, you know.... I found it ever so hard to leave a baby after four weeks, to come back — but it's one of those things—I had to come back'

She goes on to describe how these arrangements were subsequently modified.

> *Sara:* 'We did that for a while, night duties, and we found out we were Just saying 'Good morning', and, you know, going out the house. So, one of my sisters came, to go to college, so he went back on normal working, the shifts—you know, they do one week a morning, one week afternoons— and so my sister was studying at home and looked after the baby for a while, and then he went to do his normal work.... The second one, we did the same—and then my other sister came and we did the same thing— she went to college and helped us out during the day. When I had the third one, she decided she was going to get married, so I had to find a baby minder.... I used to take one to school, one to nursery...and then the other one to the minder, in the morning. But it was very hard, you know—I suppose if you want to do it, you do it.'

Geraldine left school at 15 with no qualifications and took a job as a punch operator. She worked her way up through various grades to a supervisory position, before marrying nine years later. After five years of marriage, she and her husband wanted to start a family.

> *Geraldine:* 'Now a supervisor has a lot of week-end work, a lot of overtime, so I decided to switch to be a clerk, an ordinary clerk.... I found my childminder before I was pregnant.... I used to pop over before the baby arrived, she was the first one to know when I was actually pregnant.'

When the baby arrived, in 1976, she took seventeen weeks' maternity leave. She described her feelings about going back to work.

> *Geraldine:* 'I didn't want to leave him—you don't. It's a terrible wrench. I would never advise anybody to do it—and it's hard, jolly hard, on you, because you're losing your sleep at night...of course you can't breast-feed if you're going back to work after six weeks; it's not fair on the baby, so I had to bottle-feed him.'

Both Geraldine and her husband come from large families, and have chosen to have no more than their one child. Andrea also left school at 15 with no qualifications. Her father had recently died and she considered herself fortunate to have obtained a job as a telephonist. After about three and a half years she married, and at roughly the same time was promoted to a supervisory post which involved working shifts. Her first baby was born about five and a half years later, according to plan.

> *Andrea:* 'I'd arranged that she would go to a nursery when I came here I was on shift work then, as a supervisor—we used to do different duties, like eight till four, and either my husband or myself used to take her to the nursery in the morning, and one of us used to collect her at night.'
>
> *S.Y.: 'And you never considered giving up work at that period?'*
>
> *Andrea:* 'No. I'd always enjoyed work too much.'

The birth of her child was difficult, and because of this she decided not to have any more children—as she put it: 'It's best to have one that's perfectly all right.'

The remaining three women had not planned their pregnancies in quite the same way. Valerie was married for twelve years before the first of her three children was born. After a short spell as a shop assistant on leaving school aged 15, Valerie joined most of her male relatives, who already worked for the same public sector company, as a clerical assistant.

> *Valerie:* 'I think it was just pressure from Mum and Dad. You know, "You ought to get that good little job", and all the rest of it. So I applied.... It's sort of family-orientated really.'

She married a few years later and was subsequently promoted several times. Why had she sought promotions?

> *Valerie:* 'I just felt—I mean, you sort of work here, you just get caught up in it...and, I think, well, if I'm out earning, working, I want job interest...so, it was the natural...course of events to some extent...rather than...an inbuilt desire as always wanting to achieve this.'

She described how she came to decide to remain at work when she eventually had her family.

> *Valerie:* 'It was just something at the time. We'd been married twelve years then, and you sort of acquire a lifestyle, and there was no way that we could continue doing the things we'd become accustomed to doing, if you like...and selfishly enough we weren't prepared to give that up. Although we'd wanted a family—had it been forthcoming, you know, in our early years of marriage, when we'd planned it, I would have left work like most mums do, you know, and had the children, and then come back to work But having worked all that time, I was too old to get up and start scratching around really, because—you know, it is hard when you suddenly come down to one wage, and such like...and so we just decided that, you know..., as it happened, my mum would look after them, and so it worked out like that.'

Valerie had three children, and took four months' maternity leave from her job at each birth.

Neither Sally nor Louise had planned to start their families when they did. Before her marriage, Sally was employed for six years in a variety of jobs. A routine clerical job which she left after about a year, mainly through boredom, six months abroad as an au-pair, and several more office jobs, including assistant to a buyer in a large mail order firm, and supervisor of fieldwork in the market research department of a large company, her last job before marriage. This, she felt, was 'probably the best job I've ever had— I was in charge of the interviewers around the country.' On marriage she moved to Kent and left her job. Although she tried to find the same kind of work there, she could find nothing like it, so after a couple of months out of employment she took a job as a shop assistant in a department store.

> *Sally:* 'I stuck it for two weeks—it was utterly boring—in many ways an absolute insult to anybody's intelligence, supervised by a woman who had no sort of intelligence either. The whole thing was a complete waste of time—utterly boring—I really was bored.'

Following this, she succeeded in obtaining part-time employment as a market research interviewer, and was doing this work when she first became pregnant. However, neither this nor her subsequent pregnancy (eighteen months later), nor having two small children, prevented her from continuing this part-time work. The hours (about 20 per week) were flexible—'you just sort of did it in your own time'—and it was possible to make arrangements for the children.

> *Sally:* 'I used to strap ['the children] in the back of the car...and there were quite a few friends who would have them for the odd hour or two—and sometimes, I would take them with me.

She continued in her market research work for about six years, at the same time running her own farm shop. Once her two children were at school, however, she took a full-time clerical job with a local engineering company. She explained why she made this change.

> *Sally:* 'Really because my [self-employed] husband took a [second] job in the evenings.., we did need the money—and he didn't used to get home until about half past eleven, really tired, and things got to the point where the children were both at school and realized that he just couldn't go *on* doing it And I came along here for the interview.... And I sort of took over the earnings, if you like. My husband had to take [the children] to school, and he had to pick them up and he had to make sure they were all right till I got home. That was the arrangement—if I go out to work, he'd have to accept that responsibility.'

She was still working in this clerical job when interviewed, but has subsequently, after about four years there, changed her employer, going first to work full-time as administrative co-ordinator in an advertising agency, and later, after three weeks out of employment following redundancy, taking a part-time clerical/cashier job with a building society (for 20 hours per week).

Louise went to secretarial college after leaving school and worked as a typist with a building society for six years before changing her job on marriage. She explained:

> *Louise:* 'I met [my husband] there.., and you can't work for the same company'so I had to leave...[also] we moved...to London, because he got promoted.'

She described how she came to take her next job.

Louise: It was easy because it was London...I could have had almost any job but the reason—it's stupid really—but the only reason I chose [the company] was that we'd got a flat nearby and it was the most accessible place to get to. And I could get home in the lunch hours and start—you know, newly married, I thought get home and get the vegetables ready, and all this rubbish [laughs]—that lasted for about three days, but that was the idea. I thought... I wouldn't be able to cope with running a house and going up to town... I wanted a nice local job.., it was very close to the flat, so I could nip home at lunchtime and do the shopping, that was why I chose the job.'

Louise's first child was born three and a half years after her marriage. At first she found her pregnancy hard to accept.

> *Louise:* 'I asked, you know, if it was possible to terminate and (the doctor] wasn't very agreeable—but looking back, I probably wouldn't have done it, it was just that—I went to him because I hadn't come on, and he told me that I was pregnant. It was a bit of a shock I did ask, but he—he lied in fact—he told me that I was sixteen weeks gone, and I wasn't, I was nowhere near that, I was about tenlooking back [my husband] would never have agreed to it anyway...to me, having a baby meant staying at home and washing nappies and things like that'

> *S.Y.: 'So you thought it was going to mean giving up work?'*

> *Louise:* 'End of my life, in fact—yes.'

Through discussing what she saw as her predicament with other people, Louise came to realize that having a child need not mean leaving her job.

> *Louise:* 'I thought about it before he was born. And weighed up lots of possibilities....I got talking to a girl who happened to take my place on maternity leave.., and she told me her child was at a childminder's.... She said, do you want me to put you in touch with this girl? And I went round to see her, and it was very clean, she was registered, obviously... I was happy with her and she was happy with me....he went there before, in fact, he was six months. They were short-staffed at the office, because it was holiday time.'

Louise felt confident that her decision to stay at work and take maternity leave had been the right one for her. She found the period at home with her young baby difficult.

> *Louise:* 'I was not really very happy—my husband used to come home at night, we didn't seem to have anything to talk about...my mum still can't understand it, because she scraped and saved to, you know, bring us...up, and she feels that if she could do it—and they had no money at all—she doesn't see why I shouldn't.'

Since returning to work from her maternity leave, Louise has moved from London to Kent (because her husband has been promoted in his job). When this happened she was able to obtain a transfer within her firm, and had three weeks' leave of absence at the time of removal. During this time, she was able to make arrangements with another registered childminder for her son. Louise would like to work part-time, but her employers have a full-time only policy, and as she has been unable to find suitable alternative employment, she has chosen to reduce her workload by employing domestic help at home for four hours per week These six women, whose attachment to the labour force has been virtually unbroken since they joined it on leaving full-time education, all showed evidence of an active commitment to paid employment.

They had relatively few employers and most were currently well-satisfied with their pay, working conditions and with the nature of their jobs. Most had been able to take advantage of opportunities for promotion, and all planned to remain in employment until retirement. All referred to some difficulties in combining full-time paid jobs with raising children, but with the support of either husbands and other relatives, paid help, or the cooperation of friends and employers, these had not proved insuperable, and none suggested that she regretted the decision to remain in employment The choices they made might not always be ones which other women would select, but many might benefit from a genuine opportunity to consider remaining in paid work as an option.

CASE STUDY: EFFECTS OF INDIVIDUAL BIOGRAPHY

Whilst most of the women interviewed had employment careers which followed the 'dominant' pattern described at the start of this chapter, and a minority' chose to remain in paid work despite changes in their family' lives, a further minority had employment careers which were quite• clearly affected by the special circumstances of their personal lives. None of these ten women had conformed to the norms currently governing family formation behaviour and the conduct of personal relationships. Thus for them the social processes of marriage and childbearing had differed in important ways from those experienced by the majority of my respondents.Whilst marital breakdown has become a commonplace of contemporary relationships between the sexes, and had been experienced by well over a third of the women interviewed, frequent breakdown of personal relationships (whether marital or extra-marital), the bearing of children outside of stable unions, and the failure of women to marry, continue to constitute behaviour which breaks with normative expectations.

These are the characteristics of the women in this group. Disrupted private lives can have important effects upon women's employment careers. Some women seek stable, full-time employment as a 'constant' in their otherwise changeable lives. This enables them to escape dependence on either the state or men for their economic well-being, and gives them a sense of maintaining control over their own lives. Others find that the personal insecurities of unstable and unsatisfying relationships, often complicated by ill-health (mental or physical) and unplanned pregnancies, keep them from permanent or full-time employment In four of the ten cases, attachment to the labour force had been strengthened.

These women were all living alone with a child or children, and were, in effect, employed full-time. Mavis was in her late twenties, had never married, and had an 18-month-old son. She was living in a small council flat, and gave every appearance of coping well with organizing her life and managing her responsibilities.

> *Mavis:* '[It's] not really [a strain]...because I've always sort of sailed through things, and sort of not worried. Well, I do worry a little bit, but it doesn't bother me what other people think... I do what I want to do, and I don't care what anybody says.

She had two paid jobs, working 40 hours per week for a food processing company, packing food, and 7 hours on Saturdays as a butcher's assistant. She had been doing this for nine months when I first met her, and was still doing so when contacted again a year later. In the week, her child went to a registered childminder; whom she paid £12.50 a week, and on Saturdays her neighbour looked after him. Her Saturday job was quite important to her, and she had worked for this employer. on.and off for eight years, going back there when the baby was 6 months old and she was living on supplementary benefit.

> *Mavis:* 'That was a great help...because, also, he said "You know you can help yourself off the counter, like." So, I mean, that was an even bigger help,, that was...things like butter and cheese, and your meat, and it did save me a lot.., and after...doing it about three Or four weeks, I didn't honestly know how I could have gone back to just being on Social Security alone—I couldn't—well, to think about it now, I don't know how I really did manage.

Three months later she took the full-time factory job, and although she was toying with the idea of working shorter hours, she was aware of all the factors she needs to, weigh up.

> *Mavis:* 'Well, you see, you can gain and you can lose—at the moment, I can't claim for FIS,because I am earning too much—but in November, they all go up again, so I can claim for them again.' (FIS = Family Income Supplement)

Kate and Cathy were both in their mid-thirties. Kate had four children, aged between 6 and 14 years, all living with her. She had been married three times, divorced twice, and said she was 'estranged' from her third husband. Cathy had been married and divorced twice, to the same man, and had three children. At the time of the interview she lived alone with the youngest child, a 7-year-old, while the elder two lived with their father. Neither woman was financially supported by a former husband, and both worked as hospital domestics.

Kate worked a 40-hour week and did regular overtime of about 15 hours. Cathy worked part-time as a supervisor, but usually worked a 42-hour week including overtime: Kate's first marriage had lasted two years, her second for twelve. She had one child from her first marriage and three from the Second. Her third marriage was breaking down after only a couple of years, when we met She described her estranged husband's attitude to her job.

> *Kate:* 'He doesn't like 'the idea—because of the independence side of it I suppose.... I was earning my own wage...so it gave me almost equal rights to him...and he didn't like the idea from

She was bitter about her past.

> *Kate:* 'I've always done everything myself, anything to do with the home, cooking, looking after the children, everything. I've always been the one ye even taken on the responsibilities of bills, always have done.... I don't feel at all happy about it, mainly because it should be a shared thing between husband and wife. I don't know if it's me, or if it's just the type of people I've married—it just doesn't work out that way.

Her early experience of employment was in clerical work, which she found boring, and as a supermarket cashier. While her children were young, she worked for about seven years as an agricultural worker (working about nine months in every twelve), before having to 'give this up because of an injury, and taking a job as a hospital domestic. She planned to stay in this job 'quite a few years, I hope. All the time I'm able to, I will.'

Cathy's early employment career was inauspicious. In the first two years after leaving school at 15, she worked as a supermarket shelf-filler and counter assistant, in two jobs as a waitress, and as a factory operative. She was made redundant from one of these jobs, sacked—'for being mouthy'—from a second, and left the others of her own accord. Before taking a fifth job as a trainee laundry worker, she also spent some time caring for her sick grandmother. Cathy's employment career was broken again before she completed her training, when she became pregnant and had her first child.

She married for the first time nine months later, and did not return to paid work (this time as a 'casual' agricultural worker) until three and a half years after this, by which time she had a second child. She continued in this work for about six years, although in the meantime she divorced, and three years later re-married, her husband. She then had to stop work to have a third child, but returned to agricultural work again soon afterwards.

> *Cathy:* 'I done one season of potato picking-up, after I'd had her....I've always suffered with my back, and that last spell of picking up potatoes just about finished me. I'd just about had enough. And then I decided that I would see if I could get a job inside.... I knew that there was one going (at the hospital) and I applied for it, and got it.'

Cathy's husband had no objection to her taking a more secure job.

> *Cathy:* 'He thought it was good that I was working...because then he could cut me housekeeping down, you see.., no, it's the truth' He always told me to get to work anyway—I did as I was told.'

As this second marriage came to an end, things deteriorated further:

> *Cathy:* '[my wages] all went in the housekeeping... I mean, I kept them all, from last May—because he never gave me anything at all—I was having to keep him, 'n all.'

How long did Cathy plan to stay in her present job? 'Until they get rid of me, I should think'

Susan was in her mid-forties, and had been living alone with her three children for over twelve years. Prior to that, she had been twice married and divorced. Susan's employment career began when she was 15, with a period of clerical work which lasted six years. During this time she married for the first time, giving up the job when she was expecting her first child. In the next three or four years, before her marriage broke down, she had another child and engaged in periodic seasonal work on farms, taking her children with her. After her marriage ended, she took on various casual jobs, including part-time clerical work and washing cars, before forming a relationship with the man she was later to marry.

At first she lived with him, unmarried, but when she was expecting his child, she succumbed to pressure from her family, and, against her better judgment, married him. A few years later she obtained a part-time clerical job in the firm where her husband worked. This lasted for two years, until the marriage began to break down and she felt compelled to leave. After her second divorce, Susan gradually became more fully integrated into the labour force. She worked for a while in the school meals service, and then moved to a full-time office job. Finally, she took the advice of her sister, who worked for a public sector employer.

> *Susan:* 'I applied for a job here—my sister is an Executive Officer here, and.., she'd brought up her family on her own. She said you' needed to get into a secure job, because you want a pension—you'd got to think about, you know, bringing up your children on your own—and this obviously made sense.'

Susan had been in this job for ten years when we met. She had accepted modest promotions, and had become very involved in trade union work At the time of her interview she was branch secretary of her union, and was also actively involved in Labour party politics, thus making the kind of link between her working life and her private life which is characteristic of male trade unionists. As she put it: 'What I do for the trade union here fits in with what I do in my leisure time—it's hardly separated.'

She expected to stay with her employers.

> *Susan:* 'I hope until I retire...all the time I'm fit... I mean, I shall need a pension.... We have excellent conditions of service, and because the [employers] have always worked closely with the unions, we don't have the unfairness that you get where you don't have union representation...[we have] flexi-time...we have a good superannuation scheme, we've got a welfare officer, benevolent society—this sort of thing...it's very secure.'

In many respects, the four women described here conformed closely to the stereotype of a 'male' than of a 'female' employee. Working regular overtime, taking a second job, relying upon earnings as a sole means of support, and active involvement in trade union activities are all characteristics more commonly found among male than female employees. Of course these characteristics have nothing to do with biological sex. What these women's employment careers demonstrate is that where women find it necessary to think of themselves as breadwinners, and shoulder all responsibility for themselves and their families, they are likely also to follow what has often been thought of as a 'male' pattern of employment

Three other women in this group were in paid employment when interviewed, but were only marginally integrated into the labour force. All were living alone with their children, but were not economically self-supporting in the way the four, women already described were. Jackie was receiving supplementary benefit, as well as support from two men, her former husband and the father of her second child, while both Hilary and Jane were in receipt of Family Income Supplement as well as a small amount of maintenance from their former husbands. Jackie and Hilary were both employed part-time, while Jane worked a 40-hour week, and sometimes did 5 hours overtime as well.

In what ways had their personal histories resulted in their marginal integration in the labour force? Jackie's employment career had been severely disrupted by ill-health several mental breakdowns, anorexia nervosa, and alcoholism. During the first three years of her employment career, she had three different jobs in residential homes for the elderly and handicapped, working as a care or nursing assistant: She left two of these jobs on account of her health, and the third following her marriage (when she was 21). After her marriage she took a full-time college course and qualified as a medical secretary, subsequently finding employment as secretary to a hospital consultant. She left this job after a year when expecting her much• wanted first child. She had not anticipated returning to employment for some years, but an opportunity to work 6 hours per week in the evenings as secretary to a general practitioner came up, and she took the job.

After, just two months she had to be' re-admitted to hospital. Subsequently her marriage broke down and after a short spell living alone with the baby she lost custody of the child to her husband, 'because of my drinking'.

> *Jackie:* 'When I got her back [four months later] I still wasn't working.., and I just lived here on my own with her for a while, and I didn't work until the following year, until I got sober.... I started that about nine months after I stopped drinking.'

Her next job was secretarial work for a charity on one day a week, and she was doing this when we met.

> *Jackie:* 'I don't claim my money from there—which is £6 per week—until my telephone bill comes in—so it's purely for the telephone.'

She explained that a telephone was vital to her because of her alcoholism. Shortly before we met, Jackie had a second child. She intends to stay on her own, and says that the baby's father now 'maintains him'.

Hilary, in her early thirties, with three children-aged between 8 and 14, was married for just two years, although she has subsequently lived with another man for about four years. After leaving school at 15, Hilary had a number of short-lived jobs, as a factory worker and as a cinema usherette, before joining her parents, both agricultural workers. As she put it 'I went on to the farm with Mum and Dad... I did quite a lot of farm work'

She stayed in this work until her first, unplanned, child was expected.

> *Hilary:* 'Well, it didn't upset my plans—because I never had any plans—I never plan things anyway, it's no good...it's just that I knew—this fella that I was going with—before I married him...it wouldn't work And I thought, you know, getting married, *it* might alter him...well, it didn't. And then, when I found that I was pregnant, I thought "Oh God, how are we going to manage?"...and this is what it was.'

Her husband was unemployed throughout the two years of their marriage. 'I was going to work to keep him.' After her marriage ended, and following a spell when she lived on supplementary benefit, she began living with the man who is the father of her second and third children, a self-employed builder and decorator. During the four years this relationship lasted, she was not in employment, and her involvement in a car accident meant that 'The very last year that he was with me, 1 couldn't walk.' Hilary felt that neither of the men with whom she had been involved had helped her to shoulder the responsibilities of raising a family: 'I've brought my three up on my own, really.... Really, I mean, because the two boys' father, we never used to hardly see him, anyway.'

When she had recovered *from* her accident, she took a part-time job as a hospital bed-maker.

> *Hilary:* 'I wanted to get out... I was just shut in, day after day, and I just couldn't take any more of it. It was either come to work or crack up in the end, I think.'

With help from her family with childcare, she kept this part-time job for over eighteen months. However, 'The reason I didn't stay was...because of the children, you know the seven-week school holiday.' Her next return to employment was as a part-time hospital domestic, a job which she had held for over three years when interviewed, despite a long period of sick leave, and a period of working reduced hours so that she could visit her youngest child in hospital following his injury in a road accident. She was not at the time of the interview entirely satisfied with her situation at work.

> *Hilary:* 'I have been moved about, quite a bit, just lately...they shove me off somewhere else. I fell out quite a few times with [management].... If I could find another job tomorrow, I'd go to it.'

Hilary was not finding it easy to cope: her children were difficult to manage, and she has had to call upon social services for assistance.

> *Hilary:* 'My children get me down....you know, sometimes...they really do make me cry....to think that I'm trying as hard as I can, to keep that house going and keep it nice, and they just don't care.

In the light of her past history, Hilary's expectations about her employment future seemed rather unrealistic: she thought she would stay 'until I find something else—or I get married—then I won't have to go to work' Jane was a divorcee in her mid-thirties, with three children aged between 11 and 15. She had been married only once, for about seven years, and did not do so until after her three children were born. She was divorced five years before we met.

After leaving school at 15, Jane was employed for five years in a variety of different jobs before having her first child. She worked as a shop assistant, in two factories, and as a bus conductress. She left the shop for better pay, was made redundant from one of the factory jobs, and left the other following an argument with the foreman. She left the bus company because of her pregnancy. There then followed a period of five years during which she did no paid work and had three children. How did she feel about being a single mother?

> *Jane:* 'Dunno... I just had to shoulder the responsibility, as with all three of them...it just happened....so that was that...'

At first she lived with her parents, but towards the end of the five years married and went to live with her husband. Her return to employment was prompted by the loss of her fourth child soon afterwards.

> *Jane:* 'I was getting a bit depressed, you know, with losing the baby and that, and I was sterilised—I had a Caesarean and sterilisation at the same time—so I took a job—that's about it.'

She took full-time work as a hospital domestic, but left after a year.

> *Jane:* 'I started having problems with the old man...whilst I was in hospital, he was carrying on with this woman....'

After two years without employment she started working again, as a barmaid in a pub.

> *Jane:* 'I started there a couple of dinner times, and then did three or four a week...and then several evenings a week. And then we split up completely...the marriage had really broken down, and then,. obviously, you know, I needed extra money, because of being on my own with three kids, so I took a job here.'

This time her job was again as' a hospital domestic, working full-time. She had been in this job for four years when I interviewed her. Although previously her personal life had tended to limit her attachment to employment, she now recognised that she needed to continue earning a living. I asked how long she expected to stay in her job.

Jane: 'Well, as long as possible.'

S.Y.: '[until] you come to retire?'

Jane: 'What can I say?... There's not a lot you can say about it, is there? It's a job.... The chance is, I might have to be.'

For these women, then, participation in the labour force had been, reduced by the nature of their personal relations and health. Unlike the four women described earlier, Jackie, Hilary, and Jane had not used employment as a means of structuring uneven and disrupted personal lives, but found that their employment careers were limited and fragmented by them. The remaining three women had personal histories which temporarily interrupted their employment careers. Annette was gentle and softly spoken, a woman who looked younger than her 27 years. Although she was caring for two children aged 12 and 14, she had no natural children of her own and had never married.

At the time of the interview she had been living for four years with Jim and his two children by his ex-wife. Jim's wife had 'walked out and left' the family some six months before Annette moved in. Annette worked full-time as a clerical assistant and had also taken on the role of mother to Jim's children, and wife to Jim. Her early employment career had been rather chequered. She left school at 15 and worked briefly in a factory, and then in a hairdresser's, finding both unsatisfactory. After this she took another factory job, this time wiring electrical goods. She stayed in this job for two and, a half years, before being made redundant After some weeks out of work, she obtained a job as an office junior.

Annette: 'I learnt how to operate the switchboard, and went from being a junior to doing all the credit control and the wages.'

Meanwhile, she had applied for another clerical job.

Annette: 'My sister worked there... I suppose that was really the reason I went there—plus it was more money.'

She was taken on, and stayed two years before starting to feel restless. She then gave in her notice, and took work for the summer at a holiday camp—'getting away from home for a couple of months'. Afterwards, she worked briefly as a barmaid, before obtaining clerical work again, in a small company. By the end of the year, however, she had been offered her old clerical job back, and this time she stayed for almost three years, only leaving after moving in with Jim. She was quite keen to stop working, and Jim was anxious for her to do so: 'He's a bit possessive and a bit selfish, and he just wanted me at home.' After three years out of employment, however, Annette was anxious to return to her old job:

> *Annette:* 'The frustrations of being at home all the time had set in by then... [he didn't want me to come to work at all—it was purely at my insistence—at which he is pleased now—but it did take quite a few months.'

She had been back a year when we met What were her plans for the future? She explained that she had decided not to have children of her own, but that was not all.

> *Annette:* '[I have] distant thoughts of having a little business of my own.., perhaps a little shop.... I think I like working better knowing that it's not something that I'm going to have to do for another forty years or whatever...if I wanted to give up, I can give up.'

Alice was a 40-year old divorcee. She had left her husband and three children five years previously to live with another man, but the relationship did not last. She then spent some time living with her father, and, since his death, with another man and, more recently, her elder son. Like many of the women interviewed, Alice had several jobs between leaving school and having her first child, and married during this period. She left employment to have her first baby, and during the next six years her second and third children were born.

At this stage she engaged in seasonal agricultural work and took on evening jobs—as a factory operative and as a cleaner. After the birth of her third child, she gradually began working more hours per week, at first as a cleaner but later as a laboratory assistant (at the same place of employment). She worked in this last job for about four years, and eventually left her family to set up home with her employer. She explained that she had been, unhappy about her marriage and her husband's attitudes to her employment

> *Alice:* 'It seemed to me that he would want me to work all day and all night.., my money always went straight in the house—it was expected to go in there—it was never mine.... That's where I wrong... I felt like a slave. He liked to have his drink, and I was working for him to have his beer. I would come home after working from ten till six...and he admitted he'd been up since half past four, but he'd been asleep all afternoon, and he hadn't bothered—he hadn't made the bed, he hadn't washed up, he hadn't done anything...and before that anyway—he was never capable of looking after me.'

When her new relationship failed, Alice had a breakdown. Afterwards, in her own words, 'I pulled myself together, and went to work.' The work was in a paper mill, 'cutting holes in paper' and she found it hard: 'It was bonus work...you had to do so much...you had to keep going.' After two years, during which time she was also caring for her dying father, she gave the job up and took work as a full-time hospital domestic instead. Two years later, at the time of the interview, she was still working full-time, often doing 11 hours overtime each week She had no plans to leave: 'I think I shall be working here—well. I just think I shall always be here.' Alice's affair, divorce, and nervous breakdown had not severely disrupted her employment career, but had created a hiatus in its development

Penny's employment career had been interrupted in a way similar to Alice's, although the change in her personal life which caused' the interruption was different. Like Alice's, Penny's employment career followed a typical pattern for about twenty years. She took employment, married, and left to have her first child. She then did seasonal framework before moving into full-time permanent employment in sales after her child started school. She continued working full-time, although changing from sales to domestic work when her son was in his early teens. When he was 18, however, she found she was expecting another, unplanned, child. I asked her how she had felt.

> *Penny:* 'I don't really know. I wasn't overjoyed, I wasn't bitter I always wanted another child.'

Having the child meant giving up her job, but also coincided with the breakdown of her marriage.

> *Penny:* 'It finished.... And then, the hard times hit.... I had two choices—either live on social security, and poverty, or come back to work, and get above—just a little bit above poverty.

She returned to her former job, again full-time, and was able to place her child in the workplace nursery. What of the future?

> *Penny:* 'I don't think I shall change [my job]... I don't think I'd like promotion... I think I've come to a standstill in my life—I think I just like being as I am. I don't think I could take on any more responsibilities because I already have enough... I'll keep continuing as long as can. I've got quite a lot of years left to continue work, and I still hope I can fulfil the years.'

As with Alice' and Annette, Penny's employment career was temporarily interrupted by developments in her personal life. Having a child unexpectedly late in her life had a similar effect on her employment career as moving in to be 'mother' to an existing family had for Annette, or leaving a family to establish a new relations hip had for Alice. I have tried to show here that 'distinctive' personal histories such as those described do not have any simple effect upon women's employment patterns, but may influence them in a variety of ways. Some women use employment to structure their lives, while others may find changes and disruption in their personal lives spreading to their employment careers. This chapter presented detailed discussion of the patterns of labour adopted by the women interviewed.

Although most followed variants on a pattern usually regarded as typical (employment—childrearing—employment), two minority groups whose experience differed in important ways also emerged. In the first, women did not leave the labour force at all, but used maternity leave, or made other arrangements, to enable them to continue in their jobs. The second group consisted of a number of women 'whose personal histories deviated significantly from current norms governing personal relationships and family formation; in some cases this deviation had the effect of reinforcing integration into the labour force, in others of restricting it. It is important not to ignore the significance of the two minority groups.

The former suggests a commitment to participation in the labour force with which women who are also mothers are not usually 'credited', while the latter tells us that there is no simple effect on employment careers which can be attributed to deviation from social norms concerning interpersonal behaviour. The women in the main group (the 'dominant' pattern) had all left the labour market at least once to raise a child or children, and had returned to it at some subsequent point; none the less there were significant variations within this pattern.

Between leaving school and leaving the labour force to have a first child, most of the women in the group held more than one job; in many cases, changing jobs, even at this initial stage in the employment career, meant changing from one type of work to another, although this changing of occupation was uncommon amongst those (few) women who engaged in further education after school. In establishing how women came to leave the labour force when expecting a first child; it was noteworthy that about half of first pregnancies were unplanned.

These women thus had little opportunity to plan seriously for a future combination of domestic labour 'and wage-earning. These 'unplanned' first pregnancies reflect the fact that most young working-class women view marriage and a (first) baby as inevitable steps in the transition to adulthood. These steps are not usually subjected to rational economic planning, and often a 'the sooner, the better' approach is adopted. Once they are taken the individual can then get on with organizing her life around what are seen as its essential components husband and children. Such economically irrational behaviour (which contrasts clearly with the career-oriented approach characteristic of the middle class) can best be understood in terms of the constraints and restricted opportunities of working-class life.

Even amongst those whose first child was planned, little thought had apparently been given to returning to employment in the future, although many women said that they had vague expectations about this at the time. Most women were to return to paid work much more quickly than they had expected. The return to employment represented a new experience of work, and the next few years were mostly characterised by a succession of part-time, temporary, or seasonal jobs. Most were in low paid and insecure occupations, and many would have gone unrecorded in official statistics. For the minority of married women who had more than one child and who remained outside the labour force throughout the entire childbearing phase, the average length of time between leaving and returning to paid employment was about eight years.

It was notable that these women tended to have stable marriages and relatively well-paid husbands. Most placed a high value on their mothering role, and many sought employment partly because of a sense of lost identity when their youngest child started school. After returning to employment there was a tendency to engage in several part-time jobs over a period of some years before taking on full-time employment Some women chose to remain part-timers, whilst for others full-time work was an aim which could only be achieved when the youngest child reached a particular age. Almost without exception, the women intended to remain in employment until retirement For many this intention reflected the fact that they had finally found themselves an acceptable occupation, where they were treated with some respect, derived some enjoyment from their work or working environment, and were earning wages on which they had come to rely.

An important minority of the women were more ambitious however, and they intended to seek-promotion, further training, or a higher grade occupation. Many of these were women who worked for employers offering training and a career structure to all able members of staff. They had been made aware of the contribution they could make at work, derived a sense of self-worth from this, and had gained the confidence to pursue a career. Others were not positively motivated in this way, but rather felt undervalued and discontented in their present jobs. They knew they could do more demanding work, and recognised that they would need to change their occupation if their skills and abilities were to be used. The evidence from the analysis of employment careers suggests that women may not be such passive members of the labour force as has sometimes been claimed. They have an experience of paid work which is fragmented and variable, but they also return frequently to employment, and intend to stay. Indeed, many have relatively ambitious plans for the future, and desire to be further integrated into the labour force.

7

Problems of Urban Working Women

> "I can promise you that women working together - linked, informed and educated - can bring peace and prosperity to this forsaken planet."
>
> —*Isabel Allende*

PROBLEMS AT WORKPLACE

The condition of working women in India as well as in the entire world in general is considered to be very distressing. Working women in general are subject to discrimination at various levels. The problems and difficulties of working women are multi-dimensional, varying from woman to woman at personal level, and section to section at general level and hence need to be analysed in depth. One may believe that there are two clear-cut sections—privileged and unprivileged among the urban working women. Women working in factories, mines, plantations or in electronics, garments or chemical units or banks, schools and hospitals appear to be the privileged sections among women.

However, the problems of working women at work places are multiple and differ from woman to woman according to the nature of the work and position. Ms. Aruna Broota, a phychologist of Delhi University, is categorical in stating that no girl is respected in the office if she is known to be a single woman. In fact, in India women are considered less and individual than as an object of vice by men whether she is single or married. this is particularly true for the women who are working among the males. Working women of the present generation, in the opinion of Ms. Broota, are at the cross-roads. They are aware that they are being exploited and ill treated. Yet they consciously or unconsciously adopt their mother's roles of subservience to the male. So, women, in general, have to be taught to develop their self-confidence, as well as self-respect and not accept the apologetic and subservient role instilled in them since childhood.

Relationship with Colleagues

The efficiency of a working woman is always suspected. Especially in the upper class cadres, even though other qualifications are equal, men are preferred. the authorities are doubtful whether she would be able to handle male subordinates, take independent decisions, cope with crisis and manage her duties. Even though she has proved her efficiency, they think twice before promoting her. Even if she is given a chance, there is always a remark that she has been taken because she is a woman. The male co-workers in the office cannot mentally accept the superiority of the woman's work. They take extra pains to ridicule her. The male colleagues get together and pass comments. As the woman is brought up in a protected atmosphere in the family, she is not mentally prepared to face this kind of situation. She feels helpless and often breaks down. This further leads to the misconception that women workers are not fit for outside work.

Women as Managers

It is equally difficult a situation where the woman is a boss. The male subordinates do not like to accept the authority of a woman boss. If she demands work, efficiency and discipline, she is criticised as harsh and dictatorial. She is supposed to dominate only to hide her inefficiency and inferiority complex. If she is polite, mild and courteous, she would be labelled as inefficient, talkative and what not. In any way, they do not carry out her orders and instructions, neglect their duties and take advantage of her goodness. They try to harass her in many ways.

In short they are not able to accept a woman as their head. There is another problem; while working with men, a woman tends to develop close relations with any one of them owing to prolonged and constant association. This, in the case of a married woman, creates social and psychological problems and tensions in her relationships, while in the case of an unmarried girl, it can create all sorts of socio-psychological problems if she gets involved with a married man. Sengupta in her study (1964) points towards the emergence of similar problems. In this connection Rosenquiet observes, "certain social conditions, most of them connected with recent changes in economic life, provide an environment quite favourable to divorce. The arrangement of office work, as now generally found, may be mentioned as an example. The professional men of male office worker and his female secretary, stenographer, or assistant are likely to develop personal attachments which endanger the marriage tie. More especially, this is likely to be true of one of the partners in this business relationship, usually the woman, is unmarried."

Even if the woman who is working in the office with men makes only good friends with them and has no intimate relations with any one of them, she is still liable to be suspected and often accused of having intimate relations with them. This often humiliates and annoys her a lot and creates frictions in her married life.

Office and Family

There is another type of problem which arise when she has to work over-time to complete her work. In certain government jobs the woman employee also face transfers, she finds it difficult to go, having the family behind. If she is married she can not go leaving her husband and children. In such a situation generally she has to give up the job. If she is unmarried the parents would not permit her to go alone. If she is married and working, she has to leave the job if her in laws do not approve of her working or if she is married in some other place then also she has to resign. Again if she wants to work at a new place, it becomes difficult for her to find a new job. In some cases women have to leave the job when the children are too young and there is nobody in the family to look after them. By the time children are grown up, women are out of touch with the field and are not able to find work again. Unfortunately, in our country the system of part-time jobs have not developed yet. Part-time jobs would have been more convenient to young married working women with children. But it has not been acceptable as they are poorly paid for and part-time jobs consume comparatively more time and require equally hard work from her.

Not Much Choice

Another notable problem for the woman worker is that they do not get jobs in the fields of their interest. They have to accept the work they get. But this problem is not confined only to women. Many male workers also have the same problem. The professional women have their own problems. As she is professionally trained, she aspires to utilise her skills, to put up the best performance and to earn a proper income. But the in-laws do not accept her working. In this way many women doctors, engineers and technicians leave their profession after marriage or do work for limited hours for pleasure only. Even when they work the fellow professionals, especially the males have a negative attitude.

Sometimes the work women get do not befit their qualifications. For example, it is often believed that teaching, medical practice etc. are the ones more suitable for women, and thereby they are forced to accept what is available and do not achieve the levels they are trained for. The composition of staff at the work-place also create problems. Some traditional families in India, for example, would like their women to be posted exclusively in a girls college or school. These families are afraid that in a place where the majority is men, their women will be looked upon as sex objects. The liberal-minded families do not entertain such a baseless apprehension and do not stand in the way of their women working in a male-dominated office, or a boy's school, or a co-educational institution. Sex segregation in the offices and establishments is an unhealthy pattern either for the present or for the future. It is a negation of equality with men.

Problem of Transport

The present transport system is far from satisfactory; generally women have to suffer the worst due to misconduct or eve-teasing by co-passengers. Sometimes they have to wait for hours on the bus-stop to board a bus. Even when the bus comes, due to it being over-crowded she is not able to catch it. Even in train the position is not good. At present there is only one ladies' compartment in local trains in cities like Bombay and Delhi, and that too, is often occupied by men. At the peak hours one can hardly entrain or detrain without difficulty. In some metro-cities there is a "ladies' special" during busy hours. But it is unsatisfactory and limited. So the authorities should provide for more than one ladies' compartment in local trains and more `ladies' special' to solve problems of various type for the women workers.

Wage Discrimination

The issue of discrimination in wages throughout the world is a matter of vital importance. Mencher and Saradamoni noted that it was often taken for granted that women should be paid less than men for similar jobs. Throughout the world, women are concentrated in low paid job sectors according to an I.L.O. report. Apart from lower wave rates poor urban women were rarely given any access to training schemes and their promotional avenues were severely limited. At every level of work, they are paid lower wages, defeating the constitutional position of equal pay for equal work for both men and women. There has been quite a few micro-studies that show that women workers in unorganized sector invariably get paid much less than men. G.D. Gambhir in his study on "Labour in Small-scale Industries in Madhya Pradesh with special reference to women and child labour in cotton ginning, bidi making and rice milling and shelloc manufacture" found that wages of unskilled women workers ranged between 65% to 75% that of the unskilled men-workers. Men coolies earn double that of women coolies. In Kerala, in cashew processing and coir industries women are paid less than men. Women construction workers are paid uniformly lower wages than their male counterparts in spite of the fact that she is doing equally, if not more hard work in comparison to men. In fact women in the unorganized sector as well as the organized sector are discriminated directly or indirectly. One can take a look at the wages in the organized sectors. Only 11 per cent of the country's female work-force is employed in the organized sector. The organized sector comprises units registered under the Factories Act of 1948 and covers those using power and employing ten or more workers, as well as units not using power but employing 20 or more workers.

In addition the organized sector is governed by legislation such as the Minimum Wages Act, Labour Welfare Regulations, and Contract Labour (Regulation and Abolition) Act. Strictly speaking violations of those Acts can be challenged in a Court of Law. In the organized sectors of the economy, people are selected for job-positions and their rate of emoluments are fixed primarily in relation to the nature of the jobs concerned. There could therefore, be theoretically no sex-based differences in wages in the organized sectors. It is, however, possible that some establishments try to separate some jobs carrying less pay and it may so happen that only females get recruited to such jobs. This may not "technically amount to sex-based discrimination", though "such categorisation of jobs' may also sometimes be done purposely." Even in the public sector, where employment has gone up substantially, a large proportion of women are shunted into low-paid jobs. Official agencies admit that no assessment has been done as to what extent the equal pay principle has resulted in the displacement of women workers. After examining different industries the National Committee on Status of Women in 1976 came to be conclusion that the principle of equal pay has not been seriously applied in most of industries which continue to maintain wage differentials by direct or indirect methods. Evidence for this is available in occupational wage surveys conducted by the Ministry of Labour, indicating differences in the minimum, maximum and average earnings of women in most of industries.

Though the survey reported that employees evade this principle by not employing men and women for the same jobs in the same establishments, such differentials were found even within the same establishments in some cases. A more successful method for evading this principle is by restricting women to certain jobs and prescribing lower wage rates for them. A study of 400 working women by Usha Talwar also reveals that lower pay for equal work is one of the most important issues faced by those working women. Wage discrimination is a problem all over the world, especially in the third world countries, where the process of industrialisation is still going on. A double standard on pay still plagues women workers everywhere according to ILO report. The average earning of women compared with men in non-agricultural activities in 1981 ranged from 44.8 per cent in South Korea to 86.2% in Australia. In the manufacture sector alone, these ranged from 43.4% in Japan to 90% in Sweden. According to I.L.O. Year Book the gap between women's and men's wages widened slightly between 1977 and 1981 in 7 countries—Czechoslovakia, Denmark, West Germany, Japan, Luxemburg, the Netherlands and Britain. the earnings of women compared to men went down from 55.8% to 53.5% in Japan and from 71.9% to 69.5% in Britain.

On the contrary, there was some improvement in women's remuneration in six countries—Belgium, Cyprus, France, Ireland, Newzealand and Switzerland. The increase was highest in Ireland going up from 80.1% to 83.7%. However women working in the manufacturing sector in Japan experienced further erosion of their earning compared to those of men, as they dropped from 46.1% in 1977 to 43.4% in 1981.

In India the average earnings of women are highly depressed. The average earning of regular wage/salaried female employees is about three times higher than of the females casual labourers. If the men and women are working on the same post in Government's jobs, there is not so much discrimination. But in other institutions there is a disparity prevailing. There is another aspect of wage discrimination in India that is female workers "are exploited as a piece-rate worker doing manual labour for trader, middlemen, contractors and big companies in the corporate sector." "There is a variation in the wages for identical work and skills." "Self-employed workers accept wage rate which potently do not cover their cost. It is difficult to understand why and how the difference exists and why workers accept them."

Thus the wage-discrimination is a universal phenomenon and it needs a world-wide awakening and revolutionary movement to wipe out the basic discrimination at various levels of the economy and for this not only women but also men have to come under one-banner and fight against it.

Issue of Health

Women anywhere in the world have to suffer from some in built disadvantages, compared to men, because of certain biological reasons. They have to put up with menstruation, pregnancy, child birth, lactation, child rearing and menopause and their various complications. Physically, they are less strong. they are also ore vulnerable to sexual aggression and abuse. The different cultural, social and economic situations in India have given different focus to these biological disadvantages of women.

These situations also influence the way these biological disadvantages affect the health of the working women.

One may hence analyse the status and conditions of these working women in various industries. A study done by Shahnaz Anklesaria gives us a clear cut picture. She has pointed out the defects of Factory Act which seeks to ensure protection to millions of women covered by it. It applies to any premises where 10 or more workers are employed and where a manufacturing process is carried on with or without the aid of power. The Act is enforced by the State Governments through their factory inspectorates. It was amended in 1976 to include the three sections which deal specifically with health hazards that the workers face. The Act outlines the principal health risks to factory workers, which arise from dangerous gases, acids and dust, harmful bacteria and micro-organisms, compressed and rarefied atmosphere, improper lighting, extremes of temperature, humidity and excessive strain. But it is silent on the impact of all these on women workers. The repercussions on women can be slightly different from those on men because of the additional physical and psychological factors and can be complicated by pregnancy, maternity and gynaecological issues. Further environmental factors like, heat, humidity, repetitive work, toxic substances also affect women. They can adversely condition pregnancy, child birth, lactation, child rearing and menopause and their various complications.

The law prohibits women's employment in dangerous and heavy operations in organized sector. At the same time in unorganized sector, as head-loader, handcraft puller, construction workers, women work more than men—for longer hours and sometimes for less wages.

What the Factories Act does say is that women must be prohibited from employment in dangerous and heavy operations. No women worker should be asked to clean or lubricate or adjust any machinery while it is in motion, if her work exposes her to the risk of injury from any moving part. No woman workers should be employed for pressing cotton in any part of a factory in which a cotton opener is at work. There are also specified limits on the amount of weight a woman worker can carry. This is limited to 65 lbs for an adolescent and 30 for a child. The State governments can, therefore, restrict or prohibit the employment of women in any operation which may expose them to serious risk of physical injury.

It is well spread belief that the physical structure and maternal functions of women place her at a disadvantage. But practices do not follow this. women have never shirked hard labour; whether it is farming, planting, transplanting, winowing, weeding, harvesting, grinding, pounding, nothing holds them back. It is has been seen that work which is physically very strenuous is done not by men but by by women like head-loaders, handcraft pullers, construction workers etc. Any "disadvantage" that women's maternal functions may cause is largely man-made. So these responsibilities have to be seen as vital functions to perform for which a woman must be adequately compensated. Male refusal to take on specific home and child-care responsibilities has also placed a dual responsibility of home as well as office on working women. These responsibilities cause mental as well as physical problem which ultimately leads to health hazards.

Further instead of outlining the kind of health hazards in modern industry for women, the law merely lays emphasis on the negative stereotypes of working women which restrict her access to certain kind of work. The Act also says that there should be separate toilets and sanitary, dressing rooms for women workers. It specifies the need for keeping both clean. Besides the obvious health reasons. what is not so well known is that modern industrial processes subject employees not only to dangerous dust and vapours, but a variety of diseases—breeding organisms that can be transmitted by fellow workers to one another. Hence the need for eliminating unhygenic contacts between workers. In study after study we come across the women workers' complaint of the absence or shortage of separate toilets at their work place. The fact is that the Factories Acts which are enforced by the factory inspectors, are not implemented. Thus in different industries women workers are suffering from innumerable difficulties and nothing has been done to alleviate them.

Both men and women can be working on the same jobs, but women can for a variety of reasons be affected more than their male-colleagues. A survey of the agate workers in Gujarat, revealed that lungs disease had affected 70.6% of women and 60.4% of the men. Pneumonia and T.B. affected 19.6% and 21.6% respectively of the women, compared to 17.9% and 12.9% of the males.

Lack of Other Facilities

A study conducted by M.N. Vanamala on Public Sectors in Andhra Pradesh shows that except the maternity benefits, the other facilities are poor and inadequate. Only about 20% of the women employees are provided with transport facilities, 16 per cent housing facilities and 38 per cent child care facilities. This indicated that the public enterprises miserably neglected the women in providing employment opportunities and adequate status.

In the present situation maternity leave is being revised and improved.

The provision for unpaid "special leave" of varying length in excess of the statutory maternity leave as is practised in France, may be followed.

In fact health problem of under privileged working women are worst due to exploitation, oppression, denial of social and economic justice. Hunger, poor sanitation and housing, unhealthy source of drinking water, infesting of insects and parasites, lack of protection from various elements of nature, poor educational status and limited access to media of mass communication, are some of the major consequences of these conditions which affect the working pattern of the society. Under-nutrition and malnutrition are common phenomenon among the working women in India, particularly in the underprivileged section.

Thus, besides the patriarchal discrimination, women in India suffer due to exploitation and oppression by the privileged sections. Such exploitation is also closely linked with extensive health problems that prevail among the women belonging to the underprivileged class. Because of this, they also have less access even to community financial health institutions. The struggle for health of women should therefore be a struggle for social, economic and political emancipation of the underprivileged as a class. With a platform of equal rights and status of women, women and men will have to fight together to attain emancipation of the underprivileged.

PROBLEMS AT HOME

Our advancement in science and technology notwithstanding, the women remain backward and poverty stricken. The condition of women in India in general is considered to be very miserable. Women's problems are linked with her general living conditions in society.

The women perform many functions in the society and for the society. They produce children, mothers and wives. However they are largely excluded from high status occupations and from positions of power. They do cooking, mending, sewing, washing and many other odd jobs. But in terms of the rewards of prestige, wealth and power, women invariably come off worse.

The emergence of middle class women as working women is a recent phenomena; however the society has mostly remained a traditional one, leading to the women facing many problems. The problems of working women are multidimensional and differ from women to women. The problems are different for different sections of women such as rural and urban women, the educated and uneducated ones, single women and ones with family. Women in joint family, nuclear or extended family, of orthodox and modern family etc. again, have their own problems. Even the atmosphere in the place of work, attitudes of the fellow workers and the authority, age of the women, kind of work, timings of work, distance of work-place from the house etc. are important factors in the lives of working women. Promila Kapur in her study of hundreds of working women employed in various salaried jobs and professions, found that their problems are of three types: environmental, social and psychological. In each of them the problems emerge due to the stained situations at home and work place. In turn, they are due to two factors; one is the inner conflict due to dual commitment and concern, and the other is the practical difficulty of combing the dual commitment.

Raka Sharan in her study found that the social degradation, economic subjugation and dependence of Indian women manifest in triple forms of exploitation—first, at the family level, secondly in working environment by their bosses or employers and finally by the political leaders, pressure groups and trade unions. Discrimination in the family is a major problem for women in Indian society. the example of the three girls who committed suicide in Chandigarh the day their brother was born, clearly pointed this out. Forgarty and his associates in their study on the family, career and working life of qualified women in top jobs found five types of dilemmas:

(1) Dilemmas arising from sheer overload.

(2) Dilemmas from experiencing in one's environment strongly conflicting ideas and directions about what is considered right and proper in a given area of behaviour.

(3) Dilemmas caused by conflicts within oneself about whether one is being a good person (good human being, good wife and mother, good woman) in leading a certain type of existence.

(4) Dilemmas produced by conflicts in obligations, attachments, desires, and so on relative to one's network of relatives, friends and associates.

(5) Dilemmas due to the conflicts between roles that may be variable in their demands at different times, eg., the marital role demands in relation to the work demands of each partner at different points in the life cycle.

The Problems of Married Working Women

Women as a group, specially married women, have certainly become an important part of the work-force all over the world. The march of wives into the work-place is gradually changing the family, marriage and child-bearing practices. In other words the phenomenon of career-couples is having its impact on the institutions marriage, sex, children, life-style, and the dream of home. The double income does liberate both husband and wife from financial stringency and self-denial, but it creates more problems for working wives.

Dual Responsibility

The major problems for working wives arise out of the dual responsibilities of the working women—house work and the office work. Even though the employment of women is accepted, most of her in-laws and majority of the husbands have not accepted the changing life pattern. They are not prepared to share the responsibilities of the household and of looking after children. These duties are still considered to be exclusive of the wife. It is a common sight that the women get up early in the morning, prepare break-fast, cooks the lunch, dresses the children for school and goes to office. In the evening when she returns the house job is waiting for her. She prepares tea and serves the husband and children, attends pending work and prepares dinner. If it is a joint family the mother-in-law or the sister-in-laws feel that they work for the whole day in house when she is in the office. Now it is her turn to work. If she is with her husband or children, they feel that she is not doing enough work for the house. They criticise and abuse her. They even comment loud that she is not earning for them or she is not obliging them by working, that they also work a lot. At times her share of work is kept apart. Sometimes they remark that she has a change to go out in the name of work, while the other sisters-in-law are totally confined to home. They are jealous of her freedom and the status she enjoys. Even derogatory stories are fabricated to hurt her. If the husband is sensible and sympathetic and does share some work to help her he is blamed as a "henpacked" husband. The in-laws do not like his attitude and criticise him also. However, even such husbands are only a few.

Krishna Chakraborty in her study, *the Conflicting Worlds of Working Mother* found that employed housewives all over the world have to face this problem of adjustment among their varied role expectations. They are required by their position to play a dual set of roles—one as home makers, wives and mothers, and the other as employees. Being simultaneously confronted with the dual demands of home and work, they are liable to face adjustment problems. At home, in addition to biological functions, there are other duties which they are expected to perform because of the prevailing cultural norms and values. These new circumstances and responsibilities, require a redefinition and reallocation of roles, duties and responsibilities, not merely for them but also for every member of the family. Unless and until it is achieved there is no chance of lessening the overload on working house-wives, and therefore, mitigating the severity of their problems. Whether it is out of their own choice or economic necessity that they have taken up employment outside, adjustment between their role obligations is not an easy task. It requires not only ability and goodwill but also physical endurance and psychological acceptance.

Conflict between the Two Roles

In addition to the above described burdens on the women, the dual role also demands of her two different sets of values. Difficulties arise because often these two roles make a simultaneous demand on the person whose physical capacity, energy, endurance and time have definite limits. Often the fulfilment of these two roles requires qualities of different and diverse kinds—one requiring cooperation and self-negation and the other calling her competition and self-enhancement. Women's business functions require such qualities as efficiency, courage, determination, intelligence, sense of reality, responsibility and independence. In the professional sphere they are expected to act in 'business-like' manner, to be straight forward and non-sentimental. In addition to these characteristics, and partly in conflict with them, woman who is a wife also expected to be sweet and soft, sensitive and adaptable, gentle, unassertive, good-humoured, domesticated, yielding and in most cases, not too intelligent. Hence a kind of conflict arising from a lack of adjustment between two competing roles is likely to be faced by those persons who have to comply with dual obligations at a time. This problem would not arise if job and home were considered as two mutually exclusive fields of life. The typical woman is dedicated to her family. She may feel that one way of serving her family is by earning additional money.

At the same time she might feel that her husband would prefer her staying at home, and rendering more domestic service, that and her children need her presence at home, and that her presence there would have prevented the emergence of some of their problems. She wonders whether the additional money—which she may earn by working outside and which might not be large after meeting additional expenses—is really worth and sacrifice. Often she is heard to make statements like a working woman cannot be outstanding both at home and in job, she had to make a choice or 'it is hard to stay happily married while working', or the 'quality of motherhood will suffer when the mother engages in a full-time job outside.'

Further religious rituals and customary practices are expected to be preserved and perpetuated by the women. 'Despite her heavy work burden women, more than the men, are the loudwearies of the rituals. Thus the problem of adjustment of working women becomes more serious. Krishna

Chakraborty correctly hypothesize—(i) that the changes in the position and role of women is still thoroughly ambiguous; (ii) that the dual responsibilities of home and work are likely to create some difficulties for the incumbents in fulfilling the dual obligations, and expectations with equal competence and satisfaction, and (iii) that the persons performing the dual roles, therefore, are liable to experience a sort of strain and conflict between dual obligations seemingly incompatible. That the two roles, the role of an employee and of a home-maker, are distinct and different by nature, and that there is wide possibility of role conflict and role strain being perceived by persons who want to reconcile them simultaneously, have been amply proved by sociologists and social psychologists.

Myrdal and Kelien write. "The characteristic feminine, dilemma of today is usually summarized under the headings `Career and family' ... Today the conflict has become `internalized' and continues as a psychological problem which may assume many different variations and shades; and just because there is no longer an absolute `either or' to be decided on at the beginning of adult life, the pull in two directions goes on practically throughout a women's life." In fact carrying out almost all responsibilities single handedly the women are over-strained and get exhausted. The illusion of having new experience and variation from drudgery of the routine house-work soon fades away.

All the aspirations are shattered. All these make a combined effect on her nature. They get irritated in trivial matters, get angry on children and husband. The home (family) which is expected to be better than paradise, get disturbed and thus happiness and peace vanish. The ideas of multiple responsibilities also create problems for working women. On the one hand they want to be efficient workers and try hard to fulfil the job-duties and at the same time they also want to be good wives, good mothers and better home managers. She wants to maintain her status in the society and be respected by the other members of the family. Her sincerity towards all the responsibilities is itself a cause of trouble. After finishing the home-job she runs to the office. if she is late, she is in tension. The officer authority would blame her for insincerity. If she has to put on some overtime work, she is late at home and she is worried for the children coming from school.

In some houses, of course, the working of women is appreciated. They are treated with great respect; her burdens and feelings are understood. Development of her personality and emergence into an enlightened status is encouraged. In such families working women have a comfortable position. They enjoy their work and aspire to do their best to be outstanding in their fields. But unfortunately this type of situation is found rarely.

Working Women and Children

Another type of problem experienced is the feeling of neglecting the children when the mother is working. The mothers often feel or made to feel that the children are not properly looked after, that they do not enjoy the facilities that the other children enjoy, that they have to let go many things, and that in addition they have to do some work at home to help the mother. When the mother is tired and gets angry, they feel that they are missing the mother's love and get disappointed. In this situation the working mother's experience, her psychological problems arising from inner conflict and a feeling of guilt, anxiety or tension are caused by the dual commitment and concern.

Control Over Income

Even though many women work, not many of them have any control over the income they earn. A great majority of them have to hand over their salary to their husbands or in-laws. They are not supposed to manage their own income. The amount is spent in the expenses of home. In some cases they are not given even the pocket money or the amount to buy things for their personal use. She has to demand and is given some money as a grace-granted to her. In short, the working women is always short of pocket money to use for herself despite having her own income. Thus employment still does not mean control over money or economic independence for the women.

The problem becomes worse when some persons feel that the women are working to satisfy their whims or as hobby. There are also instances when the men gradually withdraw themselves from leaving much of the responsibilities of running the house on themselves and pass them into the women. In the beginning the woman does not mind. But after some time she realizes that the husband has thrown the whole burden on her and this creates strained relations.

Impact on Marital Relations

The whole drama of the life of an Indian woman is played around the husband and his relations. Even though a man is well educated and dressed in Western clothes, has a look of modernity and even advocates women's emancipation, in his relations with his wife he is still like traditional husband, with age old orthodox attitude towards his wife. He may be a staunch exponent of equality of women with that of men. But at home he enjoys domination over his wife, who has to meekly obey him without questioning. He is not able to accept his wife arguing the truth. He likes his wife's earning but it defiles his ego to accept her as his equal. He is not able to even accept the fact that his wife can efficiently handle the man's job at her office. He enjoys to see her as weak, docile and always dependent on him. The problem becomes more difficult when the earning of the woman is higher than the husband's or she is more able and efficient in her work. He tries to hide his feelings of inferiority complex, by manifesting it in actions that express exaggerated superiority over her. This breeds very oppressive conditions for the woman, who is neither able to give up nor face this oppression day in and day out. Thus working women face a severe problem when their salary is more than that of her husband. Aware of the man's ego and the stereotyped notions of a woman being less than a man, women take extra care of their husband's feeling, never express their superiority and deliberately adopt a low self image and low posture. But the husbands are always conscious of the fact, and this aggeravates the oppression of women.

Restrictions on Movement

The finding of Urmila Patel show that in some cases the freedom of movement of the working women is also restricted. She is allowed only to go to the place of work. If she is late by half-an-hour, she is answerabled. She is not allowed to go elsewhere alone. If she wants to go, she is accompanied by younger sister-in-law or someone else. Some women express that if they have to work late in the office, they are misunderstood by their husbands or the in-laws. She is badly rebuked and a big fuss is made of it. Some women complain that even if they are physically unwell and badly exhausted and could not respond to the husband's sexual needs, they are not only misunderstood but are alleged to have illegitimate relations with some colleagues or the boss. They are inhumanly treated, tortured and even beaten. Women feel hurt by such humaliating actions of the husbands towards them especially when their integrity is questioned. There are examples where the husbands have illegitimate relations with other women and to hide their fault, they put on allegations on women and blame, so the latter may not question them.

Other Related Problems

There are other problems also. They are off-shoots of her being a worming woman. The working woman is left with little time for relaxation or entertainment or social life. Apart from leading to her own over work, burden and tension, she becomes the buff of social criticism. For the major part of the day, the woman is working in the office or the work place. After coming back she is busy with house work and her family. she has no time left to maintain relations with her neighbours, friends and relations. She is not able to visit them freely and spend time with them or join them in common programmes. She is not even able to go to their help when they need especially at the time of illness, marriages, deaths or other occasions. This is often mistaken for arrogance due to earning and the friends and relatives criticise her.

The working woman has not time of her own. She needs rest. She wants to thin of her problems or plan her future. She wants to read and write. She wants to undertake activities of her own interest, say creative arts. At times, she desires to be on her own not disturbed by anybody. There is no time for her. She cannot afford to be moody.

Again, to ease her job she has to depend more on domestic help and servants. She has to be generous to them to get work done. For that also she is criticised as extravagent. On the other side the servants very well know the difficulties the mistress and they exploit the situation. This also create problems for working women.

In all these worries the woman has no time left to look after her health. Still, she has to take care of her health and keep herself physically fit to work. She has to take to nourishing food and proper treatment when needed. Again due to hard work and over burdened by responsibilities, she gets into rapid ageing effects. The unending worries and tensions of modern life and the family also hastens the ageing process. She is criticised by her in-laws and the neighbours as an extravagent and fashionable lady. When she goes out of the house, well dressed she receives their criticism in crude words saying, 'dressed like a prostitute to attract males.

In the Sphere of Food

One more situation that is an off-shoot of the hectic life of the working woman is the use of fast food. It does help her a lot to reduce her burden at home. But it is undoubtedly expensive and less nutrious. The family members and the older generations do not appreciate its use. They naturally prefer home-made dishes. Sometimes fast-food is below standard. So it affects the general health of the member of the family and may at times be a cause of food poisoning or some other disease in the long run.

One New Way of Development and Modernity

Another note-worthy change we observe is that by working outside the four walls of the house, women are thrown in the open world. Every day they have new experiences and face new situations. Their mental horizons are widened, new aspirations aroused. Their ways of thinking is also changed. They want to give a new shape of their lives. They try to find new solutions to their problems. While the other members of the family are still having the same traditional outlook. The generation gap between the elders and the working women is increasing day by day. She is not able to cope with them though she wants to live with them. She hankers for the life of her thinking. This is a constant cause of increasing mental conflicts. If both the husband and wife are of a liberal outlook there is a free democratic family structure with the grab of autocracy fading away. The children grown up in this free atmosphere are able to develop their personalities. But when the grown up children take their own decisions and arrange their lives in their own way, the parents feel hurt. They feel, the grown up children now ignore them and do not recognise them. They comment that the latter do not take their advice or act according to it. They face the same problem which their elders used to face. They are happy to see the well developed and independent personality of the children but cannot throw away autocratic mentality inherited from the traditional culture and want to keep the children under their wing. It is a paradox which can never work. This also creates new conflicts and new problems.

PROBLEMS OF SINGLE WORKING WOMEN

Women as a group, specially single, have certainly become an important part of the work-force not only in India but all over the world. Women in general have to face so many problems, due to various factors. But being a single woman, she has to face some special problems.

Problems of Getting Employment

Most of the women work to help heir families in their economic disparities. However, the general impression of the society is to the contrary. When they search for a job, they have to compete with male candidates. The women in general suffer from some of the assumptions and prejudices which the authorities particularly the male, have towards them. The management feels that women are not serious or efficient workers. They put in less work and come only to pass time. As soon as they get married, they will go away. Again even if they continue after marriage, they will demand leave a number of times for domestic reasons. Maternity, childcare, transfer of the bands, work demands of the husband and family with make them give up jobs, play traunt or become indifferent and efficient. For many such reasons the women candidates are not preferred. Some managements even think that the women may spoil the strict atmosphere of the office. In fact this type of discrimination with young girls is nothing but a crime against entire women community.

Once they are selected, they are subjected to other types of oppression. The stares and the banters of the male colleagues, their typical curiosity and their uncivilised and unwarranted remarks, “She is charming and that is why she is selected” etc. are some of these oppressive ways. if the young women mix freely with them they are misunderstood. if they keep themselves confined to the work alone, they are labelled as arrogant. If the boss appreciates their work and they enjoy the confidence of the authorities, they are scandalised. They crack jokes at them and pass cheap remarks which in fact are unfair to the young women and hurt them.

Single Women and Status in the Family

In a study carried out by Arora, Bhattacharya and others on the unmarried working girls employed as typists, clerks, receptionists or telephone operators in Bombay, it was found that "with the majority of respondents their role of an earner in the family had not earned them a new freedom from parental control except perhaps in the area of marriage, nor were their status very much changed in the family with an exception of few where they got much more importance because fo their economic contribution towards the maintenance of family." In fact being an employed member of the family her responsibility increases and the family expects something from her without changing her traditional status.

Problem of Getting Married

The marriage of the daughter has become an acute problem for the parents of working girl. There are persons who do not like earning wives. They think that earning wives would try to dominate them. Some feel that they cannot be good house wives, with their well developed personalities. It becomes a difficult job to find a proper match for them. Their expectations go higher and they want a husband who would try to understand theirs. If they do not get a man of their choice they prefer to remain unmarried. But in our traditional Hindu society the parents would force them to compromise. Sometimes the result is discontent, quarrels, restlessness, frustration and disintegration of the family thus the women have to play a terrible price for keeping their jobs suppressing all their emotions and dreams they shoulder the responsibilities of life.

Problems of Parental Responsibility

There are families where the parents and other members of the family are totally dependent on the income of the young girls. They are mightly afraid of the girls getting married. They avoid settling the latter's marriages on one excuse or other. The young girls, emotionally attached with the parents, feel guilty in moving out and neglecting their responsibility to parents. The marriageable age passes away. This cause a great frustration to unmarried girls.

An eminent social scientist had the same opinion, when she observed in Bombay on the unmarried women office workers, that their parents were not interested in their daughters getting married; they postponed the latter's marriages because, if the daughters got married, the parents would not get their daughter's earnings, and thus they would be at a great disadvantage. Such working girls feel most insecure and uncertain of their future and have no one, who is interested in finding a suitable match for them. It was also pointed out by this sociologist that the number of abortions amongst the office girls was increasing which created both social and emotional problems for them.

Problem for Residence

A single woman, married, unmarried or widowed if alone, faces a problem of residence in India. Except in some of the big cities, there is no provision of working women's hostels. If it is there, it may not be well managed. In these hostels the working women are protected like children and these conditions restrict their freedom and ultimately hamper their wishes. While it is difficult to have a rented house in a limited income, the house owner looks at the single woman with suspicion and is not willing to rent it. Thus the unmarried women have many problems to face in housing.

Conclusion

Thus the working women, married or unmarried, belonging to middle class or lower middle class, face variety types of problems at the home level. Almost all of these problems are not of her own creation at all. Much of it is based on the continuing notions of the society, its patriarchal values as internalised by men and women, and their expectations of the women's contribution to home work. Some of the dilemmas of women are born out of the values they have inherited and which they find hard to shake off. Her duty for the children, and parents, her anxieties for the family stability and happiness etc. are borne out of the values and expectations built into her from childhood. The stability of the system of the family system, religious and caste system, of the society and State depend to a large extent on her playing this dominant role in the family up keep and children's up bringing. Hence, the dilemmas are not just her own dilemmas; they are society's and man's dilemmas which they had transferred to the women.

The responsibility of solving them, hence, should belong to the man and society, though the working woman often tends to believe herself to be responsible. A changed family relations based on a changed and egalitarian power relations within the family and between man and woman, is thus a need. Alternative arrangements, whenever necessary and possible, for child care during the early years and later, support services like creche, housing, etc. are needed if the working women have to be relieved of their avoidable stresses. Above all the men in general and male colleagues in the offices need to be educated on the equality and rights of women, their capabilities and contribution to productivity, rather than be treated as sex models and partners.

REFERENCES

Geetanjali Dash, *Status of Women Workers in Industrial Area in India,* (Unpublished M. Phi. thesis). Delhi University, p. 50.

Indra Chauhan, *Purdah to Profession*, p. 203.

K.P. Khanna and M. Mathew, *Women Workers in the Unorganized Sector of the Coir Industry in India,* ICSSR, 1979 (Unpublished thesis).

M. Vanamala, "Employment Status of Women in Andhra Pradesh State Public Enterprises" in K. Morali Manohar (ed.), *Women's Status and Development in India*, p. 87.

Promila Kapur, *The Changing Status of the Working Women in India,* p. 69.

Shahnaz Ankesaria, "Slow Death is their lot", *The Statesman,* January 4, 1984.

Urmila Patel, "Problems of Working Women in India" in T.M. Dak (ed.), *Women and Work in Indian Society*, p. 228.

8

Challenges for Self-Employed Women

There are basically two ways of earning a livelihood in an economy. Either you work for yourself or you work for somebody else. When you work for yourself to produce goods and/or services which are used for self-consumption, or sold for a price, or bartered for other goods and/or services, then you are self-employed. If you work for somebody else and sell your labour or skills as an employees, then you are other-employed. To understand the issues which face people in their struggle for existence, it is important to look at the structure of the economy in terms of the means of the livelihood of people. A historical process analysis helps us understand how the two basic ways of earning a livelihood, self-employment and other employment, have interacted with each other in the process of transforming the economy to its present day reality. Such a process analysis has been attempted below.

Donna Lero (University of Guelph) presented a multi-phase study that examined the particular challenges facing self-employed women, such as a lack of employment insurance and other benefits, difficulty balancing work and family responsibilities, and access to insurance for injury and illness.

Most self-employed women are not eligible for maternity, sickness and compassionate care benefits. More than one-third of respondents had required leave for family or health reasons but were unable to take the time off. Other challenges when taking leave included reduced income while covering ongoing operating costs, finding suitable replacements, loss of clients and visibility, exhaustion, difficulty concentrating and finding affordable daycare.

The majority of self-employed workers did not have private short- or long-term disability insurance or health or dental plans. Low-income self-employed workers were least likely to have private insurance. As indicated earlier, self-employed women earn less than their male counterparts. Women's average lower earnings were found to be attributable to a higher percentage of women than men working part time, disproportionate child-care and family responsibilities, lack of industry experience, and a high concentration of women in the service industries.

Four recommendations were discussed regarding government and private sector assistance for self-employed women:

(i) Extend employment insurance special benefits to the self-employed — Increase payable benefits to 70-75 percent of insurable earnings, raise ceilings and provide more flexibility regarding part-time work. Eligibility should be based on minimum gross earnings. Furthermore, additional methods to enable saving for these purposes is required (e.g., tax-sheltered savings).

(ii) Facilitate access to disability insurance — One approach could be to encourage collaboration among national associations to build pools of self-employed workers, as larger pools of members are required to obtain disability insurance at lower premiums. Changes in CPP regulations would also allow part-time work when feasible to keep the business going and allow a gradual return to work. Other options for short-term disability and long-term disability coverage are required, including deducting premiums as a business expense.

(iii) Increase access to financing — There is a need to identify underserviced regions and gaps in services. Recommendations included access to low-interest micro-loans, graduated loan programs for start-up and bridge financing. This requires stronger links or partnerships between government and self-employment associations. The report also encouraged private lenders to increase their transparency and to provide more loans in the service sector.

(iv) Increase access to training, mentoring and information — The report cited the need to increase knowledge transfer between providers and self-employed women. For example, information about alternative sources of financing and support should be posted on the Web sites of banks, credit unions and professional associations. The report also encouraged banks and associations to re-evaluate criteria for mentoring programs.

Work in Traditional Societies

In traditional societies, most of the work is done on a subsistence level where each family has to provide its basic needs from its own resources, i.e., food, clothing and shelter. Most of the work is also done by manual labour. Very few people work for others in an employer-employee relationship, but some work is done for the community, such as, trading, artisanship, health services and priestly services. These services are not provided in an employer-employee relationship but in a patron-client relationship.

The production and work relations in a subsistence economy are centred around the individual or family unit owning its own resources for survival. The hours of work, the kind of work done, the income or output derived from the work, all of these depend on the choice of each individual unit or enterprise. Since most of the community owns its production resources, it is self-employed. The emphasis is on direct producer-consumer and buyer-seller relationships.

Transactions of small size, few transactions with known people, face-to-face dealings, mutual trust, personal references, verbal vouching for each other to enforce the terms of a transaction between two people and accountability to known people, are the processes which sustain subsistence economics. Customary laws are enforced by the communities to maintain their own social order. the communities themselves are small in size.

Natural calamities like fires, floods, famines and epidermics lead to the destruction of resources of some or all of the people. Fighting and warring between communities lead to the resources of individuals being confiscated or plundered. The administrative policies of the head of the community lead to the resources of individuals being confiscated. These processes establish groups of individuals who do not have their own means of production or the resources to meet their own basic needs. They are compelled to work for others who do own resources. This is the reason for the emergence of a people who survive by labouring for others.

Commercialisation

These processes are reinforced by the forces of commercialisation. As subsistence communities become larger, more and more geographical areas are covered under a common administration and the formation of kingdoms, countries and nations starts. As the means of communication improve, distant areas become more accessible and trade and commerce flourish. Commercially oriented work slowly starts taking over subsistence-oriented work. The concentration of resources in the hands of a few people starts, and many who own resources are deprived of them. The processes of exploitation start as the stakes for commercial activities get higher and higher. Competition for survival starts. The interests of the people are not ensured in such a situation. The subsistence economy becomes a subsistence-cum-commercial economy. The emphasis of work relationships is still on self-employment and the modes of production are still predominantly manual.

With the same resources it becomes possible to exercise control over larger geographical areas and over a greater number of people. Large volumes of work, large outputs, large markets and large accounts become possible. Slowly, dealings on a large-scale become more attractive to people. Large-scale necessarily means dealing with more people, unknown people, and people from distant places.

From Verbal to Written Dealings

Largeness paves the way for written dealings because it is humanly impossible to keep mental and physical track of all the transactions conducted. Face-to-face dealings are replaced with impersonal dealings. It is also not in the interests of any one to trust unknown people. Written dealings are necessary to substantiate the actual occurrence of transactions between unknown people. It is a way of ensuring that commitments are honoured; it is something to fall back on when there are disagreements, disputes of differences, on the details of a transaction. The concept of documented evidence emerges from written transactions. In transactions with unknown people both sides operate with a sense of distrust. Hence, written dealings are necessary to protect both parties against this distrust. With unknown people, verbal vouching has no credibility. The accountability to known people also loses credibility because both parties, since they do not know each other, will not be able to trust the judgements of each other's people or community. Therefore, a third party not known to either side, becomes more acceptable.

Accountability to unknown people and common administration of large geographical areas leads to written laws. Written dealings are necessary as evidence for the implementation of written laws and accountability to unknown third persons. Similarly, large state administrations resort to written dealings for maintaining records. Customary laws get replaced by written laws and constitutions. The fear of dealing with unknown people and strangers dissolves when people have the backing of written transactions which are legal tender.

The Industrial Revolution and the Written World

With the Industrial Revolution the modes of production shift from work being done by hand to work being done by machines; from work being done in individual homes to work being done in factories and offices. Mass production leads to greater outputs, bigger and bigger units and cheap goods displace the individually owned means of production in a subsistence economy. Subsistence families, own account workers, self-employed people who are displaced by mechanisation and industrialisation, are forced to work for somebody else. Centralisation of decision-making and concentration of resources increase rapidly in the hands of a few owners and explitation becomes rampant. The emphasis of production work relations in the economy shifts from self-employment for the majority and self-employment for some. The formation of large organizations is encouraged. An age of very large sizes and transactions with very large numbers of people is ushered in due to the development of very sophisticated technologies. The modes of work, the volumes of work, the size of units, and the large numbers of people involved, all reinforce the system of written dealings. The formation of nations and modern governments also creates more opportunities for other-employment. The modern labour movement starts as a response to rampant exploitation of employees and the role of the State/Government is influenced to protect those in other-employment. Rules, regulations, and labour laws get formulated in written form. The employer-employee relationship also gets integrated within the system of written dealings.

In the highly industralised countries, the process of industrialisation has continued for over 200 years and slowly included most of the working population into a regular, employer-employee relationship. This form of work and of earning a livelihood has become the norm. The rules, regulations, policies, legislations and regulations of the employer-employee relationship create a world of other-employment and also ensure that the interests of almost the whole working population are taken care of. Trade unions develop to protect the interests of employees. A share of the profits of the goods and services which employees have helped to produce and demanded and made available in the form of various employee facilities, such as, provident funds, gratuities, allowances, housing, health facilities, medical facilities, child-care facilities, maternal protection facilities, educational facilities and training skills, among others. The implementation of the labour laws which are written make written dealings between employers and employees imperative. Over a period of time, the world of other-employment has developed its own characteristics of written dealings, impersonal dealings and dealings with unknown people. This is the world of formal systems of work.

The formal systems of work have gone hand-in-hand with creating employer-employee relationships for the majority of the working population. Ownership of resources in order to earn one's livelihood is not seen as desirable for the majority of the population. Selling labour to somebody else for wages or salaries is instilled as a value and has slowly become the most preferred way of earning a livelihood. This choice is reinforced by making available a lot of additional benefits and incentives to those who work as employees. Motivation and involvement in work are sought to be maintained by employers by providing ever-increasing incentives to employees. the formal system of work gets equated with organized industry, organized labour and organized services, and these become more and more significant in the economy.

The Indian Economy

Even by countries such as India, which started large-scale industrialisation only fifty years ago, the highly industrialised countries have been adopted as models for development. Large scale industrialisation and enterprises of a large size are recent phenomena in these countries. Attaining independence, nationhood, and starting industrialisation on a large scale have happened at about the same time in India. A written constitution and written laws, enforceable for the whole population, have come into existence only since Independence. the labour movement, the trade union models, the laws, rules and regulations enforcing the employer-employee relationship, the role of the State/Government in protecting the interests of the employees, have all been modelled on the highly industrialised countries. A subsistence economy (agricultural and tribal) which was only partly commercialised has now been super-imposed on by a industrial economy. The economy is still largely agricultural and tribal, but from subsistence it has been catapulted into a commercial economy because of industrialisation. The concentration of resources has made the large majority of subsistence individuals resourceless and has forced them to work for others. But the economy as a whole is not industrialised and everybody does not have regular, salaried employment.

The labour movement has developed but caters mainly to industrial labour. New technologies are constantly coming into existence and continuously displacing more and more of the subsistence-oriented people and forcing them to become labourers. In fact, modernisation has succeeded in shifting a number of people from self-employment to other-employment. But in spite of the present extent of industrialisation, only 11 per cent of the working population is engaged in regular jobs with a recognised employer-employee relationship, the protection of the law, and the benefits of employee facilities, i.e., the world of other-employment and written dealings. The process of large sizes, industrialisation and written dealings covers only a small section of the total population. All workers who need protective policies can get them only if they become recognised employees. This is the present situation of the working population in India.

The rest of the population is also working—they have to fend for themselves and earn a livelihood in whatever way they can. They are self-employed. Some of these people have become integrated into the world of written dealings and are also well-off. However, the vast majority of these self-employed people are poor. they are the sufferers of the processes of commercialisation, industrialisation, the concentration of resources, and written dealings. Their world is still one of verbal dealings, of small sizes, of face-to-face dealings with small numbers of people. But they are being forced to deal with the world of written transactions. Their illiteracy, their ignorance of the written world, of written laws, procedures, rules and regulations, is a major handicap. They do not know how to get things done in the written world and they end up exploited, helpless, inadequate, diffident and dependent.

The Working Population in India

A graphic representation of the reality of the working population in India, due to this whole historical process, can be shown if the total working population is represented by a circle and is divided into high income, middle income, and low income groups. People in other-employment fall across all the three income groups. The remaining population earns its livelihood by finding their own self-created niche in the economy and fending for itself. it is self-employed. The self-employed people also fall across all three income groups. People in other-employment from the high and middle income groups include managers, officers, administrators, professionals, such as, doctors, lawyers, teachers, architects, engineers and accountants, holding jobs. The low income other-employed include factory workers, peons, clerks etc. Self-employed people from the high and middle income groups include manufacturers and industrialists, entrepreneurs, consultants, professionals, traders, dealers, various contractors, big farmers, etc.

Self-employed people in the low income group includes small producers engaged in land-based, livestock-based, and manufacturing-based activities; vendors engaged in vending and the trade of essential commodities, such as, food, cloth, garments, shoes and household utility items; providers of services, such as, cleaning, transportation, washing, cooking; and manual labour, such as, farm labour, construction labour, contract labour and casual labour.

The low income, self-employed group comprises the majority of the working population of India.

Within this overall picture of the general population, it is also necessary to look specifically at the work of women in the economy. Of the population of working women in India, only 6 or 7 per cent are other employed and 93 or 94 per cent earn their livelihood by their own means—they are self-employed. If the total female working population in India is represented by a circle then the three horizontal sections represent the three income groups—high, middle and low—as approximate proportions of the total population. Women in salaried jobs, with an established employer-employee relationship, constitute 6 or 7 per cent of the population as indicated by chord ab in the circle, and are spread over the three income groups. Women who are involved only in unpaid household work for their own families are an additional category in this classification as compared to the picture for men. This group is represented by line cde in the circle. In the high income group, most women do not do their own household work but get it done by others. Women in the low income group cannot afford not to earn some income. So very few of them do only household work for their own families. Women from the middle income group are largely the ones who do only household work for their families.

All the remaining women are involved in some economic activity or other and are also spread across the three income groups. They are self-employed. Here too, as in the picture for the general population, the largest group is of the poor, self-employed women. This is the majority of the population of working women in India.

It is this large majority of the population (men, women and children) which is now called the 'informal sector' by the standards set by the industrialised countries. This sphere of work is seen as a discovery.

The Informal Sector

The term 'informal sector' has been increasingly used to refer to large numbers of people who are fending for themselves in order to earn a livelihood. The most commonly used definition, based on the ILO Kenya study report of 1972, lists a set of characteristics of the 'informal sector':

1. Ease of entry
2. Reliance on indigenous resources.
3. Family ownership of enterprise.
4. Small scale of operation.
5. Labour intensive and adapated technology.
6. Skills acquired outside the formal school system.
7. Unregulated and competitive markets.

This definition has, in a way, become the turning point in development work in attempts to understand the economies of the various countries of the world. Since the 1972 study, there have been several other studies in order to systematise the understanding of the 'informal sector'.

The ILO's pioneering study done on the 'informal sector' in Kenya envisaged the term 'informal sector' to extend to all the sectors of the economy. In their view it covered small scale non-farming activities in towns of all sizes and in rural marketing centres (p. 223). It could also be applied equally well to the agricultural sector. Although this is the general view of the study, when it comes down to specifics, we find that the characteristics of the informal sector, as defined by the ILO study, refer more to small scale enterprises than to farming or other allied activities. If the Kenya study were to be strictly followed, the focus of informal sector studies would become small enterprises which exist mainly in the urban areas.

This, in fact, is what has happened. Studies conducted subsequent to the Kenya study, both by the ILO and by others, have adopted the ILOS definition and concentrated on understanding the informal sector in the urban areas only. Thus, over time the term 'informal sector' has become synonymous with the 'urban informal sector'.

Some of the descriptive definitions which have been put forth to explain the informal sector are listed here.

Joshi and Joshi's book *Surplus Labour and the City* is a concrete application of the informal sector concept to the city of Bombay. They do not collect any primary data but rely on secondary sources, such as, the Census, Directorate of Employment and National Sample Survey. The consequence of this is that the 'formal sector' becomes primary in their conceptualisation and the 'informal sector' is studied empiricallhy from the point of view of the 'formal sector'. As the authors emphasise in the book, 'The standard procedure in empirical work is to estimate the size of the urban informal sector by calculating it as a residual of those engaged in economic activity in urban area, excluding those who can be identified as working in the "Formal Sector" (op. cit.). They use the terms 'organized' and 'unorganized' to connote the formal and informal sectors respectively, in their analysis. To measure the number of workers in the informal sector they rely only on the size of the estblishment or enterprise.

> The family of criteria discussed above cannot easily be used for empirical investigation. We think however, that of these criteria, the size of establishment is a good and workable one for distinguished between the sectors in practice. Most establishments employing large number of workers have organized sector characteristics, most establishments employing small numbers of workers do not. The next question concerns the employment size which would serve as a useful dividing line. Since the Directorate of Employment and Training collects data on the organized sector, defined as all public sector establishments with more than 25

> employees, this is certainly a convenient dividing line to use and we decided to use it.
>
> [They explain the heterogeneity of the informal sector as] "The Informal Sector" comprises a wide range of modes of production. Own account workers, unpaid family workers, household industries, `home workers', domestic servants, employees of small unregulated establishments, casual wage labour employed on a day-to-day basis by ephemeral employers or firmly established ones including Formal Sector enterprises. The kinds of production industries in which these workers are engaged are also multifarious. (op. cit.).

Dipak Mazumdar's paper 'Urban Informal Sector' emphasises the wages and working conditions in order to differentiate between the formal and informal sector.

> The basic distinction between the two sectors turns on the idea that employment in the formal sector is in some sense or senses protected so that the wage level and working conditions in the sector are not available in general, to the job seekers in the market unless they manage to cross the barrier of entry somehow. (He describes the informal sector as) Thus it (informal sector) can be expected to act as a buffer between employment and unemployment. Some job seekers who are unable to find regular employment in the formal sector may for short or long periods participate in the informal sector rather than be wholly unemployed. In this view, a substantial part of the workers found in the informal sector will be the 'secondary workers' i.e. those who are not the main earners in the household.
>
> To look at it another way a disproportionately large proportion of females as well as those outside the prime working age group (say under 25 and above 50) will be found in the informal sector employment, if they are employed at all. Similarly migrants would be disproportionately represented in the informal sector.

Jan Breman in his article, 'A Dualistic Labour System ? is critical of the concept of the dualistic division of the economy into the formal and informal.

> In my opinion, the informal sector cannot be demarcated as a separate economic compartment and/or labour situation. Any attempt to do so will give rise to numerous inconsistencies and difficulties, such as will be shown by even a discussion of social background, size and composition. Moreover by interpreting the relationship to the formal sector in a dualistic framework and in focusing on the mutually exclusive characteristics, we lost sight of the unity and totality of the productive system (p. 18).

He goes on further to explain how he views the economic system based on his research in a district town and its rural surroundings in South Gujarat (India).

> The results of this research show that it is fairly easy to find two extreme categories that oppose each other. On the one hand, those who earn their daily bread with the aid of poorly paid, unskilled intermittent work, which due to the considerable physical work involved, is considered of low standing; and on the other, those in permanent employment, for which formal education or trained skills required—jobs with a fairly high and often regular wage which ensures security and social respectability to the worker. However, these profiles are seen most clearly at the extremes of the two poles of the labour force. As the distance between the extremes lessens, similarities in recruitment, working conditions, and bargaining procedures gradually outdo the differences between various categories of labour, in this respect. In other words, gradations rather than watertight divisions. To split the employment systems into two sectors is, therefore, to adopt an approach which is over rigid and too little differentiated. (p. 1905).

Jan Breman tries to overcome the rigidity by postulating a fragmented labour market barring entry due to trade particularism, even within the informal sector.

S.V. Sethuraman in his book *The Urban Informal Sector in Developing Countries: Employment, Poverty and Environment* begins with the premise that urbanisation is a process which is gaining more and more momentum, in both absolute and relative terms, in the developing countries of the world. The urban labour force is increasing much faster than the work opportunities in the formal sector. 'Under the circumstances the surplus population of the labour force has been forced to generate its own mean of employment and hence of survival' (p. 8). These people constitute the urban informal sector. He tries to clarify the term 'informal sector' by focusing on the choice of unit which would help to classify an activity as being formal or informal.

> Perhaps the distinguishing feature of the informal sector enterprises is that they made their appearance, not so much in response to investment opportunities as in the neo-classifical sense, but out of necessity to create one's own employment. Thus the accent was on employment generation and not in seeking suitable investment opportunities for th sake of realizing a return on investment. The individuals/enterpreneurs associated with the informal sector enterprises are not capitalists in the classical sense of the term, seeking investment outlets. Since many of them are migrants to urban areas in search of employment and since few possess substantial capital, education or skills, the key characteristics of the informal sector would seem to be that the enterprises emerged in spite of the lack of necessary skills.

He goes on to give a definition of the informal sector as 'It consists of small scale units engaged in the production and distribution of goods and services with the primary objective of generating employment and income to their participants notwithstanding the constraints on capital. both physical and human, and know-how' (p. 17). He identifies the mode of production, the mode of organization, and the scale of operation as the three basic criteria for classifying a unit of production as apart of the informal sector. 'The search for the informal sector enterprises was thus confined to the following: all enterprises with 10 persons or less and engaged in manufacturing, construction, transport, trade and service sectors.' The selection is further refined by ...

> whether the enterprise is legal or not ? Works on an irregular basis ? Located in temporary structures ? Uses electrical power ? Depends on formal credit institutions? Relies on formal distribution networks ? Most workers have fewer than 6 years of schooling ? Needless to add, these ar but a few suggested criteria, and we could think of a number of other similar ones. the rationale behind the choice was simply that most of them can be applied without asking questions, just by visual observation of the enterprises. The essence of this additional measure was to include enterprises even though they had more than 10 persons provided they satisfied at least one of the suggested criteria of informality.

Fred Fluitman in *Training for Work in the Informal Sector* sums up the present state of the work on the informal sector quite realistically as 'Today, following more than a decade of spadework by academics and by researchers in international agencies, notably the ILO, policy makers in developing countries and labour market analysts among others, increasingly recognize the existence of an informal sector, somehow separate from the traditional rural economy and the modern or formal sector.' He elaborates further.

> Terminology has occasionally given rise to confusion and debate. Alternative labels have been proposed to highlight particular aspects or special concerns or to narrow the field; the micro enterprise, the unstructured, the unregistered sector, the hidden or the people's economy, etc. Moreover, different units of analysis have been adopted in informal sector surveys—the enterprise, the household, the individual workers. It has admittedly proven difficult if not impossible, to move from a general notion to a precise and widely accepted definition of the informal sector: a definition which applies to all countries, all sorts of economic activities and all stages of development; a definition which draws a clear line between the formal and the informal sector.

The theoretical work on the informal sector has assumed this sector to be a transitional state of the economy. It is visualised that the workforce in the informal sector will be absorbed into the formal sector in the due course of time.

Informal and Formal Systems of Work

However, the basic limitation of all these and other definitions is that they convey the message that the informal sector has been discovered for the first time. This implication of a discovery may be acceptable according to the norms of the industrialised countries about what is work and who is a worker, but by the tradition of the developing countries the 'informal sector' has been the predominant mode of functioning for centuries.

The formal sector is of very recent origin in the developing countries. However, it has become central to their economy due to the adaptation of models of structuring the economy on the lines of the industrialised countries. The informal sector is not a discovery, it has always been there, and these people are finding it more and more difficult to earn a livelihood today.

It is more pertinent to use the phrases 'informal system of work' and 'formal system of work' instead of 'informal sector' and 'formal sector' to explain the reality of the economies of the developing countries. Informal systems of work are essentially based on verbal transactions predominate. the more the aspects of an individual's work and life are dependent on written transactions for validity, the more that individual is likely to belong to a formal system of work. The more the aspects of an individual work and life are based on verbal transactions for validity, the more that individual is likely to belong to an informal system of work. Viewed in this way the economies of developing countries have been functioning in informal systems of work for centuries. This is the way of work the majority of the population is familiar with and this is the basis on which the economy is structured.

The poor population, which is the majority of the population in developing countries, has been variously referred to as informal sector, unorganized sector, working poor, marginal, peripheral, third sector, lower circuit, residual, illegal, black economy, hidden economy and people's economy, in the literature on development. They are used interchangeably even though they mean different things.

Of all these terms, the terms 'informal' and 'unorganized' are the two most critical ones when formulating a conceptual framework to explain the reality of the poor population in developing countries. They refer to different processes altogether, in an economy, even though they have been used interchangeably. Whereas the informal-formal continuum of a system of work is indicative of the extent of verbal-written transactions, the organized-unorganized continuum is a function of the extent of collective action of for common goals by a group of people.

When these two terms are juxtaposed, the working population can be viewed as organized and formal, organized and informal, unorganized and formal or, finally, unorganized and informal. Any set of people can protect their interests only by organizing. this is even more true for the poor in any economy. Because the terms 'unorganized' and 'informal' are used interchangeable, the real understanding of informal systems of work has been blurred. The relative importance of workers already organized has been over-estimated and the ways of organizing workers in the informal systems of work have not been understood properly.

How does a group of people get organized ? How does it protect its interests after organizing ? What are the pressures on an organized group to become formal ? How does an organized group stay informal or combine informal ? How does an organized group stay informal or combine informal and formal aspects ? A more appropriate under-standing of these questions emerges from the concept of an informal system of work and a formal system of work as explained here. Defining the term 'informal sector' per se then, does not assume criticality. The more pertinent question is—how does a section of the population—the poor—live, work and earn its livelihood ? Understanding the systems of work they are engaged in, then becomes more important.

The Structure of the Economy

The conceptual framework for explaining the reality of the poor population has to take into account the state of the economy, its ability to generate work and income for all, its structure and institutional framework. An economy which can provide work for the majority of the population in an employer-employee relationship with the protection of the law and with all the supportive legislation is different from an economy which can provide such work only for a minority of its population. In the world today, only the highly industrialised countries are able to provide regular jobs for the majority of their population. India is the tenth most industrialised country in the world, and yet only 11 per cent of the working population has an established employer-employee work relationship as recognised by the law. The scope of the economy to provide such work for greater numbers is very limited. The situation is the same for the majority of the countries of the world. the global economy as a whole is also not able to generate work of this kind in proportion with the need for work.

As the previous Director General of the ILO, Mr. Francis Blanchard, has written in *Training for Work in the Informal Sector*,

> It would be unrealistic to insist that a solution lies in integrating all workers into the formal sector. The formal sector in many developing countries is simply too small to absorb more than a fraction of labour forces entrants even in the most favourable economy conditions. Indeed work in the informal sector undoubtedly relieves poverty and its valuable contribution to meeting basic needs should not be underestimated. We must take care not to smother it with regulations. It would be more pertinent to look for other ways to protect its workers, most of whom are self-employed or apprentices, against exploitation; to help them to set up additional small enterprises and co-operatives, to provide them with training, credit and other support required to diversify production and to improve their productivity and income.
>
> Informal sector workers, whether they are in rural or in urban areas, self-employed or employees, must to a large extent help themselves in overcoming their difficulties. This will not be feasible unless they get together to defend their interests. Existing workers' and employers' associations should strive to meet the needs of their workers in the informal sector more effectively, by appropriate adjustment of their objectives and structures. In addition, or as an alternative, new forms of organization and participation should be explored.
>
> In short, I believe that it is of vital importance for the ILO to extend its concern to the entire world of labour, including the hundreds of millions of men and women in the fringe of, or outside, the organized, industrial, formal sector.
>
> The structure of the economies of developing countries has to be understood in the context of informal systems of work and self-employment for the majority of the population.

Informal Systems of Work and Self-employment

Everyone has to live, has to survive, has to earn a livelihood whether it is a situation of poverty or a situation of plenty. Every individual can be seen as an instrument in the hands of somebody else or as a self-propelled entity able to make life options himself/herself. Work is also then, the most integral part of everyone's life. How work is viewed, how options are visualised for each individual, how sustained interest and involvement in work is sought to be achieved for everyone, how the potential of each person is to be brought out and best utilised, are important considerations which determine the structuring of an economy. Cultural and social systems also evolve accordingly and the total ethos of a society is developed.

Informal systems of work prevalent in India and other developing countries have been traditionally structured around generating self-employment for the majority of the population. A positive social and cultural value has been attached to ownership of one's resources in order to earn a livelihood. Selling only one's physical and manual labour and working for somebody else as an employee has been seen, culturally, as the least preferred way of earning a livelihood. The economy has been structured in such a way that the majority of the population is in a buyer-seller relationship. A sense of involvement in work; maintaining high motivation; developing accountability and responsibility to do one's work well; linking productivity and work performance to income; developing a sense of identity and belonging through the primary social system of family and kinship; are all sought to be achieved by reinforcing self-employment for the majority through buyer-seller relationships. Informal systems of work and self-employment for the majority have therefore gone hand-in-hand. Representative organizations of all occupations and activities have been established in the form of trade and artisan guilds to enable people to protect their work and social interests, to deal with conflicting situations, to set norms and standards of work, to ensure quality, to negotiate and bargain with other guilds and with the State and finally, to participate in public policy formulation. Representativeness has been ensured for every group by being organized around work and occupations. hence, a highly organized economy developed on the basis of informal systems of work.

In the historical process of transformation, eleborated in this chapter, the development of formal systems of work has been described. The creation of a large majority of poor, self-employed workers in the economy as part of this process has also been explained. How can collective strength be created for this majority of people ?

Collective Strength through Representative Forums

All these self-employed workers (both men and women) also have to protect their interests. What would be a representative forum for self-employed workers to protect their interests ? In India, guilds have been the forum for establishing representativeness for various occupational groups to protect their interests and to participate in policy formulation. This form of representativeness has, however, been undergoing a transformation. In the process of industrialisation, the group of workers with an established employer-employee relationship have become more and more organized along the lines of the trade unions developed in industrialised countries. They have been able to bargain and negotiate for more and more economic strength for their members even though they constitute a minority of the workforce. The majority of the workforce, which is self-employed, has remained outside the fold of the representative forums a called trade unions. This process of exclusion of the majority of the workers has continued to such an extent that the whole labour movement itself has become confined to those workers who have an established employer-employee relationship, and only these people are called 'workers'. The labour movement, the labour laws and policies, the national and international labour organizations, address themselves to the needs of those workers who have an established employer-employee relationship. What happens to the majority of the workforce then ? Are they to remain excluded ? Will they be able to tilt the direction of the labour laws and the policy framework in their favour ? Will they be able to command the respect due to the majority of the workforce in a democracy?

This is possible only if the reality of the self-employed workers is taken seriously by the policy-makers, when the future envisaged for all these workers is seen within the perspective of strengthening self-employment in its own right instead of replacing it with employer-employee relationships. This is possible only by establishing representative forums of self-employed workers to protect their interest. Today there are very, very few representative forums for the self-employed workers because they have not been organized as workers. The traditional representativeness of the self-employed workers in the form of trade and artisan guilds has been destroyed for the poor, and it has not been replaced by other forums. The rich self-employed have been able to adapt the guild form of representative forums into the present day variations of trade and industry associations and federations, chambers of commerce, professional councils, etc. They are able to protect their interests through these forums as also to influence policy formulations to suit their needs. But these constitute only a minority in terms of the total number of self-employed people. the vast majority of self-employed workers have yet to establish their representative forums to truly protect their interests. Because their organizations as workers have been destroyed, they are presently *unorganized as workers*. But socially they are still highly organized, along caste, religious, and linguistic lines.

Representative Forum for Self-employed Workers

How can we build representative forums for self-employed workers ? The experiences of who many grass-roots organizations, working with different occupational groups of the self-employed, have shown that organizing workers is the only way to strengthen the position of these workers in the overall socio-economic political context. Organizing the self-employed workers is different from organizing workers with an established employer-employee relationship. The conventional trade unions have experience in organizing workers with an established employer-employee relationship. Their basis of organizing is collective bargaining and wage negotiations with the employers. This basis of organizing can be of very limited value for self-employed workers because there is no established employer-employee relationship and hence, no one employer with whom to bargain for improvement.

The State and public policy are the main forces which determine the fate of the self-employed in any economy. So, the focus of bargaining shifts from one employer to public policy. The direction, nature, and implementation of public policies and the responsibility of the State, affect the overall economic situation of a country. The economic atmosphere becomes either conducive to, or antagonistic to, the survival and strengthening of the self-employed. The representative forums of the self-employed therefore have essentially to bargain with the State for public policies favourable to their members so that their niches in the economy can move from strength to strength. The representative forums themselves provide a variety of services to members to set a precedent for the State in initiating appropriate policies and alternate systems benefiting self-employed workers. This function becomes all the more vital in the face of adverse economic policies and deprivation for a large majority of the population.

However, the established organizations of workers, i.e., the conventional trade unions, do not understand this form of representativeness or bargaining. Trade unions of self-employed workers are very rare. The few that do exist are establishing pioneering precedents in the world of work and the labour movement. But in fact they are really showing the way for adapting the traditional form of representativeness for self-employed workers (the trade and artisan guilds) in the present day world of work and labour. The trade unions of self-employed workers are the modern day versions of the traditional guilds. Other contemporary methods of organizing people, such as, co-operatives, societies, trusts and associations, can also perform the same function of representativeness for the self-employed. However, these forms are not yet seen in the perspective of trade unions, the labour movement, and the world of work.

When we consider the plight of self-employed women workers, the situation becomes even more complex. Women are not even perceived as workers, even though they may be spending most of their time in doing some work for an income either of cash and/or kind. Hence, it is very difficult to organize self-employed women workers and being them into the mainstream of the world of work. But it is essential for this process to be promoted in a big way if the plight of the majority of working women is to be improved. The social status of women, the invisibility of women's work, the exploitation of women as women and as workers, the fact of being self-employed in an economic environment not conductive to promoting self-employment for the average person, are the major forces which have to be influenced to affect the overall situation of women.

This study is a step in the direction of understanding the reality of poor, rural self-employed women, and to plan interventions for organizing and improving their life situations.

REFERENCES

1. Planning Commission Statistics, Census of India figures.
2. Towards Equality,' Report of the Committee on the Status of Women in India, 1974.
3. Employment, Incomes and Inequality,' ILO Report on Kenya, Genava, 1972.
4. H. Joshi and B. Joshi *Surplus Labour and the City—A Study of Bombay* Delhi, O.U.P., 1976.
5. Dipak Mazumdar 'Urban Informal Sector,' World Bank Staff Working Paper No. 22, July, 1975.
6. Jan Breman 'A Dualistic Labour System ? A Critique of the "Informal Sector" Concept' *Economic and Political Weekly*, 11 December 1976.
7. S.V. Sethuraman *The Urban Informal Sector in Developing Countries: Employment, Poverty and Environment* Geneva, ILO, 1981 (pp. 8, 17, 22).
8. Fluitman Fred (ed.) *Training for Work in the Informal Section* Geneva, ILO, 1989 (pp. xiii-xiv).
9. Op. cit. (pp. ix-x).

9

Towards Estimating the Quality of Women's Working Life

> "Life is not measured by the number of breaths we take, but by the moments that take our breath away."
>
> —*Maya Angelou*

It is significant to mention that nobody seems to know who coined the word 'quality of life' which has lately achieved a remarkable popularity among the academic communities of social scientists and more specially among work oriented organizations and their managements. The same term issued differently in different languages in the developed countries and more often the term is used in complaint made by representatives of the developing countries in the United Nations about living conditions in their homeland. Remarkably, Szalai (1978 approached eminent researchers, personally and through correspondence who were participants of two symposia devoted to the discussion, on various aspects of quality of life at the Ninth World Congress of Sociology (1978) at Uppsala.

The attempt produced some evidences that the expression first came into light in the late 1950s or early 1960s but not in scholarly context, rather in newspapers or general publications mostly in connection with problems of environmental pollution, the deterioration of urban living conditions and the like. Szalai also canned through 20 major encyclopaedias published uptil 1978 but he could not locate any mention or entry having quality of life as its subject or any direct or indirect reference.

He then argued that the expression has basic orientation in day-to-day conversation questions. "how are your?" which proves capability of human beings to keep in evidence of life, the conditions of their existence and to form integral judgement about the life. Therefore, the age old and uniquitous "how are you" type of questions have as their vaguely defined object, the expression of an interest in health, welfare and prosperity, in the goodness of life as the `quality of life' of the person addressed. Quality of life acquired sociological importance and became a topic of social research which converge largely on people's welfare and well being, then living conditions, their style of life, their standard of living. A new branch of socio-economic investigation took a formal shape called "study of social indicator system" and were applied in the processes of socio-economic planning, public policy decision making and even in marketing research.

Blishen and Atkinson (1978) also observed growing international concern about quality of life but stated that there was no agreement on specifying meanings of the term which resulted in differences in defining statistical indicators. Largely, two types of indicators come into picture about quality of life. Objective indicators, such as, money and sub active indicators, such as financial status, living standard, job etc. The objective indicators define the quality of life in terms of goods though to constitute desired states of existence by Govt. agencies to constitute desired states of existence by Govt. agencies while the subject indicators conceptualise individuals to define themselves, the quality of their life as perceived by them.

Hankinss (1978) pointed out that research work has revealed that quality of life is not simply the sum of its component units; it is much more than the resultant of interaction of welter of herogeneous forces and factors. And since, in the course of this interaction,the raw variables registered during the interviews undergo a through transformation, their ultimate meaning and significance can be determined only if they are analysed as the component parts of life-quality, considered as a coherent and integral system. Like Blishen and Atkinson he also argued that objective variables are concerned with the comparison of immediate surveys or census data which may allow important and valid inferences to the quality of life of the population. However, the immediate comparison of subjective variables, such as, attitudes, aspirations, fears, frustrations and satisfactions or dissatisfactions need more careful and controlled observation and infact with such indicators one can go beyond the surface registration of cross cultural similarities and dissimilarities.

A number of researches pertaining to problems regarding socialisation and personality development have cleared the doubts that a strong and systematic relationship exist between the personalities of individuals and social structures hat socialise and support them. General measures of socio-economic status have been shown powerfully to condition the attitudes the values of individuals, in particular, the degree of their authoritarianism (Lipset, 1960) their sense of personal efficiency, their satisfaction with their jobs and life situations (Inkels, (1960), and the values around which they socialise their children (Pearlin and Kohn, 1966).

The nature of the jobs men hold, especially the job's substantive complexity as well s feelings powerlessness and self-estrangement (Kohn and Schooler, 1973 and Kohn, 1976). In the late sixties and early seventies the behavioural scientists started looking at the concept as the subject assessment was their own responsibility. It was believed that in objective indicators the parametres show unchanged structural features whereas in the subject indicators there are fundamental differences about the way people arrive at the assessment of their well-being.

With the argument certain models were developed to view 'quality of life' from a combination of factors which were statistical and psychological. Rezsohazy (1978) also defined quality of life by calling it as ways of life and considered it as life style as an overall behaviour resultant of occasions like occurring daily (as at work) or seasonally (as vocations) or irregularly (as sickness) or even at unique occasions (such as marriage). Stone (1978) in his theoretical paper on "organic solidarity and life quality indicators" accepted the importance of psychological factors in the assessment of quality of life.

An individual has to consider the question of everything in terms of satisfying or frustrating. Certain satisfying things may become dissatisfying or frustrating at a span of time and one time scheduling may disrupt others resulting into frustration. Solomon et al. (1978) have pointed out that industrialisation has caused social and environmental disturbances. The declarations for improvement of quality of life of people as a national objective is easy to agree upon but there is little consensus on how the quality of life should be defined, measured and fostered?

According to them, quality of life is, therefor,e both material satisfaction of vital needs and aspects of life such as personal development, self realization and a balanced eco-system. They also believe that quality of life has objective and subjective components which define a unique way for improvement for different social groups, cultures and nations. Many authors have defined human needs and proposed classification schemes (Bossel, 1976; Galtung, 1975; Hankiss, 1976; Jarett, 1976; Mallamann, 1977; Masini, 1975; Maslow, 1971; McHale et. al., 1977). All of these are attempts to determine the necessity and, if possible, independent needs in order to describe all possible human behaviours.

Verwayen (1978) has reported that the Organization for Economic

Cooperation and Development, Paris had initiated social Indicators Development Programme in some of the countries to measure quality of life on the assumption that similarities of well-being and methodological principles of these surveys will be constant for all the countries under study. The areas that have been selected for this intensive work were:

1. healthfulness of life,
2. measurement of learning,
3. employment,
4. quality of working life,
5. time and leisure,
6. income, wealth and material deprivation,
7. housing conditions,
8. quality of the natural environment,
9. measurement of victimisation,
10. inequality,
11. economic accessibility,
12. comprehensive survey,
13. methodological issues in data collection.
14. presentation of social indicators and statistics, and
15. applicability of selected social concerns and indicators to particular national contexts. Sixteen projects were initiated and results of these studies are yet to be published.

Similarly, a number of other studies have highlighted various factors of quality of life which include work as most important aspect. The work provides a number of social material and psychological satisfactions because it largely yield money, either in the form of wages/pay or profits in a business organization. Work has the potential to motivate individuals in numerous ways, what seems to be more important is an individual's perception of his work and his working life. This directly indicates existence of two types of factors, one related to the conditions of work and the other as to how the individual is perceiving these conditions of work to obstacle or facilitate his work output. At individual level working life and feelings towards work conditions determine his work environment and any improvement to it will led to improvement in terms of total productivity.

Rise of Quality of Women's Working Movement

In the context of quality of life, researches have been done in abundance taking working life as one of the factors but, as an independent factor, quality of working life (QWL) acquired its importance very recently. The debate among scientists in various disciplines are putting forth their thoughts towards definition, measurement and effective utilisation of the concept in industrial settings. The managers of the recent time have been confronted with various organizational problems, out of which the most crucial is labour problem because machines materials, and the energy to run the machines don't perceive their environment, only man or workers do perceive.

A number of researches have helped in understanding the concept and other associated concepts which will be discussed to arrive at operational definition of the term for use in the present investigation. Newly acquired economic maturity appears to be one of the causes of the increased concern for improving the quality of working life. In many societies he framework of problem awareness for evaluating work experience has changed. This new awareness is generally attributed to the hightened aspirations of workers with regard to their working life, aspirations which in turn have been affected by improving living standards and higher educational levels of the work force in general.

Many of the current, against traditional problems are not the result of deteriorating social and working conditions rather, a consequence of hightened worker expectations and aspirations. Moreover, a number of aspects traditionally considered to be important are gradually giving way to new concerns. New problems affecting the QWL, fall in several categories. Some have surfaced as a result of new technological and social developments, other represent hanging and accelerating emphases on long recognised problem situations and conditions and still others relate to certain aspects of previously uncontested conditions which only recently have aroused concern regarding their compatibility with an acceptable level of QWL.

Walton (1975) pointed out that even though attention tends to be focussed on a few cases of obvious improvements which are widely publicised, demands for changes are usually not restricted to one or two aspects of the QWL. In fact, the extent of issues related to the QWL. In fact,the extent of issues related to the QWL is as broad as the whole range of labour problems Although opinions remain divided, there is some proof that unfulfilled needs and demands may led not only to worker dissatisfaction but also to alienation from work, low productivity and social instability.

Along with the individual differences in the perception of the QWL, there are also political, economic, social and cultural conditions which differ vastly among societies, they also result in widely varying degrees of problem consciousness and i different counter measures that have been devised in response to workers' needs that have recently emerged. In the past few years, quality of working life has emerged as a central issue not only in India but also in other developed nations. The growing concern is evident from the growing number of national and international conferences of managers, union leaders, government officials and behavioural scientists.

Perhaps the major cause for much of the recent concern is the alarm expressed by many about what has been termed the QWL problem facing today's workers and organizations. Yet there is currently a great deal of uncertainty and disagreement about just how serious this problem is, how widespread it is or whether it exists at all. Some argue that the problem is very real and very serious. Others view it as little more than the normal and expected growing pains of industry especially as maturity. Finally, still others view the quality of work life problem as one largely created by the media and little more than a passing interest.

There are a few valid or conclusive data that speak directly to the existence, the seriousness or the scope of the quality of working life problem much less to its sources or its effect but the importance of the problem is perceived as serious by few due to following reasons:

1. Worker alienation and job dissatisfaction are increasing primarily a result of meaningless jobs and authoritarian superiors.
2. The productivity of workers and industry is declining while counter productive behaviours (such as, sabotage, strikes, absenteeism, union militancy or alcoholism at work) are increasing.
3. The confidence of the public in large institutions in general and big businesses in particular is eroding.

The surveys conducted earlier shows that the behaviours like absenteeism, turn-over, job satisfaction and productivity are partially influenced by quality of working life. The reason is that while all of these attitudes of behaviours are indeed influenced by QWL, each are influenced by other factors as well. The other factors are: individual's expectations and values as well as what happens at work, technology, skills as well as motivation, etc. Quality of working life is both a good and on-going process for achieving it. As a goal, QWL is the commitment of any organization to work improvement, the creation of more involving, satisfying and effective jobs and work environment for people at all levels of the organization.

As a process, QWL calls for efforts to realize this goal through the active involvement of people throughout the organization. As a result of their involvement, people can make more meaningful contributions to the organization, its objectives and its ability to cope with the changing demands of a changing environment and at the same time, experience greater feelings of satisfaction, pride in accomplishment and personal growth. Importantly, QWL brings together the needs and development of people with the goals and development of the organization. QWL is also a philosophy and a concept of management.

The philosophy is broad,many facetted and varying somewhat in its specific foorm, one culture to the next or from one organization to other within the same organization. But the basic idea is same, a climate must been couraged in which the fundamental human dignity of all members of the organization are recognised, not only because they are entitled to it but also because workers are the most critical assets to the organization and its future. In France, when the main employers' and workers' organization decide in 1973 to launch inter-industry negotiations upon "working conditions," the issues to be discussed were classified under these headings: work organization; organization of working times payment by results; health and safety, and the role of supervisory staff.

All these considerations lead to the view that the concept of quality of working life should first be used in its broad sense in order to examine the total labour problems of each society. First, on the basis of past and present economic conditions of each nation, one can judge the areas in which meaningful improvements can realistically be made and at what level. Secondly, the socio-cultural background of society helps to define not only what goals should be selected but how they should be pursued. In spite of the great variety of economic, social, cultural and political situations in industrial societies, there is a broadly shared conviction that coherent and multi-facetted national policies are needed for the improvement of working conditions and of the quality of life.

There is no doubt that increased protection of the physical and social working environment, new working time arrangements, improved pay systems, new and imaginative ways of organizing work, wider application of ergonomics, and increased participation of workers in decisions directly affecting their working life. All these can make a substantial contribution to eliminating outdated and harmful methods of work and help promoting the QWL. The continuous rise in material living standards tended to fulfil workers' need to achieve on the one hand power and equity and on the other prosperity.

The goal of these workers began to rise higher and also to develop in a variety of directions. The relaxation of social control made it possible for them to express overtly their needs and problems, and to pursue personal satisfaction more directly. This liberation entailed first a general elevation of the level of aspirations, from material to psychological and from immediate to long range. The internal work environment within the organization began to prove inadequate in the light of new worker values.

Many of the previously accepted technical, organizational and social assumptions of organizations began to cause disfunctional symptoms. This was not so much due to a modified work environment as to a change in worker expectations towards that environments. As a result, productivity in same cases declined. Having experienced difficulties, managements began to take remedial measures. Improvements could be made in many areas, especially in work environment and conditions of work. Upon closer examination, a number of managements concluded that one of the most promising areas was work itself.

This decision was also much in line with some of the latest theories and experiences. Thus, the new area of management focus came into existence as the quality of working life. In India, context the QWL as a movement may be considered rising but, the concept is viewed in terms of western and context, where there are wide variation in Indian and western culture.

The set of industrial norms are quite different in both the civilisations and on top of this as compared to west, Indian's industrial growth is in developing stage. In India, inspite of efforts by the Government and the private sector, the unorganized sector is still existing which is as vast as the organized sector. In India the concept of QWL is considered useful to improve working conditions only for higher level workers. Perhaps no significant attempt has been made to explore QWl of the workers at the lower level and specially, unorganized sector has remained untouched.

This does not mean that workers in the unorganized sector do not have any perception of their life in the context of their work. Some of the objective parameters have been studied and a little glance has been made by some of the labour market studies to curb the malpractices of bonded labour in India which does not seem to be totally eradicated but their status surveys have thrown light on their conditions of work. After studying the QWL movement and interest of many social and behavioural scientist in it, it was realized that the concept should be applied for in-depth study of workers in the unorganized sector of industries. Women are the most downtrodden in the world of work, over burdened with hard and arduous work in dual role playing situation, at place of work as well as at home while performing economic responsibility and domestic discourses.

Women workers in the construction industry are being considered the lowest in the ladder of workers. It is pertinent to note that the notion of quality of working life, as an English idiom is closely related to the quality of life concept. Both emerged relatively recently in the industrialised nations where English was the primary language. Parallel concepts and innovative moves towards life goals developed, however, almost simultaneously in several other industrial countries. Humanisation of work, for instance, is often used in a number of languages as a synonym for quality of working life.

In France and other French speaking countries, the most useful expression is "improvement of working conditions," while in the socialist countries the established term is "workers protection." In Scandinavia, the central concepts are "working environment" and "democratisation of the work place." However, the English concept of "quality of working life" is broadly understood in all industrialised countries, even if it is sometimes barely used (Thorsrud, 1976). In the case of Japan, for instance, the concepts of *hatarakiqai* and *ikiqui* which gained impetus in usage around the same time, are surprisingly similar to those of quality of working life and quality of life respectively.

These developments would appear to indicate that the majority of industrialised nations have undergone certain common experience during the past quarter of a century. Sayeed and Sinha (1981) stated that from the time of Taylor (1911) researchers have over the years, dwelt upon the development of working conditions and other related aspects, falling within the realm of social sciences. Most of the work in the area of industrial and organizational psychology had one common feature or an ulterior goal, primarily aimed at improving quality of work and working life and enhancing employee motivation in order to increase organizational viability.

A variety of concepts have been used to map up the conditions of QWL Earlier, it was called morale and later termed as human relations, organizational development and redesign of work system. Presently, many researchers are inclined to describe the industrial democracy as a measure of quality of working life. Whatever way we have attempted to understand it, the question still remains whether we have made any headway in this direction in terms of integrating relevant findings to result in a new area of enquiry? Attempts at defining the concept of QWL has been made by many. Tylor's (1973) and Sprin's (1975) view point can be considered for an operational definition which describes QWL as "the degree of excellence in work and working conditions which contribute to the overall satisfaction of the individual and enhances individual as well as organizational effectiveness."

Prominent among those who have contributed to the area are Herrick and Maccoby (1972), Heizel, Geodale, Jayner and Burke (1973), Cherns (1973, 1975), Davis and Cherns (1975), Emry and Thorsrud (1976), Macy and Mervis (1976), Graen, Cashman, Ginsburg and Schiemann (1977) and Miller (1977). The psychological factors have been seen from the angle of labour problems by Delamotte and Takezawa (1974) in their report for International Labour organization on QWL.

They defined QWL as a set of new labour problems and their counter measures which have quined recognition as important determinants of worker satisfaction and productivity in many societies during the period of their sustained economic growth. Sashkin and Lengermann (1984) have taken a thread from Herzburg's two-factor theory and considered 'conditions' (C) and 'feeling' (F) towards these conditions as important determinants of QWL. The QWL—C/F is the result of a ten-year research programme that is based on classical sociological analysis of the relation between work and workers in society.

These approaches suggest that workers become alienated from their work when the work has little inherent meaning such as repetition of the same minute set of actions over and over or denies the worker control or power over this or her own actions. These conditions lead to subjective feelings of alienation that sociologists call "self-estrangement"—feelings of being cut off from one's own true working self (Blauner, 1964). In 1970, several research projects were initiated to empirically examine the relations between alienating job conditions which we now refer to as "quality of work life conditions" and workers" self-estrangement which we call `quality of work life feelings.' These working results led to a series of studies involving computer operators, clerical workers, machine operators, and medical technologists (Kirsch and Lengermann, 1971; Maurer, 1972).

Measurement of Quality of Women's Working

In view of the dearth of systematic work in the area of quality of working life the measurement of the same seemed to be a practical difficulty. Majority of the studies in this area are theoretically oriented, concerned with what QWL is or what are its dimensions that should be included in the measurement of QWL. Through the list of QWL dimensions to be considered for its measurement is quite exhaustive, with the exceptions of General Motor's Survey (as reported by Carlson, 1978). The QWL dimensions mentioned by other investigators are either speculative or arbitrarily selected. Apart from this most of the surveys have been conducted in the western countries. Boisvert (1977) identified fifteen dimensions for measuring the QWL. On the other hand, Walker's (2975) quality of working life involved the task, the physical work environment and the social environment within the organization, the administrative system of the enterprise and the relationship between life and the job. Similarly, Ghosh and Kalra (1982), Ganguli (1979), Joseph (1978), Carlson (1977) etc.

Took different dimensions for their study of quality of working life. The important of all these studies are by Carlson and Walton in American set-up and Sinha and Syeed in Indian set-up. Very little, however, has been done at the empirical level to relate QWL dimensions with various processes of the organization. Sashkin and Lengermann (1984) have taken a combination of two factors i.e. conditions of the work and the feelings aroused and the impression of the worker to each of the condition with emphasis on the productivity in an organization. The conditions of work were measured by autonomy, work speed and routine, task related interaction, personal growth opportunity and work complexity.

The feelings have been measured by asking certain questions about various activities of the work. The dimensions taken by Sayeed and Sinha for the measurement of QWL were, economic benefits, physical working conditions, mental state, career orientation, advancement on merit, job stress, effect on personal life, union-management relations, self-respect, supervisory relations, apathy, confidence in management, meaningful development, control, influence and participation, employee commitment, general life satisfaction and organizational climate.

The studies on QWL have taken various dimensions and at this stage when the concept is in its early stages of development, many more researches need be conducted to exactly identify the dimensions of QWL. The present investigation also has the same thought to explose various dimensions which are correlated with QWL and also the external factors affecting QWL. The importance of these factors are all the more necessary for the workers of the lowest order.

Changing Technology and Quality of Women's Working

We are living in a period of rapidly increasing wrenching social and technological change. Organization and job structures are undergoing change in response to these developments and because of our increased knowledge of the behaviours of organizations and individuals. Industrial society is in transition from one historical era to another and the environmental characteristics of the emerging era will led to crisis and marine dislocation, unless there is some form of adaptation. The structures of most purposive organizations based as they are on concepts of the industrial era, are becoming increasingly disfunctional because they stand at the confluence of changes involving technology, social values, economic environment and the practices of management.

The emergence of the post industrial era is stimulated by an ever increasing rate of changes in technology. The latter contributes to changes in values, not only by evoking new social systems and roles for organizational members but by stimulating the rising level of expectations concerning material, social and personal needs. They changes in technology changes the attitudes, aspirations of major segments of society. The seeming ease with which new technology satisfies material needs, coupled with the society's provision of subsistance, lend support for its citizens has stimulated a growing concern on the part of groups and individuals about their relationship to work, its meaningfulness and its values are the concerns of QWL. The high rate of change of technology has consequences for organization and job structure. On the product side, frequent new developments are leading to the growth of shorter production runs with the resulting need for adaptability of organization and workers to more changes.

On the production side, there is the phenomenon of more sophisticated machines and simpler manual activities embeded within automated complex production processes. The advanced technology presents is with a number of opportunities to develop new and more humane organizational foorms and jobs leading to a high QWL. First, although it poses new problems, highly sophisticated technology possesses an unrecognised flexibility in relation to social systems. There exists an extensive array of configurations of the technology that within limits can be designed to suit the social systems needs.

The new technology increases the dependence of the organization on individuals and groups and requires more individual commitment and autonomous responsibility in the work place. Their requirements for mutual dependence and independence provide opportunities to redress past deep-seated errors in social organizations and member's roles. The introduction of technology in the unorganized sectors, specially in the construction industry has affected deployment of heavy equipment for which the workers require basic skills. The training opportunities are limited and if we see gender differences, women are considered out of place.

The employment opportunities in agriculture fields are also replacing the women folk as they are unable to handle modern equipments. In this way, the immediate employment to women both in agriculture fields and construction industry are gradually reducing and so is the case with the work force participation rate. This factor would definitely be influencing change in perception of QWL by these workers. All attempts of enhancing the QWL by these workers.

Gain From Improve Quality of Women's Working

There are various elements which influence the individual's work experience. Therefor,e it is certain that an improved QWL will affect these variables. As the perception of QWL differs from individual to individual so is the gain perceived in various terms. QWL programmes incorporate a number of critical elements including a commitment from top management—acknowledgement from both management and employees that a voluntary desire from both sides to co-operate is essential. From the organizations, point of view the gain of QWL improvement is significant because there is:

- improved quality,
- increased output,
- reduced absenteeism,
- higher turnover,
- better labour management relation etc. and to employee; the gains are:
    - job satisfaction
    - greater control over one's own job
    - recognition
    - increased self esteem
    - a sense of accomplishment
    - fewer mental health problem, improved physical and phychological health.

To sum up, we can say that a higher quality of working life can often lead to decreased absenteeism, and higher turn over, few accidents and higher quality and quantity of output of goods and services. The most direct and immediate gain from an improved QWL is higher job satisfaction.

These two phenomenon are so closely related that they are often assumed to be one and the same and people sometimes use to interchangibly. But the term job satisfaction refers to an individual's affective reactions or feelings, toward his job and the term QWL refers to the individual work experiences. Job satisfaction is determined largely by how well an individual's actual rewards and experiences on his job are compared his desired or expected rewards and experiences, it is based largely on job. Quality of work life is a broader concept than job satisfaction in the sense that it includes both the job content and job context.

Generally, the workers having high QWL experience high job satisfaction. Individuals whose important needs are being satisfied by their job related activity, invariably experts positive feelings about these jobs and hence, there is increase in individual productivity. Individual productivity and quality of work lie are closely related, specially when productivity is defined in terms fo the individual's internal work standards. High productivity is both a cause and an effect of a high quality of work lire. The term productivity is much more than merely the quality of the individual's work output.

It also includes such work behaviours as poor turnover, absenteeism, defiance of rules and authority, grievances, strikes, union activities sabotage, theft, accidents and specially the quality of work output. All of these behaviours have been shown to be directly influenced by the individual's job satisfaction, involvement or commitment and these attitudes are directly affected by the quality of the individual's work life. Although, QWL is not the only determinant of individual productivity, yet it is the most important determinant. So, in any attempt to improve productivity the other various factors, both inside and outside the organization, must also be taken into account. A high QWL does not always or necessarily assure a high level of productivity but the poor QWL definitely discourages the productivity to some extent. Improved quality of working life improves the organizational effectiveness on the whole. If the interests of workers and goals of the organization are mutually supportive, improvement in the quality of work life will result in gains for both parties.

As for example, improvement in job design will produce not only more intrinsically motivating and enriching tasks but also higher individual productivity. However, there are many areas where the interests of individuals are not clear and inevitable conflict with the goals (economic goals) of the organizations that employ them or with the interests of the other groups in the organization. The worker's demand of more pay or greater security are in direct conflict with the profitability of most organizations and similarly, the demand of increase in power or autonomy of non-management workers because it will cause reduction in autonomy and authority of managers.

If these cases significant benefits can be gained from improvement of QWL, which has an impact on the ability of inter-dependent individuals and groups to work together toward organizational goals, to communicate effectively with each other, to co-ordinate their activities and to resolve their conflicts. There is fundamental difference in female and male work roles which need extensive examination of he nature of these socially accepted sex-bound roles.

Although, no society is a sex based division of labour, there is an extraordinary variety of sex typing of occupations across cultures suggesting that the sex typing is not based on unchangeable, genetic, physiological or psychological differences between the sexes but is and has been a social construct. The industrialisation brought about a revolutionary change in the occupation expansion with varying degree of basic human input required from the workers. This gave impetus to misplacing women socially and in the labour market.

The women are still considered inferior to men in terms of skill, pay, prestige and authority. The female role has to face two conflicting situations in the world of work as responsibility at work place and at home as care taking mother, performing perfect domestic and social activities.

This is common for all the societies, irrespective of occupational category. The quality of working life of women has to undergo various stages in the life cycle. After being prepared to under-take work and coming out of the domestic situation, the marriage brings about numerous changes and extra responsibilities on the part of women workers. At times women have to withdraw themselves from the world of work due to their marriage. Many studies have proved that like men, women are also motivated to work for money.

Working women's income is of considerable economic importance even when it is additional to the husband's income which determines sufficiency or deprivation in the family. The QWL of the women workers has so far not been assessed by any of the research study. In India, the efforts were not significant. The need is to undertake indifferent research works to study QWL of women workers.

Since quality of working life is a relatively new concept, most of the work in this area are on a theoretical-descriptive line concerned with how QWL should be defined and measured. However, a few empirical studies have been reported from India which tried to relate QWL to job satisfaction, work performance or managerial expectations or to some demographic variables. In an attempt to study the relationship between job attitudes and QWL, Joseph (1978) collected data from 96 skilled and semi-skilled technicians in a public sector enterprise, following a questionnaire approach. Conceiving QWL as an evaluation process of one's life in the work context. Job attitudes operationalised in terms of work, pay, promotion, co-workers and supervision.

The findings of the study indicated that

(a) attitudes towards the nature of work is clearly associated with QWL. The more one feels that his/her work is interesting, challenging and that it gives him/her a sense of achievement, the higher would be his/her perceived quality of working life;

(b) associates or co-workers have the potential to make QWL high or low, and

(c) attitude towards supervision and pay appear to be least associated with QWL even though supervision seems to be a general factor influencing other job aspects.

Singh and Maggu (1980), while studying the corporate quality of working life, operationalised QWL in terms of five dimensions and collected data from 251 managerial level employees representing 42 organizations. The results showed that QWL was considerably low across all the categories of respondents and across all the parameters of work system, perceived QWL being the poorest in the case of democratisation of work process.

It was further observed that he variation in managerial hierarchy, income and experience do not significantly influence the perception of the QWL. In another study, Ghosh and Kalra (1982) collected the importance ratings of 15 QWL factors from 70 managers in public and private sector organizations in their attempt to study how the different factors associated with the concept of QWL are influenced by variables like age, income, qualification, experience etc.

The results of this study revealed significant perceptual differences only in relation t four factors; employee welfare, advancement base don merit, absence of under job stress and union-management relations. The enquiry further showed that 'employe welfare' was influenced by age and income, 'advancement' based on merit, was influenced by education and experience, absence of under job stress' was influenced by professional, non-professional categories and the perception of 'union-professional categorisation of respondents. However, "various QWL, factors are likely to be perceived differently by different groups." In a more comprehensive study, Sayeed and Sinha (1981) examined the relationship between QWL and job satisfaction and performance taking data from 184 class III employees working in two organizations.

For measuring QWL, they used the inventory developed by Sinha and Sayed (1980). For Job satisfaction, they used the same dimensions as used by Joseph for measuring job attitudes. And performance measures were obtained from worker's self and supervisor ratings. Overall, the results indicated that higher QWL leads to greater job satisfaction and better performance. Emery (1976), Srivastava (1975) and McGregor (1960) in their studies stressed that the organizational structure played a significant role in developing human personalty.

All these studies have demonstrated beyond doubt that a bureaucratic culture severely inhibits human growth and that it is inadequate for inducing commitment to work, Friedlander and Newton studied the impact of organizational climate on the individual's job values and job satisfaction. They found organizational climate to be a significant determinant of individual job satisfaction. Lyon and Lvaucvich observed that the organizational climate had the most significant impact on self-actualisation a lesser impact on autonomy and only slight impact on esteem. In spite of the awareness of these findings and many other researches which clearly high-light the role of the corporate culture and quality of working life in determining human behaviour. Kapoor has concluded that about 25 per cent in the satisfied group and remaining 45 per cent in the neutral zone.

In a survey of 2821 American managers, Tarnowieasi concludes that 70 per cent of the managers were satisfied with their present career. The same study reveals that within the preceeding five years nearly 50 per cent of the executives surveyed had either changed or seriously considered changing their line of work for more meaningful career. Based on the study of the middle level managers, from 500 organizations Tasrnowieaski further reported that the middle level managers were highly dissatisfied with the contemporary organizational work life.

According to Mehta (1976) work amenities including economic compensation, interpersonal support, autonomy on the job and respectful supervisory behaviours are important factors in work related satisfaction. Studies also suggest the importance of general life satisfaction in promoting work satisfaction and efficient functioning in work organization (Mehta (1976). Repeated studies done by Mehta (1976) and Veccho (1980) on several categories of people including government officials, managers and supervisory staff show that perceived availability of influence and autonomy are the major source of satisfaction or dissatisfaction.

Similarly, influence and autonomy were another important indictors of dissatisfaction at the work place is the employee's perception of lack of amenities such as general welfare amenities and inadequate economic compensation including inadequate salary. In several cases, non-availability of adequate water and canteen facilities, inadequate medicine and health care provided to be a major source of work related dissatisfaction (Mehta, 1976). In developing countries, various kinds of developmental activities, following political and social freedom have led to very significant rise in the people's aspirations. Such rising aspirations are bound to effect the sense of life satisfaction among the workers. Similarly, socio-economic factors also play an important role in shaping attitudes towards work and related matters in the context of rising aspirations.

For instance, studies identified economic factors like income, promotional opportunities, social security as important factors in employee's sense of life satisfaction. Factors like working hours and nature of job did not find same importance as salary, security and advancement (Ganguli 1976). Another important finding in various studies ins related to age of the employees. The young entrants to organizations and younger employees showed greater work related dissatisfaction. Such dissatisfaction tended to decrease with increasing age of the employee (Mehta 1976). Mehta also fund that older employees felt more satisfied with life related issues in comparison to the younger ones. Although, it is not clear why the older employees feel so.

With the increase in age, they are expected to have greater family and social responsibility and therefore, greater concern for salary increments than younger ones. The dissatisfaction among the younger employees seems to be realistic to a certain extent because they have rising aspirations and expect more from the job than they actually get at the work place. In another study Ahmed (1971), Ashraf (1975) find that lowly educated younger employees show greater sense of dissatisfaction with their life conditions.

As a rule, lesser educated employees also get lower pay and lower benefits as compared to higher educated employees. Dissatisfaction due to economic factors is enhanced by rising aspirations. Such employees carry their disatisfaction with life conditions with them to their work and work place. Singh (1982) in his study of quality of corporate work life found that perceived QWL was considerably poor in Indian industries and perception did not change with the change in the managerial hierarchy. The findings of his study further revealed that the income did not significantly influence the perceived quality of work life. In another important study, Mehra (1984) found the relationship of job involvement to background factors, perceived importance of needs and need satisfaction.

Although, his study was not directly related to individual need fulfilment, yet individual's job involvement has its roots in the principles of need satisfaction and motivation. Job of an individual is of great importance and the individuals involvement in job depends on satisfaction f needs derived by individuals on the job. His study throws light on income and length of service having significant correlation with need fulfilment among other factors. The subjects with more income were found more satisfied with their needs and were more job involved. Level of education and place of birth did not make any difference to the need satisfaction and job involvement. Livneh (1978) in his study on quality of work experience found that patterns of changes in work values, job reward are contingent on specific facet of work involved, rather than age being uniformly a significant determining factor.

He also found that education has the most important relation t various work values followed by occupation. George (1984) studied lower, middle and upper managerial workers to study QWL in Public Section Undertakings. Along with the background variables quality of life was correlated with QWL. The results indicated that high quality of life will have high quality of working life, older employees have lower QWL, no relationship existed between length of service and income with QWL. Mishra (1985) studied quality of working life of managers and Research and Development personnel of two Public Sector Undertakings to find relationship between age, length of service, education, income and need fulfilment. The results indicated that age and length of service did not affect QWL perception. QWL was a function of income of the employees, the high income leads to high QWL, higher the educational level, higher was the QWL perception. QWL was significantly related to need fulfilment.

Appendices

APPENDIX–I

ORGANIZING AROUND CREDIT: THE CASE OF THE WORKING WOMEN'S FORUM

The women's movement in India had a new lease of life in the 1970s, after nearly two decades of lull after independence. However, it should be noted that the term women's movement is an abstraction. In reality, it comprises heterogeneous groups, some engaged in consistent and some in sporadic action—action itself ranging from a wide variety of militant struggles with a focus on structural change to welfare-oriented social service agencies that do not question the status quo. The period of the 1970s saw an increased participation of the urban masses, drawing particularly the educated middle class in the urban areas. The declaration of Emergency in 1976 was preceded by one of the most militant working class struggles in the post independence period on a countrywide basis—namely, the railway strike exposing state brutality in its most powerful form. The post-Emergency political awakening in the country led to a re-examination of the true nature of democratic polity in the country. This manifested itself in the emergence of numerous civil liberties organizations and women's groups.

The UN declaration of the decade of women strengthened these newly formed women's groups by providing both moral and material support as well as a rationale for their existence that could, in some instances, camouflage their own political origins.In many instances, political awakening among a certain section was synonymous with a disillusionment with party politics. It was generally felt that political parties were deviating more and more from the grassroots, and the genuine needs and aspirations of the people found only inadequate expression in their political agenda. The leadership of the parties was not only estranged but contained very few from the oppressed sections of society, (such as women, poor or the depressed castes).

In the case of women, the disillusionment with party politics led to the formation of independent and autonomous women's groups, drawing, in some instances, women from political parties, and coopting others who would otherwise have been drawn closer to the parties. These independent and autonomous women's groups may be termed 'non-party political formations' and do not constitute a homogenous lot in respect to ideologies or strategies. Some of the groups are the outcome of dissatisfaction with the left parties' traditions and have a conscious class-based political and feminist approach with struggle as their focus, while others that are the outcome of non-left political and trade union practices have a developmental approach rather than struggle.

This developmental approach to the mobilisation of women and collective action has received a fillip from international agencies. Whatever perspective on development the agencies might have, there is no denying the fact that such developmental organizations have served the useful purpose of promoting consciousness among women during periods of what may be called 'normal levels of exploitation'. Unlike periods of intensified oppression (such as the Emergency, with consequent actions like the suppression of civil liberties when spontaneous collective actions emerge which, at times, lead to militant struggle), periods of 'normal levels of exploitation' have, by and large, been accepted and internalised by the masses as a 'way of life'. Politicisation and consciousness-raising during this 'normal' period serves the long-term strategic interest of creating a highly developed and emancipated consciousness among the masses. This provides the *raison d'etre* for development organizations with a focus on empowerment and consciousness raising. In what follows, I shall examine the experiences of one such organization, recognised the world over as a very successful experiment.

The Working Women's Forum (WWF) in Madras city is a grassroots organization, exclusively involved in mobilising poor working women. I have called this an experiment in collective action as it exhibits a case of such women coming together, mobilising their resources, and achieving their objectives with whatever methods are- suited best. These women have, not only provided the leadership, but are also the potential agents of social change. The primary objective of the Forum is to empower poor working women both in their productive and reproductive roles. Empowerment is understood as providing a sufficient degree of control and decision-making power, access to resources and raising the level of consciousness of both their class and gender status. Using credit as a point of entry, the WWF mobilises the 'micro entrepreneurs' in the urban informal sector, and the home-based producers in the rural areas of three southern states. It has now extended its activities to two cities in the northern state of Uttar Pradesh, and hopes to venture soon into another northern state—Bihar. The manner in which credit intervention is conceived transforms it from an end to a means of forming a collective. Neighbourhood collectives of women drawn together for credit purposes, also take up numerous other issues affecting their work and lives and become, over time, conscious participants in collective action.

The activities of the Forum can be listed under three broad groups: the credit programme, the family planning and health programme, and social conscientisation activities. When the President of the Forum and her allies decided in 1978 to break away from the women's front of the Congress party, which had by then split with the dominant Congress (I) party, they decided to form a women's organization that would be apolitical (that is, non-party oriented and women-intensive). This was based on their conviction that grassroots development organizations, though no substitute for political parties or political solutions, could lead to political action. Thus, when the organization was formed, they had to decide on the focus and the activities. Credit was theft identified as an instrument of mobilisation.

Credit Programme

The Forum has two channels of credit for women informal sector workers—through nationalised banks and through its own cooperative credit societies. Since its modest inception in Madras city in 1979 with about 800 members, the Forum's credit activities have grown both intensively and extensively in such a way that it now has a membership of nearly 200,000 and covers the following women workers: informal sector workers in Madras city; agricultural labourers and shandy (wholesale market) workers in Dindigul taluk, Madurai district, Tamil Nadu; fisher women in Adirampattinam, Thanjavur district, Tamil Nadu; Beedi workers in North Arcot district, Tamil Nadu; agarbatti workers in the slums of Bangalore city, Karnataka; lace makers of Narasapur, Andhra Pradesh; rural non-agricultural workers in Bidar district, Karnataka; silk weavers in Kancheepuram, Tamil Nadu; chickan embroidery workers in Lucknow, Uttar Pradesh; and night schools for migrant workers in Kanpur, Uttar Pradesh.

The objective of credit intervention is to relieve women engaged in subsistence occupations from the clutches of moneylenders and middlemen by providing them working capital at low rates of interest. Individually, it reduces the interest burden as well as provides women with a certain autonomy, access and control over resources, and enhances their contribution to household income. These individual effects are the outcome of supplying cheap credit. The most striking impact, however, is the 'collective consciousness' and 'collective action' generated by the manner in which credit intervention is organized.

The core of the organizational structure consists of its members constituted into groups, with a group leader nominated from within. The group leaders of the neighbourhood loan groups report to the Forum's organizers (who are full-time employees on a monthly salary) on all matters relating to the Forum. The initiative for the formation of groups in a neighbourhood is obviously local. The entire credit intervention system revolves around the neighbourhood loan groups. Loans are not given to individuals but to groups, with group leaders providing the guarantee as well as the responsibility of collecting the dues. Thus, when an individual approaches the Forum for credit, she is asked to identify nine or ten others like her in similar occupations and in need of credit, and form a group. The neighbourhood loan groups provide both peer group support and peer group pressure.

Loans for groups are negotiated with nationalised banks under the Differential Rate of Interest Scheme, whereby loans carrying a 4 per cent rate of interest are given to weaker sections of society (weaker sections refers to those households with a low annual income, the limit of which was specified in 1985 as less than Rs. 3,000 per annum). Alternatively, the Forum has its own cooperative credit societies in all centres where, for a share of Rs 20, the members can obtain a loan ten times the value of the share. The initial capital base of these societies is met through grants. Here, too, loans are given only to groups. However, the rate of interest on loans from credit societies is high (13—15 per cent per annum).

There are different sets of people involved in the entire credit programme—members, groups and group leaders, organizers, Forum staff, staff of the cooperative credit societies and banking personnel. Relations between these different people determine, to a large extent, the success or failure of the credit programme. The fact that, in the last seven years, there has been a manifold increase in membership confirms the strength and success of the group system. This is not in any way to brush aside the constant tensions and contradictions that surface everyday, most of which get resolved through the 'collective process'.

It is also the responsibility of the group leaders to cultivate among their members the spirit of the women's collective. Different leaders, depending on the extent to which they themselves are conscious, try to promote this in different ways. The most common is by interacting closely with members' families and listening to their problems in a concerned way. Quite often, group leaders have brought to the attention of organizers instances that they have encountered on such visits of desertion, dowry harassment, suffering at the hands of drunken husbands, wife beating, and the 'other woman' syndrome. Obviously, on these matters, there are no guidelines by the Forum on bow group leaders should achieve their goals, and this is largely left to their discretion, temperament and the situations in which they are placed.

In a slum clearance tenement in Madras city, I was witness to a massive confrontation between the members and group leaders. Members complained that group leaders very often threatened them that they would not get their loans if they did not attend the Forum meetings or participate in processions, and it is because of these threats that they attended. The group, leaders countered that there is a tendency to view the Forum as Only a loan giving agency, and that the ideology of the Forum and the spirit of the women's collective is not understood. Given the terms of reference of both groups, each group's arguments seemed valid. A younger member of the group intervened to say that this kind of problem would not come up if the Forum arranged more meetings in that area. Infrequent meetings have kept the members at a distance and without complete identification with the Forum's ideology.

The task of the organizers is to extend the activities of the Forum to other rural areas and urban slums, to screen the new groups formed, inform them of the rules and regulations of the Forum, assess their genuine credit needs by probing into the economics of their occupations, and to negotiate with the banks for loans and help the groups in repayment. Thus the organizers serve as a vital link between the groups and the Forum. All problems in the area are brought to the attention of the organizer who, in turn, brings it up for discussion at the meetings where all the other organizers and office bearers are present.

Clearly, the extent to which the organizers can understand and appreciate the work and lives of the members and their ability to maintain a good rapport with the groups determine the kind of results they can achieve. In this context, the socio-economic background of the organizers becomes important. A majority of the organizers come from working class households with prior occupational experience in the informal sector. A little over a quarter of the organizers have themselves not been engaged in any occupation, but the personal crises in their lives have cemented their solidarity with the working women. Personal crisis here could be a state of dependence forced on them by the death of a father or husband, desertion, inability to procure a marriage partner owing to excessive dowry demands, harassment due to the presence of 'the other woman' or alcoholism. Such crises do enable the woman to dovetail with the class-based oppression of other working women also.

The following case study is a hood illustration of this point. Sivagami, a young widow with two children, recalled that soon after her husband's death in an accident, she approached *amma* (meaning mother, and refers to the President of the WWF) for a job in the Forum. Married after her school final to a bank clerk, Sivagami had led a protected and cloistered life till then. She was emotionally and economically shattered when she went to work as an organizer among the fisherwomen of Adirampattinam, but she soon realized that there were people worse off than her, and now she moves around with confidence organizing the fisherwomen.

Joining the Forum creates, in women like Sivagami and others, a new awakening, and they begin to perceive their own specific oppression as one amongst a wide range in a class, caste and patriarchal society. However, as in the case of group leaders and members, here, too, there ate tensions and challenges. Bangalore city, with its two ethnic groups—Tamil migrants and the local Kannadigas—offers a striking example. Conflicts between these two ethnic groups have, in recent years, led to some major conflagarations. Thus, the Forum was stepping into troubled waters, as it is an organization based in Tamil Nadu. It, naturally, attracted a number of Tamil organizers and members in the beginning and created suspicion among the Kannadigas. These suspicions were further exacerbated when the few Kannadigas who joined the Forum found that the sanction for their loans through the bank was getting delayed. Now the Forum has its own cooperative credit society in Bangalore.

I have traced in detail the nature of the relationship between the members, group leaders and organizers as they constitute the core solidarity group. The most noteworthy aspect is that most of them are drawn from poor working class households—households engaged in informal sector occupations. Apart from these, the staff of the cooperative credit societies and the Forum workers who are involved in the credit programme are generally women below 30 years of age with a school education and sometimes with a diploma in cooperative training. These women are generally from lower middle class households.

The Credit Programme in Different Areas

The coverage of the credit programme under the credit scheme in all the centres. In each of these centres, the dominant occupation for which credit intervention is aimed at is different, and I shall, in each instance, examine the efficacy of such an intervention as a means of mobilisation and its effects on increasing the awareness of oppression faced by the women.

Madras City: Within the Municipal Corporation limits of the city, there were 107,553 women workers in 1981. About 30 per cent of them were engaged in informal sector activities, both as self- employed and as casual wage labourers in low paid, low working capital low skill and low absolute surplus generating subsistence occupations. These self-employed women workers can, in fact, be called micro entrepreneurs as they are clearly very innovative in devising adaptive strategies for survival. But, most often, even these survival strategies are severely constrained by the lack of working capital finance, very high interest payments, lack of markets, lack of space and lack of mobility..

The organization first concentrated its activities in Madras city where a large number of women in the informal sector are engaged in petty trade such a vegetable and fruit vending, selling of snacks like *idli* and *vadais* in the urban slums or selling cut-piece (pre-cut) cloth and sarees. They approached this section of women to find out their foremost needs. These retail vendors felt that their low absolute returns each days were further diminished by interest payments on loans taken either on a daily or weekly interest basis to meet their working capital requirements. These survival enterprises are largely dependent on the extent and availability of working capital. The women suggested that if loans at a lower rate of interest were given to them to meet their business requirements, they could free themselves from the local moneylenders. Thus, they perceived themselves, to be in an immediate antagonistic relationship with the local moneylenders.

Till 1985, the Forum had identified and provided credit assistance to 79 different occupations in the urban informal sector, though cut-piece, vegetable and *idli* sales accounted for nearly half of all the loans provided. I give below an account of these occupations.

All the vegetable vendors have to go to the wholesale bazaar in the city in the morning. Their loan requirements, as observed, range from Rs 100—Rs 500. In one of the retail markets I visited in north Madras, a rental of Rs 2 in the forenoon and Rs 2 in the afternoon was collected. Because of the renovation of the market, they had to pay an advance of Rs 5,000 per shop as well as a daily rent of Rs 12. A large number of women vendors, whose scale of business is rather small and who cannot afford to pay the rental for the market space, are seated outside on the narrow streets leading to the market, spreading their wares on the side of the street. Apart from passing cycles and autorickshaws squashing a few tomatoes, they are constantly harassed by the police by the constant threat of eviction. With the Forum mobilising the women and through their constant pressure, in the opinion of the women there has been a perceptible decrease in the number of police cases registered in certain areas.

A few profiles of those who have benefited under the credit programme in Madras' city are revealing. Sundari, a vegetable seller in Pattalam market, notes that prior to her joining the *sangam* and obtaining credit assistance she used to borrow on an interest rate of 10 per cent per month (120 per cent per annum) with payments to be made every day or weekly.

This money was largely rolling cash for her business, which did not roll with a one shot injection of a stock amount owing to unexpected market or personal losses. So far she has borrowed five times from the *sangam* starting with Rs 200 to the most recent Rs 800. She has even repaid that, and is waiting for her next loan.- Now Sundari does not take money from moneylenders on *thandal* but when contingencies arise (particularly during periods when loans are fully paid and the next one gets delayed), she pawns a few items to the pawn broker.

Lakshmi, her husband, their 17-year old son and 9-year old daughter were all engaged in making cardboard boxes for a jewellery shop. With an initial investment of Rs 100 they could make a profit of Rs 50 if the entire family worked for a full week. Earlier, they would take money from moneylenders but, with the Forum's loan coming, their survival constraint was eased. But that was only for a very short period before they were caught up in a severe trap. Recently, her husband was hospitalised for a month with a heart attack and he is still unable to work. It was not only the hospital expenses that burdened them, forcing them to borrow from moneylenders but, more severely, their entire occupation was affected. Her husband was the only one who knew the measurements and the way to cut the cardboard for the boxes. The rest of the family did only the sticking. Lakshmi is now thinking of setting up an *idli* stall. Hesitant to take up this new occupation, she is forced into such a venture as debts with moneylenders mount everyday. She is now dependent on the Forum for the initial capital.

Summing up the impact of the credit assistance programme in Madras city, in most areas women who were previously indebted to usurious moneylenders for their working capital requirements now seemed to be relieved of them. However, delays in procuring the next loan and other unforeseen business and personal contingencies sometimes force them back to the pawn brokers, though there has been a clear decrease in their involvement with *thandals*. Secondly, the loan amount had, in many cases, provided the initial capital for a business or helped in expanding their scale of operation. In some cases, it helped in clearing old debts and meeting other household expenses. Women also reported that they were now eating better. Apart from these direct benefits relating to their occupation and income, the women could also perceive an enhancement in their status. Earlier, most of them had never stepped into a nationalised bank and those who had gone narrated how they were treated by the officials. These unseemly women chewing *pan,* and most often stinking after a day's work in the vegetable market, would be a nuisance factor to the more elite bank customers. Now, when they walk into the bank, they are offered chairs to sit on. With the starting of the Working Women's Cooperative Credit Society, their realization that it is their own bank has enormously increased their self-confidence.

Dindigul: In the Dindigul taluk of Madurai district, two groups of women have benefited from the credit assistance programme— women from landless agricultural labour households and women shandy workers.

Natchikonampatti is a small hamlet with sixty households, where most of the members are hired agricultural labourers. A variety of crops are grown—paddy, sugarcane, cholam, tomatoes, sunflower, chillies and cotton. However, women here have work for only about 60 days scattered over the year. This is a dry taluk, lacking well irrigation, where agriculture depends largely on rainfall. Agricultural wages in 1985 stood at a very low Rs 3 for women and Rs 6—Rs 8 for men. During the harvest they are paid in kind--3 measures of paddy, which amounts to 2 kilos of rice. For cutting sugarcane, the leaves of the cane are given as wages. Fodder for cattle is very scarce in this dry region and so the leaves, which elsewhere command no price, are a substitute for money wages. Similarly, for plucking cotton, the inferior rejected balls are given as wages.. None of the women were aware of the existing minimum wages law. Here women and men face the problem of both availability of work as well as low wages. Some households had availed of goat loans and some others had dairy cattle on a *varam saram* basis, (that is, the landlord would buy the cattle and the labourer would rear it, and milk would be shared on a 50—50 basis).

Prior to obtaining these dairy loans, women would take loans both for purposes of consumption and to meet unforeseen contingencies, both from moneylenders and landlords. Harassment from moneylenders is known. When these women took loans from the landlord, they had to send their child to the landlord's *pannai* (farm) to work until the debt was cleared.

In this context, the kind of credit intervention the Forum launched in collaboration with the women agricultural labourers was to provide them loans for obtaining dairy cattle. By negotiating with a local nationalised bank, the Forum was able to provide dairy loans for 251 members in the district, Of these, 228 members got loans for the first animal and 23 got a second loan (either for a second animal or to replace a dead one). Twenty-two of the 60 households in Nachikonampatti had obtained dairy loans. The Forum had also arranged for milk marketing through a depot in Dindigul.

Keeping dairy cattle and making a living out of it is not an easy affair. Firstly, only some of these households had any experience in rearing dairy cattle, and many women had to be-trained by the animal husbandry officers. Secondly, with the scarcity of fodder in a dry region and the lack of access to grazing land owing to privatisation and encroachment of all village commons by the landlords, feeding the cattle becomes a costly affair when both fodder and husk have to be bought. Invariably, the loans were fully repaid after the second calving.

The impact of these dairy loans on the work and lives of women has been manifold. The women who are -now engaged in looking after the cattle do not take up agricultural work at such low wages as before, causing some annoyance to landlords during times of peak labour demand. They are often known to remark, 'Your hands have now been strengthened. You won't come and work in our fields.' Thus the landlords are now forced to draw labour from other hamlets, a threat the landlords had used for years whenever the local workers asked for higher wages. Now they are forced to carry out this threat—not because the landlords are powerful but because their power has been whittled down. The bargaining power of the cattle recipient has obviously improved. Yet their income from agriculture has not significantly improved, nor has their nexus with the landlord been severed.

First, in a household with more than one adult woman (of whom only one person is engaged in looking after the cattle), the others do take up agricultural work. Secondly, during dry-milking periods, even those otherwise engaged in looking after cattle seek agricultural work. During the cotton picking season, all the women go to work as it has to be done at the dawn, after which they come back to look after the cattle. Thus the labour supply situation for the landlords, due to the existing nexus and availability of labour from other hamlets, is not altered significantly. However, for the women, agricultural wages have increased over time from a low Rs 1.25 to Rs 3.00 today. The women recalled that a year ago they refused to take up agricultural work if the wages were not increased. But their struggle, which was only in the nature of a small pressure group, did not succeed.

Even if these small increments in wages were due to the presence of an alternative income-earning opportunity, they were still very much lower than the legally stipulated minimum wages. Thus, both on the wage front and of altering dominance—subordination relations at the village level, there is need for a major thrust by the Forum.

Shandy Loans: There are a number of women in and around Dindigul selling items such as flowers, fruits and vegetables, tamarind seeds, banana stalks, ropes and old iron pieces. For four days in a week they traverse up to 10 kilometres to the larger villages and towns where the shandies are held. On the remaining days they sell their wares on the streets, or door-to-door. For vending in the shandies a rent is collected. Most of the women moving from the village to different shandies are shelterless.

Kotturavarampatti, a hamlet in Dindigul taluk, has a large number of womenfolk employed as shandy workers. This extremely isolated hamlet, with no public transport facility, lies in a drought- prone village. Little agricultural work is available during the year. Dairy cattle, as alternative employment, does not appear to have much scope owing to the non-availability of fodder and water. Thus a number of survival mechanisms have been adopted. Bananas, banana leaves and banana stalks are bought by the village women from the landlords and, sold in the shandies. With a low agricultural wage of Rs 7 for men and Rs 5 for women per day coupled with the extreme irregularity of agricultural work, women did not even have the funds to procure these items. Most of them pawned whatever jewellery they had with the cooperative bank and obtained loans on interest rates of 10 per cent per annum. Those who could not avail of this option invariably pawned whatever household items they possessed to the moneylender. As the professional moneylenders were not present in the village, the better-off families performed the moneylending role.

The Forum, through its credit programme, gave loans to these shandy workers once they formed credit groups, and has eased their survival constraint to a significant extent.

While these are the direct effects, the indirect but articulated effects are striking. All the women are now confident about speaking up in meetings and articulating their problems. This has been made possible by the numerous discussion meetings organized by the *sangam*. Further, their isolation, caused by spatial immobility, appears to have totally broken down. Those who were able to visit large cities (like Madras and Madurai) and towns (like Dindigul) recalled what a tremendous learning experience and exposure to the world it was. Particularly, though not surprisingly their disillusionment with the functioning of political parties as well as their total understanding of the power relationships in the system, the role of politicians, the bureaucracy, landlords and moneylenders have totally transformed their perception of their own selves. Whereas, earlier, their powerlessness was matched with ignorance and a positive acceptance of fate, now their understanding of their powerlessness is accompanied by a strong and articulated resentment. Hopelessness had given way to attempts, however weak or meagre, at achieving a greater solidarity among themselves.

Adirampattinam: In Adirampattinam and twelve nearby coastal villages in Thanjavur district, the WWF has formed credit groups of women involved in fish marketing. The role of women in fish marketing can be understood only in the overall context of the fishing economy of the region. The entire catch is auctioned off, and no individual can sell directly to the market or hand over his catch to his wife. The village auction system evolved out of a necessity to generate common village funds as well as to have a regulated market for fish where the village collective could have greater say. Village funds are generally used for the purposes the community decides on (such as temple functions/renovations or inter-village litigations). Women not only support and strengthen these community decisions directly and indirectly but, very often, draw a lot of their social and cultural sustenance from these activities as well.

On the economic front, however, the emergence of the auction system has been adverse for women. Whereas, earlier, men used to give their catch to the women in their household to sell (thus enabling women to obtain a cash income along with some degree of control), this has now passed on to the men completely. Deprived of this as well as the fact that if women wanted to sell fish they also have to buy it in the auction, for which they needed cash, women's involvement in the auction system became-both compulsive and difficult. Women were forced to take loans from moneylenders at usurious rates and under humiliating conditions. The Forum's credit intervention enabled the women engaged in fish marketing to carry on their occupation outside the hold of the moneylenders. Apart from the fish sellers, the Forum has also mobilised other women peripherally engaged in the fishing economy (such as basket makers, salt sellers and those selling food items near the fish landing spot).

In several villages in Adirampattinam, the women pointed out that through the credit assistance programme of the *sangam* they have now been able to relieve themselves from the clutches of the moneylenders to a great extent. Almost all of them also indicated that the loan amount was grossly insufficient. Whether or not they were prompted by their menfolk, all of them wanted loans to buy nets. All the women are very clear that it is only the ownership of the means of production that can give them greater economic power, and for fishing households a larger number of nets mean a larger catch. This is in spite of the fact that women realize that not all of the higher earnings got thereby are going to percolate down to the household.

As in the other centres, one of the indirect effects of the *sangam* of raising the class consciousness of these women through their credit scheme has been their holistic understanding of power relationships (namely, the conflicts between the launch operators and the traditional fishermen, between the boatowners and others among the traditional fishermen, of their compulsive involvement in the auction system, and of the other dominance—subordination relationships, such as caste, in which they are caught in a total state of powerlessness.

Vellore: Most of the women workers in the household industry in Vellore (numbering 4,422, according to the 1981 Census) are beedi workers, of whom a little less than 50-per cent have been brought within the fold of the Forum. Most of the women and a large number of the men are engaged in the piece-rate putting- out system of work, though there are beedi factories predominantly employing men. The put-out piece-rate system is a hybrid one, also involving a sale and purchase transaction. The beedi workers buy the *tendu* leaves and tobacco and sell the rolled beedis to the beedi *mandis* (merchant-cum-factory owners) at a rate that amounts to only piece-rate wages. Most often, the 'sale-purchase' transaction involves a loss to the workers because of the bad quality of raw materials or fraudulence in the quantity measure. In order to ensure for themselves the stipulated piece wages, the workers are forced to meet the deficit raw materials. Further, during the monsoon period, the beedi *'mandis'* do not give out work at all and the workers are forced into a consumption loan trap. It is here that the credit of the Forum plays an important role. The credit assistance programme of the Forum found an enthusiastic response with women beedi workers.

The effect in terms of raising consciousness is noteworthy. No doubt these women on the put-out system were, to an extent, already sensitised on class issues, given their formal subsumption under merchant capitalists. Though not formally members of any trade union, these women workers are sufficiently influenced by the activities of the trade unions in the beedi factories, employing predominantly men. At the times of struggle by the organized beedi workers, the put-out women workers were laid off, and also during lock-outs in the factories no work was put-out. However, successful wage struggles in the factories found the put-out piece-rates increase only marginally.

The Forum's activities, while sharpening the class consciousness that existed, carried the women to a new height of consciousness. For instance, the articulated resentment of a Muslim woman against the refusal of Muslim *mandi* owners to give raw materials to women, while giving them only to the men of households on the put-out system, was seen as a way of reinforcing their cultural subordination in the domain of work. The resentment of working Women against the functioning of the bureaucracy after their ordeal in getting *patta* for their homestead land, against elite researchers and against postmen who would visit the low-lying shims only on dry sunny days, are instances of their consciousness with respect to their class and gender status vis-à-vis others in the totality of the society.

Bangalore: According to the 1981 Census, of the 13,007 women workers in household industry in the Bangalore urban agglomeration, 3,337 women had been covered under the credit programme of the Forum in *1985.* In a span of two years, this is a no small achievement in an environment of suspicion and hostility between the two ethnic groups—the Tamil migrants and the local Kannadigas.

The organization of the *agarbatti* (scented incense sticks) industry is on similar lines as the beedi industry mentioned earlier. It is characterised by the coexistence of factory, workshop and put-out production. Most women on the put-out system were home-based producers, dependent upon the exploiting merchant capitalist for raw materials. The credit programme of the Forum, in effect, transformed them from dependent home-based workers status to independent home-based producers by enabling them to purchase raw materials and sell independently. Though the increase in income was only marginal and the survival struggle itself was not overcome, the women felt less harassed now than before. More importantly, with their own working capital, during the monsoon period when they stop work due to the peculiarity of this activity, they are left with a part of that capital to meet their consumption requirements.

While the earlier attempts at unionisation focused only on the factory-based agarbatti workers, the Forum made the first attempt, as pointed out by the women themselves, at bringing together the home-based workers. The attendant trials and tribulations of bringing together two ethnic groups that were mutually suspicious and hostile has been an enormous learning experience for the Forum. For the women themselves, where these bridges of communication have been built, it has brought about an enduring solidarity among the poor women as one oppressed group.

Narasapur: Narasapur is situated in West Godavari district in the southern state of Andhra Pradesh. This is an agriculturally prosperous and highly commercialised region. With the green revolution came the capitalist farmer replacing the precapitalist forms of sharecropping tenancy. The tenants are now agricultural labourers.

While men previously cultivated the land as sharecroppers, their women were confined to domestic chores. In the late nineteenth century, these women learnt the art of lace making which has now become a flourishing export trade for the state. The lace making industry is predominantly in the hands of merchant exporters. They employ contractors to go around various villages distributing reels of thread along with export orders to the women lace makers on a piece-rate payment of Rs 4 per reel of thread woven. Apart from these contractors, the lace makers who are quick at work and have additional members at home, and for whom the thread given by these contractors is insufficient, prefer to make lace on their own and sell it in the weekly Palakol shandies. However, not all the lace makers go to the shandies to sell. In most villages, tradeswomen have emerged.

The lace makers, under the capitalist agricultural regime, belong to the agricultural labour households. The obvious display of communist party flags in the region may represent a strong tendency to unionise the agricultural labourers, but has apparently bypassed this section of the working class—the women lace makers— perceiving the, lace making activity as the leisure-time work of the women. Consequently, the political parties have missed the misery of the women lace makers of Narasapur. The Forum's intervention in the West and East Godavari districts has been threefold. First, through its credit assistance programme it provided scope for the women to be independent lace makers selling for shandies, or to combine contract work with independent work. Second, through the Commerce Ministry, it sought to procure export orders directly and began to distribute thread to women on its own at a rate of Rs 10 per reel. The quantitative jump from Rs 4 to Rs 10 which proved feasible under the Forum's assistance, laid bare the exploitation of the merchants. The lace makers perceived this so clearly that they forced the merchants/contractors to increase the piece-rate to Rs 6 or Rs 8 per reel. Third, the Forum, through its credit programme, actively encouraged the not-so-good lace-makers, largely selling to the shandies, to shift to other occupations (such as coir rope making). The credit scheme, by attempting to transform the women into independent producers, has forced them into another set of problems—that of marketing in the shandies. The demonstration effect of higher piece-rates through direct export orders runs into difficulties because the orders are erratic, the organizational resources are small and so the activity cannot be expanded, and the supply of quality thread recently (referring to the time when fieldwork was done—March 1985) has been affected by a lock-out in the major thread unit.

In the case of occupational diversification, the Forum is constrained by limited resources. This does not enable the setting up of mechanised coir rope making units on a cooperative basis, which would pay the women Rs 5—Rs 10 a day. The activity, therefore, is done manually in their homes involving even the children of the family.

Bidar: Bidar district, in the north-eastern corner of Karnataka, is one of the most economically backward regions in the state. In order to promote rural non-farm employment opportunities in this dry region where agriculture is solely dependent on the rainfall, the Karnataka government in 1981 initiated the Bidar Integrated Rural Development project also known as the BIRD project, specifically with a view to improve the quality of life of rural women and children with a substantial resource allocation of nearly Rs 6 crore. Under this project, it sought to provide non-farm employment to women by assisting in both technology and credit through the village technology centres and rural cooperative banks. The local Mahila Mandals were involved in the credit scheme. Each Mahila Mandal was given Rs 5,000 and had about thirty or forty women members. Through this initial capital, loans from commercial banks were sought for the members as start-up finance for new economic activities.

By 1985 this scheme ran into a number of difficulties. Invariably, the presidents of the Mahila Mandals were high caste women belonging to the Lingayat and Okkaliga castes, and these women were reluctant to reach out to the low caste women of the Scheduled Castes, and Muslims. Thus the sections that most needed assistance were deprived of it. Many of the members, not having had prior experience in this kind of activity, found themselves flush with money but did not know how to go about starting an economic activity, despite the technology centres. The banks did not advise them either. Those who bought themselves dairy cattle with the loan found no veterinary care. The animals often became sick and they found themselves helpless. Under these conditions the Karnataka government, on the advice of UNICEF, (which had invested nearly 90 lakh into this project), invited the WWF(I) to take up this section of the BIRD project, and requested them to start a cooperative society as part of their Karnataka society under which the agarbatti workers from the slums of Bangalore city were already organized. The Bidar branch of the WWF(I) has been functioning since January 1988.

The Forum restructured the membership of the Mahila Mandals into group systems, and did away with high caste leadership. Harijan and Muslim women in the region now engage in a number of non-farm activities (like poultry rearing, blanket weaving and making caps). When the Forum started its operation in Bidar in 1988, it had a membership of

2,000 women. By mid-1990, membership reached 5,000. The Forum has been able to reach 92 villages in all the four taluks of the district. The example of Bidar again proves the strength of grassroots initiative vis-a-vis the top-down approach.

Kancheepuram: This ancient temple town in southern India could justifiably compete with Patliputra (today known as Patna), acclaimed to be the oldest town in the country, for a share in that unique historicity. Silk weaving has been carried on here since ancient times. Today, even though the prized silk sarees of Kancheepuram sell for exorbitant prices, the lives of the weavers, as in other parts of the country, are a tale of woe. The government, as part of its policy of protecting and developing the handloom industry, offers assistance to the weavers through its cooperatives.

This scheme is not without its share of difficulties. First, it admits only weavers as its members and, therefore, only men become members. Even though women and children as household members are involved in the various activities of this industry, they cannot formally become members of weavers' cooperatives. 'Secondly, government cooperatives offer assistance in both cash and kind. Assistance in kind is in the form of supply of gold thread (or *zari)*. Often the weavers, taking the assistance of the cooperative society, pledge the gold *zari* with moneylenders. They fritter away that money, and wait until the sale proceeds of the finished sarees are realized to purchase *zari* on their own. Thus, cooperative assistance is transformed into a consumption loan used solely by the men, rather than a productive one. As a consequence, the male weaver's contribution to household income is also correspondingly reduced, though the women of their households contribute to that productive activity. The ILO agreed to support the WWF in starting its own cooperative society for the women in the weaving households as an experimental measure. This support from the ILO was linked with the third phase of the family planning programme. Thus, this was conceived as a credit-cum-family planning scheme. The scheme sought to provide credit assistance to the tune of Rs 1,000—Rs 1,500 to each woman to help redeem the pledged *zari* from the moneylenders and enable them to do the weaving themselves. It also attempts to replace the widely prevalent child labour force in the industry. Reports from the field indicate that most children in weaving households do not attend school, and do not evince much interest in doing so either. These children appear to be quite confident and content with their earning potential. While the Forum is aware that its credit assistance may not be quite sufficient for each household, it is quite wary of increasing its assistance. The Forum's enquiries in the town have revealed that in bigger cooperatives where male weavers have access to larger loans, it has often enabled them to bond the services of a couple of children to themselves. This is done by the weavers lending out the money under the bondage contract. By giving assistance to women, the Forum hopes that child bondage can be restricted. It is also in the process of organizing night classes for the children.

Lucknow: The cool and comfortable Lucknowi kurtas with chikan embroidery are very popular during the hot summer months in all parts of the country. For the many thousands of poor Muslim women engaged in embroidery work, it is a life of sweat, and toil. This is shocking but true. On most pieces of work the women net only 10 paisa. They want the piece-rate to be increased to 25 paisa. The Forum has started its credit assistance programme to this section of the workers, and its membership today is nearly 1,000. As in the case of Vellore, Bangalore and Narasapur, the Forum hopes that through its credit programme, it can provide visibility to these workers and thus enable the piece-rate wages to be pushed up. For the home-based workers, the Forum believes that Increasing the piece-rate wage is more important than organizing marketing. Many organizations that help in marketing function more or less like the merchant-contractors themselves, and do not after the exploitative relations. In all the areas where the Forum's credit intervention programme was aimed at home-based workers, wages have increased over the years.

Jamshedpur: In and around this steel city, where the TISCO plant is located, are large sections of Harijans, Adivasis, Rajputs and Muslims. Though not strictly employees of TISCO, the male members of many of the households are engaged in some activity relating to the industry. Adivasi men are often called in for some months in a year as coolie labour. While the steel industry provides large employment opportunities, it is the people from outside and not the local population that get these attractive jobs. A large number of Adivasis are engaged in bamboo work, Harijan women are involved in making cowdung cakes, Rajput women in selling bangles and flowers, and Muslim women in some kind of home-based work. Adivasi women spend six months here in the town seeking some kind of work. For the remaining period they go back to their villages. However, this is true only of the older Adivasi women. The younger women do not want to go back to their village for agricultural work for part of the year.

The Forum has conducted a pilot study to explore starting a credit programme for these sections of the women workers. The Adivasi women are already organized in a cooperative society, but do not get loans for working capital requirements to pursue their occupations. The TISCO community centres train women for batik, embroidery, tailoring and candle-making in addition to providing creche facilities. The Forum feels that through its credit programme it can reach out to the vast tribal settlements in the villages in that region. However, it is interested in organizing the women into credit groups for productive activities for which the TISCO centres offer training, and only if TISCO undertakes the marketing or guarantees to buy all the output. This is the first time the Forum is negotiating with the private corporate sector, and it will be to its credit if it succeeds in this venture. For the moment, the pilot study team,' comprising of Forum workers from the southern states, have come back with exposure to working class lives in other parts of the country.

In its efforts towards mobilisation, progress is perceptible. But, at the level of consciousness, varying results are obtained across occupation groups. I shall reflect on this below. In occupations such as vending, where the women are self-employed, credit intervention is viewed as an end rather than a means, whereas in occupations where women are on a put-out system or under some form of wage labour system, women perceive the intervention as a means of mobilisation. In the case of self-employed vendors, they perceived themselves as being in an immediate antagonistic relationship with the local moneylenders, and once the moneylenders were eliminated from the scene through the credit programme, they themselves begin to function with a merchant mentality, albeit on a small scale. Their occupational situation does not enable class consciousness to be developed beyond a point, though they gain in their understanding of the state machinery (such as the police and banks).

Some self-employment activities are contexted within a collective, such as fishing which is an activity of the village community with a unique intertwining of the sphere of production with socio-cultural spheres. In these contexts, despite the self-employment status with no identifiable employer—employee relationship, Credit intervention appears to reinforce the already existing collective spirit with the added gender emphasis. If this perspective is kept in mind, the apparently contradictory statements of the fisherwomen, (namely, their grievance that with the introduction of the auction system, men who now have access to cash earnings give very little for the household, along with their request to the Forum to provide loans for nets which would be used only by the men) is easy to resolve.

In occupations with an identifiable employer-employee relationship, credit intervention sharpens their class consciousness and enables them to raise a number of issues in their work sphere (such as child bondage, implementation of factory laws, minimum wages act, and bonus issues). While transforming them, in some instances, from dependent to independent producers can be construed as similar to the case of self-employed vendors, it also exposes in the process the exploitative system constituted by the hierarchy of middlemen. Further, it does not completely eliminate the merchant or capitalist from the picture and, to that extent, the antagonistic elements are still retained.

These insights drawn from the experiences of the women, and gathered during the course of fieldwork and later interviews, is substantiated to a great extent by the actual evolution of the Forum itself. The Forum started in 1978 and concentrated its activities amongst the self-employed vendors in Madras city. As the Forum spread to other areas involving agricultural wage labour and home-based workers, the class character of the oppression of women took a sharper focus as the antagonistic elements in the sphere of production and circulation were clearly perceivable by the women themselves. With the sharpening of this focus, the Forum also realized that its original grassroots development character could not be sought to be achieved without it at the same time assuming the character of a trade union to protect the rights of its members and to ensure for them their subsistence. With that end in view, the Forum registered itself as the National Union of Working Women in March 1981 under the Trade Union Act.

Family Planning and Health Programmes

Earlier, I had noted that the objective of the Forum is to empower women both in their productive and reproductive roles. The relationship between the two roles is well recognised. Empowerment in the reproductive sphere essentially means that women be given the knowledge and accessibility to methods of birth control, personal hygiene, and health care institutions. Further, empowerment also means that women be given the confidence and strength, that it is their right, to decide and to promote 'informed consent' on all issues of reproduction.

With this objective in view, the Forum sought to adapt the state sponsored family planning programme into a women centred grassroots health care project. This was done by retaining both the grassroots and, neighbourhood concept, as under the credit programme. So far, the programme has been conducted in three phases, with funding from the ILO, UNFPA and the Government of India for the third phase. The impact of this programme has been at two levels—the recipient household level and the women, and the trainees and their relationship with the health delivery system. At the house- hold level, there has undoubtedly been a breaking down of inhibitions in discussing intimate/personal affairs and, to that extent, what is deemed to be a private domain becomes narrowed down. The women do recognise that it is their right, and that they would take decisions pertaining to family planning. Numerous instances were cited of the struggle within households the women had to wage, and the kind of support provided by the Forum. Correspondingly, a certain degree of sensitisation among the male members of the household also appears to have taken place. Clearly, women's empowerment has been achieved to a significant degree.

The lacuna that one perceives is the dual level of consciousness of the women. Most women insisted that they need to have control over sexuality and fertility, and many others felt That an additional child was, given the existing context, an income augmenting and survival guaranteeing mechanism. Women in fishing households indicated a strong preference for sons—a minimum of four sons to own a boat—irrespective of the total number of children they would need to achieve the norm of four grown-up sons. Very few women attributed their household poverty to the number of children; the most striking manifestation was their criticism against the Chief Minister's Noon Meal Scheme for all school children. They say that those who have borne the children also know how to feed them. Yet, at a macro level, the women have absorbed the rhetoric of the state that the country's poverty is solely due to its population size. This contradictory nature of consciousness is due to an incomplete understanding of how the politics of reproduction within households is enmeshed with the state politics of reproduction. To that extent, while the private domain has narrowed, it still has to move to a stage where the private becomes political,

The constant tussles between the state health personnel at all levels and the Forum's health workers has, as in the case of the credit programme, sensitised the workers to the functioning of the bureaucracy.

At a conceptual level, the introduction of the family planning programme into its activities has reinforced the fact of a dual existence—a collective existence and an individual one—and how both these features can be used for mobilisation. In the work sphere, the collective existence assumes dominance. Here, I had noted earlier, a difference in the level of consciousness of women in occupations with an identifiable employer and those who were self-employed. Thus, credit as a means of mobilisation has a limited applicability, especially among the latter. The Forum has circumvented this limitation by using the individual existence of women as a means of mobilisation. Thus, the family planning programme brings together all women as individuals, and the differentiation noticed in their collective existence as defined by their work status gets camouflaged.

Social Conscientisation Activities

In the two sets of activities described earlier, I had mentioned the aspect of change in consciousness. Activities are undertaken by the Forum specifically as a part of social. conscientisation. These include inter-caste marriages and group activities like role-plays, group singing and dancing, and group-eating.

Issues in a Nutshell

The experiences of the Forum raise a number of issues.

The Forum uses the appurtenances of the existing system to raise the consciousness of women. Its use of the DRI (Differential Rate of Interest) loan scheme, of the family planning programme, and so on, serve as examples. This leaves it with two sets of difficulties. Often, it can be dismissed as an exercise within the system without really challenging it or attempting to change the status quo. When probed deeply, it is clear that what has been achieved in terms of raising consciousness cannot be belittled. The growing consciousness, in the course of time, will bring the Forum in conflict with the existing system. The system will then put pressure on the existing modes of operation of the Forum. The possibilities of radicalisation within the system as well as the limits to such radicalisation is an area of concern.

This takes us to the next issue of whether the experiences of the Forum are taking the collective to a critical juncture where it gains a certain autonomous momentum of its own. The success of a collective can, in the long run, be judged only by the extent to which it has gained an autonomous status.

The experiences of the Forum in organizing the informal sector micro entrepreneurs and the home-based producers have effectively demonstrated that new forms of mobilisation and forms of struggle for this section of the working class are possible and under way. To that extent, it challenges the more conservative trade unions where forms of mobilisation and struggle are limited to factory gates, shop floors and wage issues.

At the experimental level, the formation of neighbourhood groups, promoting grassroots leadership, and using peer group support and pressure tactics, thus minimising alienation, are inputs that are not region or culture specific and, to that extent, the organizational structure, and the structure of leadership and decision-making are replicable.

NOTES

1. Field work was first conducted in March—April 1985. The update on the Forum's current activities are based on interviews with the Forum staff in Madras in April 1992.

2 For a quantitative analysis of these aspects, see Kalpagam (1985) and Naponen (1987). For a general account of urban poor households' income earning and pooling strategies in Madras city, see Chapter 7 in this volume. Also see Naponen (1991). For another experiment in organizing around credit, see the work on Annapurna (Bombay) by Everett and Savara (1984).

3. For a more elaborate historical account, see Mies (1982).

4. For a further understanding on this read, Arunachalam (1991).

APPENDIX–II

THE SEXUAL HARASSMENT OF WOMEN AT WORKPLACE (PREVENTION, PROHIBITION AND REDRESSAL) ACT, 2013

The Sexual Harassment of Women at Workplace (Prevention, Prohibition and Redressal) Act, 2013 is a legislative act in Indiathat seeks to protect women from sexual harassment at their place of work. It was passed by the Lok Sabha (the lower house of theIndian Parliament) on 3 September 2012. It was passed by the Rajya Sabha (the upper house of the Indian Parliament) on 26 February 2013. The Bill got the assent of the President on 23 April 2013.

Text of the Act

The introductory text of the Act is:

> An Act to provide protection against sexual harassment of women at workplace and for the prevention and redressal of complaints of sexual harassment and for matters connected therewith or incidental thereto.
>
> WHEREAS sexual harassment results in violation of the fundamental rights of a woman to equality under articles 14 and 15 of the Constitution of India and her right to life and to live with dignity under article 21 of the Constitution and right to practice any profession or to carry on any occupation, trade or business which includes a right to a safe environment free from sexual harassment;
>
> AND WHEREAS the protection against sexual harassment and the right to work with dignity are universally recognised human rights by international conventions and instruments such as Convention on the Elimination of all Forms of Discrimination against Women, which has been ratified on the 25th June, 1993 by the Government of India;
>
> *AND WHEREAS it is expedient to make provisions for giving effect to the said Convention for protection of women against sexual harassment at workplace.*

Background and Provisions

According to the Press Information Bureau of the Government of India:

> The Act will ensure that women are protected against sexual harassment at all the work places, be it in public or private. This will contribute to realisation of their right to gender equality, life and liberty and equality in working conditions everywhere. The sense of security at the workplace will improve women's participation in work, resulting in their economic empowerment and inclusive growth.

The Act uses a definition of sexual harassment which was laid down by the Supreme Court of India in Vishaka v. State of Rajasthan (1997). Article 19 (1) g of the Indian Constitution affirms the right of all citizens to be employed in any profession of their choosing or to practice their own trade or business. Vishaka v. State of Rajasthan established that actions resulting in a violation of one's rights to 'Gender Equality' and 'Life and Liberty' is in fact a violation of the victim's fundamental right under Article 19 (1) g. The case ruling establishes that sexual harassment violates a woman's rights in the workplace and is thus not just a matter of personal injury.

Under the Act, which also covers students in schools and colleges as well as patients in hospitals, employers and local authorities will have to set up grievance committees to investigate all complaints. Employers who fail to comply will be punished with a fine of up to 50,000 rupees.

The legislative progress of the Act has been a lengthy one. The Bill was first introduced by women and child development ministerKrishna Tirath in 2007 and approved by the Union Cabinet in January 2010. It was tabled in the Lok Sabha in December 2010 and referred to the Parliamentary Standing Committee on Human Resources Development. The committee's report was published on 30 November 2011. In May 2012, the Union Cabinet approved an amendment to include domestic workers. The amended Bill was finally passed by the Lok Sabha on 3 September 2012. The Bill was passed by the Rajya Sabha (the upper house of the Indian Parliament) on 26 February 2013. It has come into force and has been published in the Gazette of India, Extraordinary, Part-II, Section-1, dated the 23rd April 2013 as Act No. 14 of 2013.

Major Features

- The Act defines sexual harassment at the work place and creates a mechanism for redressal of complaints. It also provides safeguards against false or malicious charges.
- The definition of "aggrieved woman", who will get protection under the Act is extremely wide to cover all women, irrespective of her age or employment status, whether in the organised or unorganised sectors, public or private and covers clients, customers and domestic workers as well.
- While the "workplace" in the Vishaka Guidelines is confined to the traditional office set-up where there is a clear employer-employee relationship, the Act goes much further to include organisations, department, office, branch unit etc. in the public and private sector, organized and unorganized, hospitals, nursing homes, educational institutions, sports institutes, stadiums,

sports complex and any place visited by the employee during the course of employment including the transportation.

- The Committee is required to complete the inquiry within a time period of 90 days. On completion of the inquiry, the report will be sent to the employer or the District Officer, as the case may be, they are mandated to take action on the report within 60 days.
- Every employer is required to constitute an Internal Complaints Committee at each office or branch with 10 or more employees. The District Officer is required to constitute a Local Complaints Committee at each district, and if required at the block level.
- The Complaints Committees have the powers of civil courts for gathering evidence.
- The Complaints Committees are required to provide for conciliation before initiating an inquiry, if requested by the complainant.
- Penalties have been prescribed for employers. Non-compliance with the provisions of the Act shall be punishable with a fine of up to ₹ 50,000. Repeated violations may lead to higher penalties and cancellation of licence or registration to conduct business.

Penal Code

Upon the act's presidential approval, section was added to the Indian Penal Code that stipulates what consists of a sexual harassment offence and what the penalties shall be for a man committing such an offence. Penalties range from one to three years imprisonment and/or a fine. Additionally, with sexual harassment being a crime, employers are obligated to report offences.

Criticism

Brinda Karat, serving in the Rajya Sabha as a Communist Party of India (Marxist) member for West Bengal initially complained that the Bill does not cover women in the armed forces and excludes women agricultural workers, "a gross injustice to agricultural workers who are the single largest female component of work force in the country." However, the final bill includes the clause "No woman shall be subjected to sexual harassment at any workplace" (clause 3.1), and is considered to have addressed those concerns.

In the May 2012 draft Bill, the burden of proof is on the women who complain of harassment. If found guilty of making a false complaint or giving false evidence, she could be prosecuted, which has raised concerns about women being even more afraid of reporting offences. Before seeing the final version of the bill, lawyer and activist Vrinda Grover said,

> "I hope the Bill does not have provisions for penalizing the complainant for false complaints. This is the most under-reported crime. Such provision will deter a woman to come forward and complain." Zakia Soman, a women's rights campaigner at ActionAid India said that "it helps to have a law and we welcome it, but the crux will lie in its implementation once it is enacted."

Manoj Mitta of The Times of India complained that Bill does not protect men, saying it "is based on the premise that only female employees needed to be safeguarded." Nishith Desai Associates, a law group, wrote a detailed analysis that included concerns about the role of the employer in sexual harassment cases. They called out the fact that there is no stipulated liability for employers in cases of employee-to-employee harassment, something upheld in many other countries. They also viewed the provision that employers are obligated to address grievances in a timely manner at the workplace as problematic because of potentially uncooperative employees. Furthermore, the law requires a third-party non-governmental organisation to be involved, which could make employers less comfortable in reporting grievances, due to confidentiality concerns.

Bibliography

Audrus, J. Russel, *Burmese Economic Life,* Stanford, 1948, p. 291.

Boland, Mary L. *Sexual Harassment: Your Guide to Legal Action*. Naperville, Illinois: Sphinx Publishing, 2002.

Bossard, James H.S., *The Sociology of Child Development,* New York: Harper, 1954, pp. 282-86.

Cormack, Margaret, *The Hindu Women*, London pp. 5,160.

D'Souza, Victor S., *Social Structure of a Planned City Chandigarh,* New Delhi: Orient Longmans Limited, 1968, p. 73.

Gore, M.S., *Urbanisation and Family Change,* Bombay: Popular Prakashan, 1968, p. 159.

Harper, Colin. *Why I can't take 'no' for an answer...* Bridge Publications, 2001.

Hauser, P.M., "The Labour Force as Field of Interest of the Sociologists", *American Sociological Review,* 16 (1951), pp. 530-38.

Husain, A.F.A., *Employment of Middle Class Muslim Women in Dacca.* Dacca, 1958, pp. 60, 65.

Kapadia, K.M., "Changing Pattern of Hindu Marriage and Family," Part II, *Sociological Bulletin,* 3 (September, 1954), p. 153.

Klein, Viola, *Britain's Married Women Workers,* p. 59.

Koyama, Takashi, *The Changing Social Position of Women in Japan,* Unesco 1961, p. 109.

Langelan, Martha. *Back Off: How to Confront and Stop Sexual Harassment and Harassers*. Fireside, 1993.

Leaflet, 11, "Why Do Women Work?" 1951, as quoted in Ray E. Barber, *Marriage and the Family,* New York, McGraw Hill, 1953, P. 348.

Lewis, W.A., *The Theory of Economic Growth,* London, 1957, pp. 16-17; Nath, Kamla, "Urban Women Workers—A Preliminary Study," *The Economic Weekly,* 37 (September 11, 1965), p. 1412.

Lundberg, Ferdinand, and Farnham, Marynia F., *Modern Women: The Lost Sex,* New York: Harper, 1947 as quoted in *The Employed Mother,* p. 7.

Mukherji, R.K., "Caste and Economic Structure in West Bengal in Present

Times," *Sociology, Social Relations and Social Problems In India,* Saxena, R.N. (ed.,) Bombay: Asia Publishing House, 1961, p. 157.

N. Sokoloff (1992). *Black Women and White Women in the Professions: Occupational Segregation by Race and Gender, 1960-1980* (Perspectives on Gender).

Nye, F. Ivan, *The Employed Mothers,* p. 279.

Patai, Daphne. *Heterophobia: Sexual Harassment and the Future of Feminism*. Lanham: Rowman and Littlefield, 1999.

Penina Migdal Glazer and Miriam Slater, *Unequal Colleagues: The Entrance of Women into the Professions, 1890-1940* (Douglass Series on Women's Lives and the Meaning of Gender).

Ranade, S.N., and Ramchandran, P., *women and Employment,* Bombay: Tata Institute of Social Science, 71 AS, 1970, p. 7 and p. 3.

Roberts S., Barry Mann A., Richard- "Sexual Harassment In The Workplace: A PRIMER".

Rowe, Mary & Corinne Bendersky, "Workplace Justice, Zero Tolerance, and Zero Barriers," 2001, in Negotiations and Change, From the Workplace to Society, Thomas Kochan and Richard Locke (editors), Cornell University Press, 2002.

Rowe,Mary "People Who Feel Harassed Need a Complaint System with both Formal and Informal Options," in Negotiation Journal, April, 1990, Vol. 6, No. 2, pp. 161–172.

Rowe,Mary, "Dealing with Harassment: A Systems Approach," in Sexual Harassment: Perspectives, Frontiers, and Response Strategies, Women & Work, Vol. 5, Margaret Stockdale, editor, Sage Publications, 1996, pp. 241–271.

Trentham, Susan; Laurie Larwood (1998). "Gender Discrimination and the Workplace: An Examination of Rational Bias Theory". *Sex Roles* 38 (112): 1–28.

Index

■■■